DANGEROUS WATERS

DANGEROUS WATERS

Wrecks and Rescues off the BC Coast

Keith Keller

HARBOUR PUBLISHING

Harbour Publishing
P.O. Box 219, Madeira Park,
BC Canada
V0N 2H0

www.harbourpublishing.com

THE CANADA COUNCIL | LE CONSEIL DES ARTS
FOR THE ARTS | DU CANADA
SINCE 1957 | DEPUIS 1957

Cover, maps, page design and composition by Martin Nichols
Cover illustration by Graham Wragg
Photo at the beginning of each chapter—taken during a 60-knot
storm off Cape St. James in Queen Charlotte Sound—by Peter A.
Robson
The text of Randy Morrison's description of his ordeal in
"Randy's Story" is taken from a telephone interview done by
CBC broadcaster Del Phillips, the first reporter to speak with
Morrison after his accident. "Southeasterly" is from *Southeasterly*
(Thistledown Press Ltd., 1987).

Printed and bound in Canada

We acknowledge the financial support of the Government of
Canada through the Book Publishing Industry Development
Program for our publishing activities. We further acknowledge
the support of the Canada Council for the Arts and the Province
of British Columbia through the British Columbia Arts Council
for our publishing program.

National Library of Canada Cataloguing in Publication Data

Keller, Keith, 1958–
Dangerous waters

ISBN 1-55017-168-2 (bound). — ISBN 1-55017-288-3 (pbk.)

1. Shipwrecks—British Columbia—Pacific Coast. I. Title.
FC3820.S5K45 1997   910'.91'6433   C97-910759-8
F1087.K45 1997

This book is dedicated to
Mabel Elizabeth Keller

Contents

Their Own Stories, Their Own Words

Late one afternoon in the closing weeks of 1995, CBC radio broadcast an interview with one Lieutenant Larry Littrell of the United States Coast Guard. The night before, under harrowing circumstances, Littrell had been part of a helicopter crew that snatched a stranded Canadian fisherman from his precarious perch in the aptly named Graveyard of the Pacific, off the southwest coast of Vancouver Island.

It was a great story: danger, daring, salvation. My first thought was that it had *Reader's Digest* written all over it. But later, as I reran the interview in my mind, it struck me that the story didn't require *Reader's Digest*. What it required was Littrell. And whoever else had been on hand: rescuers and those rescued. They could tell their own stories in their own words.

The next morning I called CBC to ask for Littrell's phone number (see "Making History With the Velcro Grip"). A year and a half and seventy-seven interviews later I had compiled accounts of twenty-four marine rescues that have taken place on the B.C. coast. Twenty-one of those accounts appear in this collection.

My sources for these stories were many. I wrote to lightkeepers and sent letters to the editors of most newspapers in coastal BC. I read mariners' magazines, newspaper clippings and accident investigation reports. I drove around much of Vancouver Island, speaking to people on or near the waterfront. Some of these accounts are the result of persistent research, others the gifts of chance.

I neither began nor ended this project with any specialized knowledge about boats, oceanography or the intricacies of search and rescue procedures. I am a sea kayaker and I did a little commercial cod fishing back when east coast cod existed in more than relic numbers. I have at times—while paddling in confused chop at the mouth of Porlier Pass, say, or wallowing through Labrador Sea swell in a heavily loaded boat—silently pondered the question that must occur to most people who venture forth on the ocean: "What if...?" What if being on the water suddenly deteriorated into being *in* the water? Our species may have evolved from the oceans, but as we find out when we're inadvertently returned to salt water, it's no longer our element. When misfortune separates us from the little islands we call boats, we become one of those people qualified to answer the question, "What if...?"

These stories repeatedly tell us that when the worst happens, people who can help, do help. They at least try. The search and rescue specialists respond because that's what they do—which in no way diminishes the risks they take on others' behalf. Those who just happen to be in a position to help—vessels of opportunity, as they're known—also respond, often at their own significant peril. I have read the piece "The Most Popular Guy in the Pub" at least two dozen times, and I still get a lump in my throat at the point where Ken Datwiler, alone and knowing his boat will soon founder, tells seine boat captain Bruce Rafuse to carry on and at least save himself from the hurricane conditions they're both fighting. And Rafuse, at the helm of a boat which has previously turned turtle with him aboard, responds that he will not abandon Datwiler. He keeps his word; they both go home.

When I interviewed Rafuse, a thoughtful, soft-spoken man, he said that despite the obvious danger to himself, leaving Datwiler that ferocious night "was never an option. I've owed my life to others, and when you see something like that, it's not an option." He added, "It's an interesting crowd, fishermen. Compared to most of society I guess you could say they're at the rougher end of it—independent spirits. And yet when anyone's in trouble, I doubt there's any of the fishermen that would just let you drown. I know lots of them, and the ones that you think are the really rough, tough fishermen...if you were in trouble, they'd be there."

◆ ◆ ◆

I am not aware that this book contains any lies. It undoubtedly contains errors, most of them attributable to the limitations of perception and memory. Wave height, elapsed time, actual sequences of unfolding events—these cannot be reported objectively when people are fighting for their lives. Wave height is difficult to calculate at the best of times, let alone from the deck of a boat tossing in those same waves. And does it matter whether the waves were twenty-five feet or thirty or forty feet? People who have survived such events report the numbers truthfully rather than accurately; what they say is, "The waves were godawful big and from all evidence were about to annihilate me." Good enough.

Given that each person involved in these events experienced them from his or her own perspective, both literally and figuratively, it shouldn't be surprising that some differences of recollection occur in many of these pieces. "I know in all three of us the story's a little bit different," says Kurt Guilbride ("Three Men on a Raft") after describing how tugboat skipper Paul Bottomley inadvertently tipped their life raft—an occurrence that Bottomley recalls not at all.

In "The Law of Gravity Shouldn't Allow It," I included George Moore's version of the rescue which went briefly but almost fatally awry when the life raft streamed from the rescue vessel back to his stricken *Concreta* flipped, nearly depositing his family into the waves. Audrey Samuel, Moore's wife at the time, remembers these events unfolding in exactly the reverse manner—father and daughter being caught in the raft while she watched helplessly from the *Concreta*'s deck.

Resolving these differences proved a challenge at times as I attempted to meld several individual accounts into a single narrative. Every survivor, every rescuer, every chronicler would compile a different account. It has been a humbling challenge to act as gatekeeper, selecting from among several possibilities the nuance or the point of view making it into print. I have trod as lightly as possible.

These are sacred stories, and I have great respect for the people who entrusted them to me. The ordeals they described often became transforming events in their lives. I recall sitting across from George Moore at his dining room table as he explained how he, his wife and three-year-old daughter came to be drifting helplessly in the mounting fury of Chatham Sound. Moore's expression was intent as he spoke. I don't think he was seeing me; he was revisiting the events of twenty-two years earlier, when he and his family were on the verge of dying. At one point, as he was describing the "awful fear" presented by the prospect of imminent death, he paused, his face shattering like a slowly exploding jigsaw puzzle. He rose from the table and walked into the kitchen, taking time to gather his composure. He stood in front of a refrigerator whose door was almost invisible beneath a papering of family photographs. He later identified some of the faces for me—young faces, for the most part, faces he could easily never have known. "Those twenty-two years," he said, "have been a gift."

Acknowledgements

Working this project through from inspiration to termination has involved the collaboration of a great many good folk.

Winding down one summer evening I paddled my kayak, as I often do, to the south end of Denman Island. I circled tiny Chrome Island before heading home, and met by chance Chrome's principal lightkeeper. We chatted briefly, ship to shore, as it were. I described the project I'd embarked on and asked if he had any leads I might follow. You should talk to my father, he said. Hence the piece "The Loss of the *Bruce 1.*" Thank you, Chas Thomson.

Driving just outside of Sointula one agreeable winter afternoon, I stopped to ask directions of a woman out for a stroll. Rush hour had not yet developed on Malcolm Island; I shut off my car in the middle of the road. We chatted. I described my mission. You should talk to my husband, she said. I never did talk to her husband, but I did get to hear about "Daryl's Ghost and the *Salty Isle.*" Thank you, Shirley Sampson.

To the many other people who directed me toward specific incidents or helped me make essential contacts, I offer sincere gratitude. My phone bills attest to the fact that you are legion.

Thanks also to Mike Mitchell, light station services officer, Canadian Coast Guard; Norbert and Kathi Brand, Cape Beale light station; Stan and Judy Westhaver, Egg Island light station; Ed and Pat Kidder, Nootka light station; Jim Abram, Cape Mudge light station; David ("Heavy Weather") Hegstrom, Bamfield Coast Guard lifeboat station; Scott Price, historian, US Coast Guard Headquarters, Washington DC; Tove D. Johansen, librarian, University of Oslo; Captain Alf Mørner; staff at the Comox and Courtenay branches of the Vancouver Island Regional Library; staff of the Researcher Services Division of the National Archives of Canada; Barbara Sayle (for gentle, persistent, influential prodding); Kyriakos Katsanakakis (for the translation—it was all Greek to you); Murray Leslie of Moonstone Design (a steady beacon piloting me through the perilous waters of computerdom/cyberspace); Sol Mogerman (for counselling—editorial and otherwise—and, when distraction was the best medicine, unlimited access to the woodworking tools); Captain John Mein, senior investigator, marine, Transportation Safety Board of Canada (for responding to my phone calls, faxes and unannounced personal visits, and for explaining in triplicate the arcane logic of the investigation report filing system). Thanks also to Scott Crowson of the *Prince Rupert Daily News*, Rob Giblak of the *North Island Gazette*, Des Kennedy of Pickles Road and Linda Diver of Little Burnaby.

If any single person cheerfully bore the brunt of my incessant prodding for names, dates, files and reports, and went to or slightly beyond the limits of professional obligation, it was Captain Dennis Johnston, deputy officer in charge of Victoria's Rescue Coordination Centre. I owe you one, Cap'n.

I am grateful to Peter Robson of Harbour Publishing for thoughtfully guiding this project through to completion, and to senior editor Mary Schendlinger for the skill, sensitivity and grace she unfailingly demonstrated while transforming my material into a publishable manuscript.

My thanks to Graham Wragg for his meticulous, painstakingly researched illustrations.

At the very top of a freelance writer's list of essential qualities—above writing skills and the nose for a good story—should be the ability to deal well with rejection. I do not. When it came time to approach the publishing world with this project I made one pitch, a pathetic attempt to bribe the founder and president of Harbour Publishing with all the free coffee or beer he could drink in exchange for his hearing my idea. His reply: I get a thousand book pitches a year; I can't drink that much; write it in one page and drop it in the mail. I did. He bought it. Thank you, Howard White.

To my wife, Heather MacLeod. For never ceasing to inspire and amaze, my gratitude and admiration.

Finally, to the people who gave of their time and their souls to tell me their stories, a heartfelt thanks.

Wrecks and Rescues
off the BC Coast

SOUTH
COAST

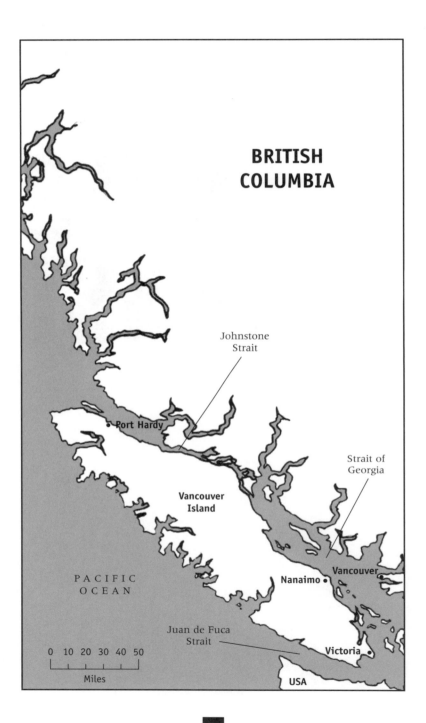

BRITISH
COLUMBIA

Johnstone
Strait

Port Hardy

Strait of
Georgia

Vancouver
Island

PACIFIC
OCEAN

Vancouver

Nanaimo

Juan de Fuca
Strait

Victoria

0 10 20 30 40 50

Miles

USA

The

Most

Popular

Guy

in the

Pub

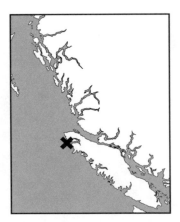

The Most Popular Guy in the Pub

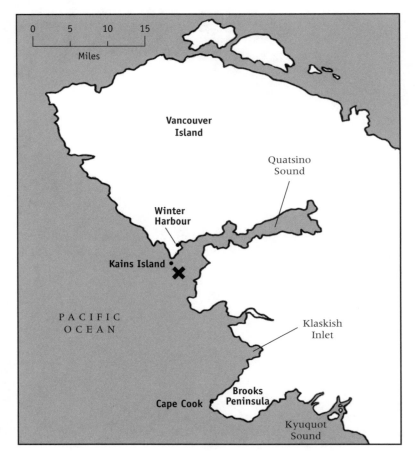

WEATHER ON THE WEST COAST OF
VANCOUVER ISLAND had been unsettled for two days
leading up to the morning of October 11, 1984. In
Nootka and Kyuquot sounds, a fleet of almost 400 sein-
ers and gillnetters were gathered, taking part in the
annual salmon harvest. Fishing closed at ten o'clock on
the morning of the 11th, at which point crews turned to
the task of delivering their catches to packers and
preparing for departure.

The forecast that morning called for winds increasing to 20 to 30 knots with a further outlook for strong to
gale force winds by the morning of the following day.
The next salmon opening was to take place shortly in
the Qualicum Beach area on Vancouver Island's east
coast. Most fishermen decided to get at least partway
there before being forced to seek shelter, if necessary, at
some point along the route.

Among the fishermen who chose to leave the
grounds was Ken Datwiler of Courtenay, owner of the 36-
foot troller/gillnetter *Lady Val II*. Travelling with him were
two other small vessels, the *Silver Triton* and *Miss Robyn*.

Bruce Rafuse was also travelling north that day.
Rafuse, skipper of the 57-foot wooden seiner *Miss Joye*,
was bound for Port Hardy with deckhand Mike Wallace,
his other deckhand having left the vessel earlier in the
day. Accompanying *Miss Joye* was a second Port Hardy-
based seine boat, Murray McGill's *Western Hunter*.

Datwiler: I'd delivered and I was waiting for somebody to
travel with because I didn't want to go by myself. I waited until
these other two boats were ready to go. One, John Secord, I
knew personally—that's the *Silver Triton*. As soon as he was
ready to go, him and I took off, and then his friend came behind
us.

The storm was supposed to come up the following afternoon. I think it was about nine hours that I had to travel, so I

The *Lady Val II*.
Photo courtesy Ken Datwiler.

wasn't concerned about the time. By the time we got to Cook Island it was still quite calm but the breeze was coming up a bit. I didn't have my stabilizers in the water. Then it started to get a bit rougher so I put my stabilizers in the water. And of course it got worse.

Rafuse: About ten o'clock a wind started blowing from behind the boat but wasn't strong—it didn't seem to be going faster than the boat. By eleven o'clock the winds were 15 to 25 knots but travelling was still not bad although the boat was rolling a fair bit. Mike would steer until he'd feel seasick, then lay down. After about eleven I decided to just let him lay down as he was getting quite sick.

Datwiler: John said maybe we should go in behind Cook Island. I said, "Okay, but I don't know my way in there." John said that I should just head in there and he'd show me the way once we got there. Well, by the time I'd got my boat turned around the bow was going right under the water. So I told him that I couldn't go in there and that I'd have to keep going toward Winter Harbour. At normal speed with my boat it would take about three hours from there. But the wind was pushing me and I couldn't give it any acceleration because the boat was listing so badly. Then when the gusts would come you'd go right over. At times the pole would go right under the water. I thought it would never come back, but it kept coming back.

By the time I got outside of Quatsino ... I guess the wind come out of the lee there—it came right out of Quatsino Sound. They're in behind asking me what it was like, and I told them that I wouldn't make it, but I didn't know what to tell them to do. They were telling me that it was flat calm but that the wind was so strong it was going to blow their boat over. John, he hit bottom I guess with one of his stabilizers. I think he said he ripped a pole off. He broke it, anyways. He didn't know what to do, and I said, "Well, I'm not going to make it, so I don't know what to tell you to do." He had phoned the Coast Guard and they said it was blowing about 50 or something but a big tug come on and said it was blowing more like 70.

Rafuse: I was going past Cape Cook about midnight. The seas were pretty heavy by this time but not enough to throttle back. I noticed a couple of boats in the lee of Cape Cook and found out later it was the *Silver Triton* and *Miss Robyn*. The boats behind Cape Cook were quite concerned about their situation. They asked me if Klaskish Inlet would afford any better shelter and I replied that I had never been to Klaskish.

Not long after I passed Cape Cook I met a boat with a spotlight on. It seemed strange, 'cause most people don't travel with spotlights on. He turned it off and turned around, which seemed very strange. I thought he must be looking for something. Still, it's not my business.

I heard on the 78 channel, from *Miss Robyn*, that there was a boat in trouble in the waves and he wondered if we could stand by. I asked if it was the one with the spotlight and he said, "Yeah, but he's on another channel." His name was Ken.

Datwiler: John's friend on the *Miss Robyn* had phoned this Bruce Rafuse on *Miss Joye*. They happened to see a seine boat go by but they didn't know it was him. They asked Bruce Rafuse to look after me. He called me—I was standing by on a certain channel—and asked me how I was doing. I said, "Not very good, actually." He said, "Don't worry. We'll find you, and we'll stay with you."

Rafuse: He had turned around and was going to go to Winter Harbour. I idled back because he was going so slow. Pretty soon he was out of sight—out of sight of the radar, 'cause when the waves are big like that you don't get a reflection from a boat. The seas were so large they reflected as well as any boat.

I called and asked him to put his spotlight on again. He wasn't that far away but I had to turn around and go back to him. This was the first time I realized the size of what we were in, 'cause we had been going with it and it wasn't so bad, especially when you're going slow. We turned around and it's like this huge cliff of water coming at you—gives you quite a thrill.

Datwiler: He'd turn around and come back, but he told me he didn't know how many more times he could do it, because he was taking water halfway up the mast. So I told him to not worry about me and keep going. And he said that he'd never leave me—they were going to stay with me.

Rafuse: I kept talking to him, trying to get him to turn to starboard, into Winter Harbour. But the waves were too bad, and he wasn't able to. As we got closer to Kains Island light I'd tell Ken, "We are eight miles now, five miles now, three miles, two miles, one and a half miles."

The total ten miles we went together took about four hours. It was getting worse, and he kept thinking he wasn't going to make it. I'd tell him, "Sure you'll make it." What else could I say?

It must have been close to four in the morning, I found that if I put my bow in the wind and kept him on one of my sides and just idled, I'd go backwards as fast as he was going forwards. I had to have enough throttle to be able to steer the boat, so every once in a while I had to turn around. I realized by this time that he might not make it and if I was ahead of him when he went over I'd not see him and I'd never find him in those seas.

Datwiler: According to reports it blew between 70 and 100 miles an hour. The sea was thirty to forty feet high. You couldn't see very much because of all the water. It was like being in rapids—everything was foaming. I'd look out the back and say, "No way my boat can handle this." I went out once because I'd heard something bang on the side of the boat. The boat had gone over so far it lifted my life ring off the side of the boat and put it in the water. I went out to try and get it and I thought I was going to go over so I said, "To hell with it—whatever happens, happens." And I left it.

I kept carrying on, then I told them that this was it. I knew that this time I'm not going to come out of it. My pole was under the water, the wind isn't quitting, and he said, "Okay, we're right behind you."

Rafuse: He called me "Seine boat." This one time, about 4:30 a.m., he said, "Seine boat, I think it's going over." His stabilizer pole was in the water. He said, "My prop's out of the water. I think it's going over." And then all this crackle, crackle. Then the lights went out. And I couldn't find him. I put my spotlight on, but he'd disappeared. I was only a few boat lengths away when he rolled over, otherwise there wouldn't have been a chance of finding him. The waves were over thirty feet. I would have had no idea, but afterwards, at the inquest, they talked about the wave height.

Datwiler: I had the window on the one side open so I could get out, and I'm talking to him on the phone while the boat's filling up with water. When I climbed out, that's when I knew how bad it really was. I couldn't hang on. The water would come totally over the boat and me. I hung onto a chain that was hooked to the pole. I kept going up with the water washing over the boat, but hanging onto the chain. Then I'd come back down. I figured this wasn't very good, so I stuck my legs in the fish locker, wrapped the chain around my arm and hung on. I couldn't get the hood on my survival suit with one hand.

Then when the *Miss Joye* actually came up to me he didn't see me. Every time he'd turn his searchlight toward me, that's when a wave would come up between us and he'd miss me.

Rafuse: When Ken turned over we were just about straight out from Kains Island light. I'd imagine a mile, two miles. I don't know how long I looked. It wasn't that long—a person can't live in that water very long. I thought, Well, maybe we should just head for harbour too. I thought I might have searched too far to the right so I told Murray I'd try one more pass to the left. I told the Lord that I knew we'd never find Ken unless we had help and for all our sakes we needed help. I made one more pass, and as I turned around I saw the debris in the water. Talking to Ken afterwards he said that several times my spotlight had shone right on him but the waves came between us.

My stabilizers were in the water. They had been for most of the evening. With the boat I was on you didn't want to take too much of a chance—it had rolled over before. I came up, maybe thirty or forty feet from him. He was on top of his boat. It was on its side and he was up on the hull. There was junk all around. I took it out of gear. I had to think twice about doing this but I knew we couldn't pick him up with the boat still going forward. I thought he'd swim to my boat and then we'd pick him up.

Datwiler: He was hollering at me, but the wind was so strong going through his stay wires, I can't hear what he's saying. But I know he wants me to go into the water. And I can't swim. I didn't want to go into the water all that bad until he got close to me. There wasn't much of my boat above water, but it was still floating. But I let go.

When I got into the water he lost me. He had turned around again and was coming back toward me. I think that I kicked myself off the bow of the boat. I was going to grab onto his stabilizer pole.

Rafuse: My deckhand Mike suggested the life ring. He tied it to our bowline and heaved it to Ken. The wind blew it right back, but Ken left his hull and slipped into the water and started drifting away from the boat, but not as fast as us. He had his survival suit on, but improperly, and it was filling up with water.

When he got far enough away I came up upwind from him and drifted down on top of him. I took it out of gear, ran outside and we drifted down sideways. We just came rushing toward him. And as soon as we got to him I threw him the life ring, told him to get in it.

Datwiler: He saw me and threw me a rope—about an inch and three-eighths, this huge rope that the seine boats use—with a life ring on it that's too big for most human beings. It was a great big one—quite a bit bigger than the one on my boat. I got in it but I was having trouble staying in it because my arms weren't long enough. Then the rope came off.

Now I'm in the life ring that I can't really stay in, but I'm in it. And I'm floating away.

Rafuse: I gave him the rope and said, "Tie it back on." He said, "I can't, I'm too cold." The current was already pulling him around the bow. I said, "You *have* to put it on." He said, "I'm too cold." I said, "Just put it through the ring and give it back to us." He said, "I *can't*."

He was up by the bow. I said, "We have to pull you back here." He said, "I can't hold on." I said, "You *have* to hold on." He held on. We pulled him back, he got the rope through somehow. I realized that he was weak enough by that point that he could slip back out of the ring. But I figured we'd put this much effort into it we weren't going to lose him. I said, "Kick your feet. Help us in." He said, "I *can't*."

Datwiler: They couldn't lift me out of the water because I was too heavy—my suit's full of water.

A wave took me and threw me up on his boat to about my ribcage, right up near the bow of his boat. I was able to reach behind to a stay wire. He said something like, "Come on, Ken, you've got to help us." And I said, "I'm not going anywhere."

Rafuse: I grabbed his suit and rolled him somehow. I think the rocking of the boat actually helped us get him in.

I said, "Okay, now, come around and get inside the cabin." I didn't know at that rate how long it would be before we'd be up on the beach. He said, "I can't. I can't move." So we coaxed him in. Somewhere along the way I slit the boots on his survival suit and let the water out.

Datwiler: I crawled—I looked like Sweet Pea, actually, in my nice red suit—into the cabin. The deckhand was really sick and said he was sorry but would it be okay if he went and lay down. I said, "That's fine—I'm not going anywhere now. I'm staying right here."

Rafuse: We got him in the cabin and I told Mike to get Ken out of his suit and get him comfortable. Mike came up and said, "He wants a shower." He'd be beat to death in a shower. I said, "Take my quilt and wrap it around him." Mike said, "I'm really sick. Can I hit the bunk?" I said it was okay.

Pretty soon Ken came up and said, "Do you mind if I smoke?" I said, "I don't have any cigarettes." He said, "I figured if I was going to survive I'd need two things: my cigarettes and my wallet."

Datwiler: Before I went over I felt that Bruce was religious and he didn't smoke. I knew I was going to need a cigarette in the worst way so I put two packages of unopened cigarettes in my pockets. When I got on board Bruce said that he couldn't give me a cigarette but he had lots of matches. I said, "Well, I brought my own cigarettes." Bruce said, "That's a true smoker."

Rafuse: By this time we'd drifted to some islands that were downwind from Kains Island. Murray was on the scene by then, and we had to go back to the left, around the light, sideways to the storm. You couldn't see much, and the radar didn't help

Ken Datwiler aboard the *Lady Val II*.
Photo courtesy Ken Datwiler.

much, but you could see the surf all around and you weren't sure if it was surf or just the waves.

It was probably about daybreak that we came into Winter Harbour. I lit the stove for a hot drink, Ken had a shower, and Murray and I phoned home and our wives came and picked us up. It was quite a joyous group that travelled back to Port Hardy that afternoon. We were going to put Ken up for the night but by the time we got to Port Hardy the Seagate looked pretty good to him. He figured he needed to celebrate a little bit. One of my friends, Bobby Charlie, called up about ten o'clock that night and said, "Hey Brucie, you're the most popular guy in the pub!"

In an ironic twist of fate, Ken Datwiler owes his life at least partly to the fact that he was unable to follow the *Silver Triton* and *Miss Robyn* into what turned out to be the illusory shelter of Brooks Bay; all four hands aboard those vessels perished during the night. The body of Datwiler's friend, John Secord, was never found.

In a further irony, Datwiler's rescue was accomplished from a vessel that had been involved in one fatal accident and would, after this incident, capsize twice more. Bruce Rafuse had been aboard the *Miss Joye* in 1977 when it capsized in Seymour Narrows and three lives were lost. The vessel, part of James Walkus's "Joye" seine fleet, subsequently capsized near Seymour Narrows in 1986 and again off Egg Island in 1994—without any more deaths. Both Datwiler and Rafuse have left the commercial fishing industry.

A Ministry of Transport investigation concluded that the weather forecast for October 11, 1984, had been inaccurate. The storm that caught the west coast salmon fleet unawares struck earlier and more fiercely than predicted. By the morning of October 12, seven vessels and five lives had been lost off Vancouver Island. Conditions were such that the Coast Guard cutter *Ready* and the fisheries patrol vessel *Tanu*, two of the many vessels to participate in the extensive air and sea search, were both forced to seek shelter at various times owing to "high seas and extreme storm force winds."

The
Loss
of the
Bruce I

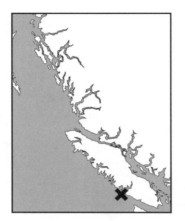

The Loss of the
Bruce 1

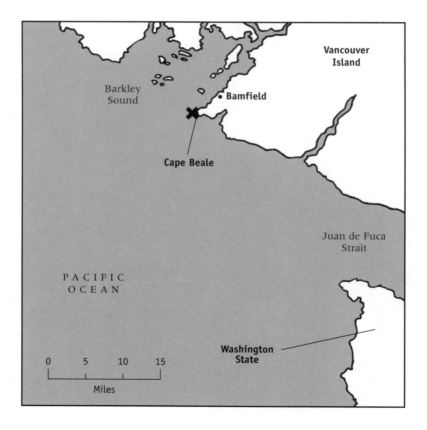

IN LATE FEBRUARY 1976, AS A
LARGE GILLNET fleet was assembling for the annual roe
herring fishery in Barkley Sound, reports indicated that
the roe was maturing more quickly than anticipated.
Clearly there was a good economic opportunity for any
packers—vessels that transfer the catch from fishing
boats to processing plants—that could reach Barkley
Sound ahead of the pack. Stanley Beale, a fisherman living in Vancouver and working for the Cassiar Fishing
Company, was anxious to be one of them.

The seine boat *Bruce 1* left Vancouver's inner har-
bour with four hands on board: Beale, his nephew
Randy West, and two of his friends, Rusty Waters of
Texada Island and Reid Dobell, a lawyer.

Dobell: Stan and I had been friends for years and years. We
went to St. Michael's University School together and we've kept
in contact ever since. I phoned him one evening to see if he
wanted to go out for a beer but he wasn't home. His wife Dianne
said, "I think he's meeting the rest of the crew. He's going out on
a boat, a fish boat, tomorrow I think, and he's meeting them at
The Anchor." Something like that.

So I went down to have a beer with them and we got chat-
ting. It was a Thursday and I was taking Friday off. I'd never
been out on the fish boats, but I'd had my own sailboat for quite
a while and I know a bit about boats, and Stan was short one
crewman—he was going to meet the crewman in Port Alberni.
So I said, "Well, I've never been out on the west coast. I'll come
along and give you a hand, and that'll give me a chance to see it.
I'll take the bus down from Port Alberni."

Beale: We left Vancouver. It was blowing—the outflow winds
coming out of Squamish created some of the first problems for
us. We discovered, perhaps from layup, the battery system, the
radar were not functioning all that well. But we continued on.
We didn't ice up in Vancouver because the ice shed was closed.
We thought we'd pick it up in Victoria.

We went around and got to Mayne Island. We had no radar functioning at that time and we went into the Esso station in Ganges Harbour [Saltspring Island]. So we stayed overnight. Something was not functioning correctly. The batteries and charging system may have been separated. We resumed running and the radar was working fine. We went around to Victoria the next day, where we put ice on board, tied everything down. As soon as that was done we left to go around Cape Beale, which would bring us into the Alberni Inlet where they had an off-loading station in Port Alberni itself.

Dobell: The water was like pee on a platter. The sun was out, there wasn't a cloud in the sky, and we were sitting out on top of the boat having lunch and joking about how they call this the Graveyard of the Pacific.

As we kept going up the coast—and there's virtually nowhere to put in—it got worse and it got worse and it got worse. 'Til finally it's really raging, and blizzarding.

Beale: The weather deteriorated as it got dark and we ended up off Cape Beale. We were now in a snowstorm, the radar was not functioning again and the red-green light that comes off Cape Beale—it's quite obvious, it's a very strong light...I felt that we were too close in, so I turned the vessel around, went back out again and lined up the red-green light changeover so I knew what position I was on in relationship to the light and to the entrance into Bamfield, where we were going to go for that night.

I then proceeded on a compass course in there. It would appear that we were either set off or made some miscalculation on that end of it, and under heavy weather with snow conditions totally obliterating any kind of view, the sounder ran up very quickly to all of a sudden two fathoms. A wall of rock appeared directly in front of us, with water washing off of it.

I threw the machinery into full reverse. The weather—waves—were such that it basically picked the boat up and tossed it onto the rocks, where it stayed. At that stage the engine also quit. I tried to restart it and it did start, but that didn't last for very long and there was no effect in trying to get the boat out. When the engines quit the batteries quit and the whole thing was now pitch black.

Dobell: Stan tried to get off a signal; we didn't know whether it got off or not. We all went up on top and we were all trying to launch this rubber life raft in one of these great big drums. We launched it and got it over the side. But nobody realized that it had in fact inflated, 'cause it was pitch black.

It apparently inflated, floated around the back of the boat and right around to the other side. I distinctly recall us all being very methodical about going from the top of the boat and getting down to the deck of the boat. We took our gumboots off at that stage and we all were very orderly. None of this "every man for himself" bullshit. That's not how you react in that situation. I was amazed that nobody did.

> Principal lightkeeper Alec Thomson was in his house perched atop Cape Beale's rocky headland as the *Bruce 1* groped toward the security of Trevor Channel on that dirty February night. Assistant keeper Mike Slater lived next door.

Thomson: I was sitting in our living room when a boat went past our window and turned in to the inlet, and I knew it was going in the wrong place. It should go out around the breakers. So I went outside with a radar light and I was flashing it at them. They didn't see it. Then I saw their searchlight go on. The light was playing around, then I saw it flip up in the air. I thought they'd found their way so they'd turned it up out of the way or something and shut it off.

Then Mike Slater come over, knocking on the door. He had taken his dog out for its last run of the night, and the dog started to bark, then Mike heard something. He says, "There's some guy calling for help down here on the rock." I says, "Oh Jesus, it was that boat—it hit something." So we went down there with flashlights and the little radio and prowled around. And we could hear someone hollering for help. And we couldn't see them. In the meantime I'd told my wife to phone the lifeboat— tell them to get out quick.

> The lifeboat Thomson referred to was the Coast Guard's *Banfield III*, a 37-foot, self-righting vessel stationed at nearby Bamfield (originally called Banfield). Coxswain David Christney and his crew of three soon were

steaming toward the cape where Beale and his three-man crew were fighting for their lives as their vessel was demolished by an insistent sea.

Beale: The boat was laying with its starboard side against the rocks, where it was being pounded. The raft went underneath the back of the boat and came up on the starboard side and Randy, I believe, was the first person to get into the raft. I was standing on the back of the drum, which was eight or nine feet high, hanging on there.

I was ultimately swept off the boat and fortunately hit the life raft. Randy and I were both on it, trying to get the attention of the other two to get into the water and get onto the raft. We were free from the boat, and we were then washed over the rocks and turned upside down, entangled with this small nylon line which had a knife attached to it but which had us both well trapped inside the life raft.

This passage over the reef, in fact, punctured most parts of the raft. It was probably good luck that we got untangled and ended up on top of the dome of the raft. It was slowly sinking. Randy was trying to get to the shore, or wanted to, and I refused to let him go. I had left with his father's instructions to look after his son. I could see that striking out was a doomsday scenario, even that close to shore. So we clung together there like lovers. He was getting quite cold. He was a slight lad and he was certainly more hypothermic than anybody else. I just had on a heavy wool turtleneck sweater and long underwear. He did have on, I think, a Floater coat. Rusty had on a Floater coat which I'd bought for him. I don't know what Reid had on.

We were now on the inside of the reef and out of the main surge of the waves. There is a light that goes on at the top of these rafts and stays on and I was blinking it in an SOS pattern, hoping that somebody who came by might see it. We were basically there until the Coast Guard cutter came alongside.

Christney: It was snowing. Seas were probably around thirty feet. It was not a very nice night out there, that's for sure. It was blowing 25 or 30, I guess.

When we first got on scene we found a life raft right in behind the west breaker. There were two people in it. The skipper of the boat, Stan Beale, was in pretty good shape. He just sort of jumped up onto our boat. The other crewman was laying in the life raft. He was in an advanced stage of hypothermia and we had to lift him up into the boat. He had a chunk of parachute cord wrapped around his leg and that got caught around the prop, so there was a bit of a struggle there for a while until we managed to get a knife out and cut this line free. We let the raft go— never did see that again.

The skipper said there were two more people, two people missing, so we started searching. I had a 13-, 14-foot outboard-powered inflatable with me, so I had two of the crew in that, Martin Charles and Clifford Charles, sneaking a little closer in. Bob Amos was on the cutter with me.

Bob was pretty busy through most of this, trying to get this other guy back around. This was back in the days when we didn't

Lawyer Reid Dobell: "Well, hey, we're not going to make it anyway..."
Photo courtesy Reid Dobell.

know as much about hypothermia and how to treat it—didn't have the equipment that we have at the station now. So we were trying to pour hot tea into this guy. Bob could make the tea so hot that you'd have to hold it with a tea towel—you couldn't hold the cup. You could just pour it down this guy's throat. He still didn't seem to be restoring very well. It was like there was no bones in his body. He was sitting on a settee there, and you had to hold your hand against his chest or his body would just sort of slither down onto the floor.

I remembered that our engine room runs at about 140 degrees air temperature, so I said to Bob, "Can you get him in the engine room?" Something clicked in my mind that really warm air is what he needed to help him come back as quick as possible. So Bob got him in the engine room and lay him on the floor between the two engines. Bob had to stay with him because it was pretty rough and he could have got hurt in there pretty easily. After about fifteen or twenty minutes in the engine room he started coming around.

The guys in the other boat managed to get in close enough to the big rock. They came back and notified me that there was at least one person on the rock but they couldn't get close enough to hear what was going on—whether they were both there or not. The sea was breaking right to the top of the rock, and it's a big high rock. I guess he got washed up there somehow. He hit something solid and just started climbing.

I passed this information on to Rescue Centre [Rescue Coordination Centre (RCC), Victoria], and that's when the US Coast Guard got involved. They'd heard about this and they'd volunteered their services. They flew one of their helicopters up from the Port Angeles station up to Neah Bay. They had a Sikorsky sitting there but they were a little reluctant to come up because it was snowing and conditions were bad, plus it was an area they'd never been in before. But when they heard that we knew where somebody was, and there was somebody alive, they said to hell with the weather and came up anyway.

Dobell: Because we didn't know this rubber life raft had inflated, we were going to launch the big wooden herring skiff on the back. The waves were crashing over top of us, and you just had to hold on to anything you could while a wave crashed over you. By this time your hands are so cold you can't untie anything. It was just impossible. There was nothing to do—it couldn't be done.

I grabbed hold of the boom. The first wave took off my socks, and I held on with my arms around the boom. Holding on like that, every time a wave came over me I floated a little bit farther up the boom, toward the mast. I assume that Rusty must have done the same thing, because he floated up to the mast before I did. He was climbing the rat lines up to the top of the mast and I was climbing up after him. The waves are still coming over top of us, and after a very short time I couldn't hold on—your hands are absolutely frozen—and I just washed off the boat.

I was wearing a thigh-length down ski parka and it was unzipped, so when I washed over, it flips up over top of my head. I'm thrashing around trying to get this thing out of my face. I don't know how long I do that—for a few minutes at least.

While I'm flailing away like this I feel something solid and I think it's a piece of wreckage, so I grab it. And it's in fact a rock. So I grab hold of this rock. It's just a tiny rock, and then there's about five feet of water and then there's a tiny islet. Not very big at all—maybe thirty feet, forty feet out of the water. Something like that. It was one of the hardest things I had to do: get back into the water and go that five feet, ten feet to get to this bigger rock. But I did it and climbed up the side of this and I got to the top, and I found a little hole in the top. And I just curled up in a ball and sat there.

I had bare feet and ice was forming on the tops of my feet. Pretty soon I was feeling pretty warm. I had read something not that long before, probably in *Pacific Yachting*, about hypothermia. And I realized that I was going into hypothermia. So I was forcing myself, every little bit, every ten minutes, fifteen minutes, something like that, to stamp my feet, keep moving, stuff like that, 'til I could get the blood moving again.

First of all I was scared because I didn't know whether we were at low tide or whether high tide was going to drown me. That was one of my concerns. The other concern was, I didn't know whether I would ever be found, whether we ever got a signal off or not, so whether or not anybody would even be looking for us. And third, because I had absolutely no feeling in my feet whatsoever, I was dead certain that I was going to have both feet amputated. I was sure of that. I didn't have any feeling in my feet for maybe three months afterwards.

I think we went down about eight o'clock at night. That would be my guess. After about a couple of hours I see this light coming toward this islet. So I'm up there waving, and they shine the light directly on me, and then they start shining it down around the wreckage. And I think they're goddamn salvagers and they don't care a damn about me. So I'm swearing a blue streak at these sons of bitches that are more worried about what they can salvage than saving my life.

Then the boat buggers off. And I'm just cursing and swearing and I get back in my hole. I guess about an hour or so after, I hear this whap, whap, whap. It's a helicopter, and they come over with what they call a Midnight Sun light and it lights up everything. I'm up there waving and they sit right above me indicating they know I'm there, and then they bugger off. And I don't think much of them, either.

About fifteen minutes later they come back. I presume they were looking for the other people. They already saw me and they went off to see if they could find somebody else. Back comes the helicopter, and they've got this toboggan out, and they're lowering it as they're coming toward me. And they bang it on the rock, which is very smart, because these things build up tremendous static electricity and can easily electrocute you if you grab it without them grounding it first.

It bounced off the rock and I grabbed it and jumped into it. And up I go. I get hauled in there. They strip off all my clothes down to my red underwear, and they give me a nice pair of matching neoprene booties from their wet gear, their diving suits. They wrap me in a blanket. And it's nice and warm in the helicopter because of the warmth from the engines. And they go searching. They're backing this helicopter into tiny ravines along the shore, scaring the Bejesus out of me.

When I had first washed up on the rock I heard Rusty yelling. I yelled that I was okay, I was on a rock. He said that he was on a rock, and he yelled at me, "Come on over to my rock." No goddamn way! I was quite happy with the rock I was on. I wasn't going back in there.

So when they got me in the helicopter I told this to them— that I'd heard him yelling. It wasn't far from my rock and I had a fairly good idea of where he was in relationship to the Cape Beale light.

They gave me a pair of headphones so that I could listen to their conversation and also direct them while they're searching around in all these ravines. They can't find the rock that Rusty was on. The pilot can't see anything—he can't turn on any lights 'cause he gets vertigo from the snow. So what's happening is that one of the crewmen from the helicopter is leaning out the door with the spotlight and telling him how far he is from the water. I'm listening to a conversation that goes something like: "A hundred feet, fifty feet, thirty feet, UP! UP! UP! UP!" Up would go the helicopter. They're just scaring the shit out of me.

We go through this, I guess for probably half an hour. Then they're running out of fuel.

Christney: The closest place the helicopter could get fuel was the Tofino airport. They came up with a course, but all they had with them was an aeronautical map that didn't have much detail as far as elevations and so on. They charted a course direct from there to the airport and had me check that on the marine chart. I told them that there was a bit of a hill—I forget how high it was—and that they'd better be flying at least that high or they were going to smack right into it on their way to the airport.

Dobell: We get up to 200 feet, we get snow in the intake and the helicopter falls out of the sky. It comes crashing down and I think, Oh my God, here we go again. From what I understand they let the blades freewheel all the way down, and then just before they hit the ground they throw on the collective, which grabs the air. So we go all the way down, and then all of a sudden we start going up. And I think, Shit, they got it going again! And then plunk, in the water. Just as a matter of interest, they told me they'd tried that manoeuvre one week before and had broken the tail off a helicopter. But this time he did it right.

So there we are sitting just off Cape Beale, which is sheer rock cliff, in these waves. The inflation goes immediately into effect and they send out an SOS. It's bobbing quite nicely and the doors are wide open—we're not taking on any water at all. They give me one of these inflatable life jackets and instructions about when the helicopter capsizes: go underneath the bottom rather than up where the blades are, otherwise the blades are going to slash your flotation and you'll drown. I was saying, "Well, hey, we're not going to make it anyway..."

Christney: They hit the water and Alec Thomson, the lighthouse keeper, called me. I had no idea what had happened, because they were around the corner from me, and you can't hear anything with the big diesels running in the boat anyways.

Thomson: We called the chopper and he said, "We conked out. We're immobilized." Something like that. The lifeboat was way out on the outside, so I called them and said, "Hey, you'd better get in here." They said, "Can we get in through here?" I said, "Yah, come on in—I'll guide you through the reef." So they come in, and I was telling them to go to the left, go to the right ...

Christney: We didn't have much choice as far as I was concerned. There was people who needed help so we went in there and picked them up. It was a little dicey getting in. We took a breaker broadside going in—just lifted me right up on the rocks. At one point the boat was up on the curl of the breaker right flat

A US Coast Guard Sikorsky crashed at Cape Beale shortly after plucking Reid Dobell from his wave-pounded rock pinnacle.
Painting by Graham Wragg.

on its side. I was looking straight down through the window and all I could see was bare rock. And all I thought was, This is going to be one hell of a crush. Just then the water flowed in underneath us and kicked me sideways for forty or fifty feet. No contact.

I had a spotlight on the bow, and a wave had hit that and kicked it up in the air so I couldn't see worth a darn. My crewman Clifford had gone out to bend it back around—get it aimed right. He was halfway back to the cabin door when we got caught in that breaker. I thought he was going to get washed overboard. When we came out of there he was hanging on to an antenna and the rail on the front of the boat for dear life.

But we still had to get out of there. I knew that these boats were not made to take breaking seas on the beam, but they certainly are built to take it head on. So I just turned right into it and popped up through the breaker. Then I was clear of that and could see the helicopter.

Martin and Clifford got back in the inflatable—I was towing it again at this time—and I remember as they were jumping in on one side I looked up and saw one of the helicopter blades. It's above the foredeck. I've got my bow underneath this thing, and it's heading straight for the wheelhouse window. So I had to holler at them that I was going to have to reverse. They sort of hung on and I backed away, then got their boat away.

On one surge the helicopter had actually gone up and caught one of the landing wheels on the shore and hung on for a second until the wheel broke off and they surged back out. They had the side door open and Clifford just drove the boat right into the side door.

Dobell: We bobbed there for, I guess, half an hour anyway. Then all of a sudden this Zodiac pulls up to the door of the helicopter and we just dove into it: bang, bang, bang, bang. Get in the Zodiac and go to the Coast Guard lifeboat—the main one. Get in that, and they just gun it right over the reef, the same way they got it in.

Christney: A big seine boat, the *Nucleus*, was coming up the coast and the skipper was a fellow I knew. He phoned and asked if he could be of any assistance and I asked him to stand by out there. He asked me, "Are you getting out of there now?" And I said, "Yah, as soon as I can figure out which way's out." I was so disoriented from crashing around in those seas.

I called up Alec Thomson and said, "This is your front yard. Can you see us now?" And he said, "Yah." I said, "Can you see the lights of the *Nucleus* out there?" And he said, "Yah." I said, "Can I just go straight for him?" He said. "You should be able to." He'd actually helped guide me in through the breakers as well. So I headed straight out into the sound.

I was concerned about the guy who had hypothermia because he still wasn't very good. I really wanted to get him in for medical attention. I was also concerned that I was getting an awful lot of people on board the boat now, as far as carrying on the search. I asked permission from Rescue Centre to go back in to Bamfield and drop them off at the hospital. They said, "Sure," so I went in, dropped them off and came back out again to carry on the search for Rusty Waters. By this time, as we're heading back out, the Buffalo aircraft from [Canadian Forces Base] 442 Squadron in Comox was there dropping flares and they've got

The *Banfield III* lifeboat.
Painting by Graham Wragg.

the whole place lit up, so now I can see and get into all kinds of places.

I went into Mud Bay with the lifeboat, and I went to reverse out of there and there was only half power. Bill Amos went down into the engine room, and he came back up and said, "You might as well shut it off." I said, "Why?" He said, "Well, you broke a hydraulic line and you've got a fine spray of hydraulic oil spraying all over the hot manifold."

I shut that engine down and went to back out of there with the other one, then notified Rescue Centre that I was having mechanical problems. They stood me down and said, "Get back into Bamfield." As soon as I got out of there into clear water and went to speed up again with number one engine, everything started shuddering and shaking. We had part of a life jacket and about forty feet of rope all wrapped up in the prop. The stuff was everywhere. We managed to get in to Bamfield. We still had the old wooden lifeboat, so we turned around and went back out with it. By this time it's just starting to break daylight.

Thomson: They had to go back to Bamfield for the old boat. And this guy's still hollering for help, getting weaker all the time. You could hear it getting pretty weak. We couldn't do a thing— you're stuck on land, you can't move. I'm sure it was on the cliffs. After that I got a trail cut to the cliffs so you could get right up to the edge.

The lifeboat came out, prowled around some more, and then no more voice. The next day they found a green life vest or jacket pulled inside out. They never did find Rusty Waters.

Christney: I forget what time we broke off from there, because the aircraft had spotted a 34-foot gillnetter upside down about five miles off the lighthouse. So we went out, found that and brought that in. We didn't get back in until about eleven o'clock that night. It was a pretty slow tow. We were twenty-two hours from when we originally went out—twenty-two hours underway.

Dobell: Two things I learned from that. One is that when push comes to shove, when you're in that kind of situation, it's not every man for himself. It just doesn't happen. Nobody was trying to get any advantage over the other.

The second thing is that even when you know there isn't a prayer of surviving, you fight for every last second. I was single—still am single—and I had no spouse, no kids, no one that I had to live for. I had no obligations to anybody. But you fight for every last second, no matter how ridiculous it seems.

Beale: To me this had a dramatic impact on my life. It's something that's with me every day. But if any good can come out of this I would suggest that anybody at sea at any time should always have with them, on their person, a light of some nature. Because when all the lights go out on the boat and you're out there, it's as black as it can ever get. You can't see anything. Even the smallest little penlight would have brought attention from others to Rusty.

Bamfield Coast Guard coxswain David Christney and his three crew members all received lifesaving medals from the American military and Stars of Courage from the Canadian government. Christney recently retired after thirty-two years of Coast Guard service.

Alec Thomson is now retired and living on Vancouver Island. He was commended by the Canadian Coast Guard for his role in the rescue. In addition to alerting Bamfield Coast Guard to the shipwreck and guiding Christney through the Cape Beale reef line, Thomson, with the help of his wife, Phyllis, played impromptu host to the seventeen-man salvage crew which the American military sent in to recover what they could of their downed, drowned Sikorsky. After helicoptering in to Cape Beale light, the salvage crew was pinned down by a snowstorm and spent the night in the Thomson home. From what the Americans recovered, it appears that the Sikorsky crashed as a result of mechanical failure.

Stanley Beale did not return to fishing after the loss of the *Bruce 1*. He is now the president of Consolidated Van Anda Gold Ltd. of Vancouver. Reid Dobell, now semi-retired, lives in the Fraser Valley. On the twentieth anniversary of being rescued, he phoned the Bamfield Life Boat Station's answering machine and reminded the people there that he hadn't forgotten their service to him.

Thirty-Seven Hours in a Skiff

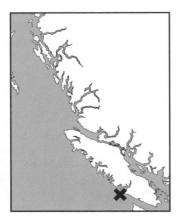

Thirty-Seven Hours in a Skiff

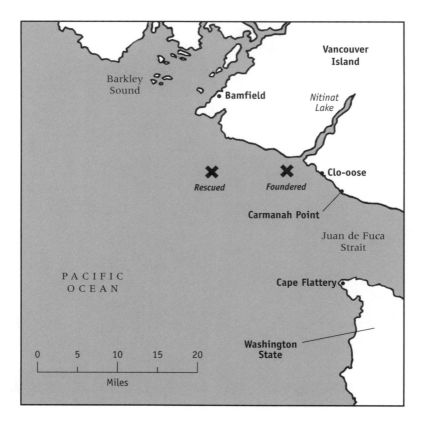

SEARCHERS WERE STILL SCOURING
THE RUGGED CAPE BEALE shoreline for Rusty Waters of
the *Bruce 1* when, only miles away, the 35-foot gillnetter
Star Shine was overwhelmed by mountainous stern seas,
forcing skipper Harold Wulff and deckhand Trent
Hansen to abandon ship. It was the beginning of two
calamitous weeks in the 1976 west coast roe herring
fishery—two weeks during which fourteen fishermen
lost their lives.

Hansen was making his first excursion as a commercial fisherman; Wulff got his start commercial fishing
early enough that he can't put an accurate age to it. He
bought his first vessel when he was fifteen, "a 26-footer,
an old wreck of a boat," named *Quetzacoatl* in honour of
the legendary Aztec plumed serpent. His father, also
Harold Wulff, began gillnetting salmon as a twelve-year-
old; at seventy-eight, that's what he still does.

Hansen: I'd known Harold all my life, and I'd been wanting to
try this. He said, "Well, we're going out on the herring. That
would be as good a place as any to start, I guess. Why don't you
come out on this trip?" I said, "Fine." So away we went.

Wulff: We were travelling with some other guys. Not the real
buddy system, but there was a whole bunch of boats travelling,
some ahead, some behind. One of the boats we'd met in Victoria
was having some engine trouble, and was going to continue on
that evening. We went on ahead in the morning.

It was normal, nice weather, and the forecast was good.
After dark we got up by Port Renfrew. As soon as dark came it
began to blow, I suppose it would be southeast, on our stern. We
got past Carmanah, and the wind kept picking up and up.
Eventually I believe it was over 55, 60 knots, against the tide.

We got off Clo-oose and the weather picked up. It was really rough seas, and we took a wave over the stern. Gillnet boats
have a real open, low stern, so you can hold a lot of water if you

take water in there. That filled the stern up. And of course you lose buoyancy if your stern's way down. Trent was sleeping at the time. I woke him up and said, "The boat's not responding right. It feels heavy."

I looked outside, and the next wave came right up the deck and into the wheelhouse. Time to abandon ship.

The first thing I thought about was ... we've got a one-inch towline—probably a 50-, 60-fathom poly towline to the skiff. I was worried about the boat sinking and dragging us down. I grabbed a knife. In hindsight I should have grabbed a flashlight and a knife. I waded out to the stern, up to my waist in water. And of course the waves are breaking over it. The line was tied quite low, so I had to reach right down underwater to grab the towline.

Harold Wulff.
Peter A. Robson photo.

The deck would go dry, then the waves would break and the next one would come over and through the boat. I just started pulling the skiff hand over hand up alongside the boat—in record time. I was really, really pumped up with adrenaline. Everything's going up and down—our boat's up, the skiff is down, and so on. I told Trent, "The next time the skiff is down, dive in." We were up on top of the hatch coaming; it's about a three-foot coaming.

He dove in, head first into the skiff. On the next swell I dove in. At that time the boat was almost completely submerged. We got ahold of the towline. The wind's just screaming. I'm yelling at him, "We've got to get the towline!" I was concerned about the boat going down and dragging the skiff under. That was my major concern.

When we got the line—it was really, really hard to hang on to the line—between the two of us, between the swells, we tied it around a stanchion. We figured we'd just let it go or cut the line if the boat decides to sink. By the time we did all that just the top of the wheelhouse was showing. We could see the waves smashing against the wheelhouse. The windows were coming out. You could smell propane—the propane tanks had been washed right off the roof. They were bolted down; it just smashed them right off.

The swell was so heavy, the line was jerking like crazy. The skiff would bang at the end of the line, then ride up. Then bang again. 'Cause basically the boat was just a stationary thing in the water—a sea anchor. I don't know what the time frame would be. We were maybe half an hour banging like that. I realized the boat wasn't going to sink. I thought we were doing okay—at least we were still alive. I figured in the morning somebody would come by. But even with all that towline, it still broke. I thought, Oh boy—here we go.

There was no outboard on the skiff. In those days—and some guys still do it—when they travelled they'd take the outboards off and all the fuel tanks and everything. After that we always did, and still do, leave the outboard on the skiff. If we had had the outboard on there we could have been into Bamfield in about half an hour.

We had a coffee can for bailing. That was our total equipment. I was wearing a T-shirt, one of those lumberjack shirts, blue jeans, socks and no shoes. I have a habit, when I'm steering the boat, of always taking my shoes off—it's nice and warm with the oil stove on the boat.

It's blowing very, very hard, and the wind was pushing us farther and farther out to sea. Possibly an hour later I could see a boat coming. I didn't know at the time, but it was the boat that had stayed behind in Victoria, good family friends. I could see running lights—both red and green. Once in a while it would go red, and once in a while it would go green: the boat was wallowing, because it was blowing so hard.

I thought, If he keeps coming he's going to smash right into us. But I thought, Oh well, the skiffs are pretty wide and low. It'll probably just hit, the skiff will spin around, and they'll come and get us. Just at the last second the boat took a big wallow. I could see the name of the boat: the *Premier*. At the time it was Eric Arkko's vessel. I still fish with his son, Glen; we travel together.

Eric's since retired. At the time he had a deckhand with him whose name was Bert Lamden.

We were screaming at the top of our lungs. If we'd have had anything to throw we could have thrown it right through the wheelhouse window, no problem. But it's pitch black, blowing, raining. I think there was sleet, too. Terrible conditions. They passed us within forty feet. They were gone.

Later in the night we could see another white light coming—big. Same thing. This time it was a freighter coming. By this time we'd been pushed out more, into the freighter lanes. Trent and I were talking back and forth. I said, "This is really not good. If we get hit by this freighter ... they don't see nothin'. They wouldn't even know it."

Hansen: We saw these lights coming. I looked up and I thought, Are we getting closer to shore? I thought maybe it was a lighthouse or something. We kept looking and looking. This thing kept getting closer and closer—really fast. Then all of a sudden, out of the gloom, this freighter shows up. It was headed straight for us. I thought it was going to hit us.

Wulff: It was the same thing: we could see the red and the green wavering back and forth. They just slid right by us. They passed us I'd say about 300 feet away. I remember a big black hull, wheelhouse amidships, booms fore and aft—older style.

Hansen: I remember we went up on a wave and we could look in through the portholes and see pipes running along the ceiling. We were that close.

Wulff: It was very, very cold. I was saying to Trent that with the hypothermia we wouldn't last all that long. We had to get warm. We were on the outside of the skiff. We stayed there. We huddled down where the guys stand to shake [the net] in a herring skiff. We put our arms around each other, trying to conserve warmth.

A little bit later that evening we could see flares going off. I didn't say anything to Trent, but I thought, That's strange, did somebody find the *Star Shine*? But I thought that was crazy, 'cause it was over and a few miles away. It didn't make sense. At that time I didn't realize it was the *Bruce 1*. At the time it just didn't seem right.

We were drifting and getting colder. In the bow of the skiff there's a flotation tank. It's a pretty little room, but it's got a little opening in it for storage. You can throw life jackets and stuff in it. Of course there were no life jackets there.

I says to Trent, "We'll climb up inside there. At least we'll get out of the wind." He put his arm in, and his head and shoulder, squeezed in there—he got up inside. That's fine. I'm pretty hefty right now, and I was even heftier then. I was 312 pounds or something like that. I thought, I'll try to get in there. I got my arm in. They say once you get your shoulder and head in you can get in, and I squeezed up in there. It was pretty cozy then— cramped. That's what saved our bacon. It got us out of the wind. There was a little lid. I took the lid inside, turned it around and hooked it up—just left enough for an air space.

The only cold part then was that you're against aluminum that's against cold water. But it wasn't so bad. We were huddled together. I had my arms around Trent, his around me, and we were just huddled as tight as we could hug each other, to conserve heat. You're trying to think of all this stuff—survival stuff. It's amazing what you can do when things happen like that. That was the first night, up in there.

Although Wulff and Hansen couldn't have known it, the crew of a passing aircraft had spotted the *Star Shine* drifting eight kilometres off Cape Beale. David Christney and the crew of the *Banfield III*, having been called off of the *Bruce 1* search for Rusty Waters, ended a twenty-two-hour shift by towing the gillnetter to shore. Divers verified that neither man's body was trapped inside the overturned hull.

That night, while Wulff and Hansen shivered in the skiff's minuscule bow compartment, the Coast Guard's on-scene commander, Captain Monty Montgomery, spoke by phone with both men's families. He explained that he was preparing to declare an all-out search the following day. Both fathers advised Montgomery that, should more emergencies develop, he should not risk others' lives by continuing to search for their sons if he concluded that further searching was futile. True to his word, the following day Montgomery expanded the search area and threw every available vessel and aircraft into the operation.

Wulff:　　Come daylight we got out. The wind had gone down. By this time we were quite a ways off shore. We could look and see the mountains down Barkley Sound. We could see Cape Flattery. We're going a long ways off shore. I thought, Okay, they should be looking for us.

I could see search aircraft in toward land. Being a fisherman I knew they fly grid patterns, and I could see them flying a grid, but way inside of us. I think it was a Buffalo. I guess we were probably on the next grid out. He was coming right for us. I'd say they came within two and a half miles. If they'd have kept going for another ten seconds or so they'd have flown right over us. I took my red mackinaw and flapped it. Then it did a steep bank, and they flew away—kept flying the grid pattern. That was really painful to watch. An aluminum herring skiff's very hard to spot from the air—I've been told that. I could see how they could miss us from a couple of miles away. But at least I knew they were out looking.

An oil-soaked duck came along, so we grabbed him, threw him in the skiff—we rescued that. So that was the second day.

I thought, Okay, they've gone through that grid, tomorrow they'll fly the next grid out. The wind had gone down, and it switched to I think northwesterly, and we started to get blown in a little bit. I thought, At least we're not going out to sea any more.

We tried to get as much warmth as we could. There was a little bit of warmth from the sun, so we sat out, trying to get our body temperature a little warmer. Stayed down low out of the breeze. As soon as it got darkish we went back up inside to keep warm again. The second night was uneventful. We'd peek out once in a while—couldn't see any ships or anything. The next morning we could hear a helicopter: thump, thump, thump, thump. As soon as I heard it—Trent's a lot more slender than me—I said, "You get out first."

Master Corporal R.J. (Soup) Campbell, airborne in a helicopter from Canadian Forces Base Comox's 442 search and rescue squadron, was the first to spot the drifting skiff. Campbell, now retired and living in Sidney, recalls the weekend of this rescue as "a pretty rough one—boats sinking all over the place. At the time we didn't know just how many people were missing, and how many boats."

Wulff: Trent skinned himself getting out. He got out there and started waving. I squeezed my way out. The wind was picking up more and more. But the chopper came—a Labrador—and they saw us. We were waving to them. We could see the guys looking out the little portholes, waving. They dropped smoke flares all the way around us—four points. The Buffalo came, and he did a few passes over. I can tell you it was quite a feeling; I cried for a long time.

Campbell: We were really just running a pattern from a little bit of altitude. Of course the skiff was pretty low in the water, and from a distance you don't see nothin'. I just seen—like a log in the water—you just see a little bit of a line, like a tideline or a windline.

I just happened to look a way off in the distance. I said, "We've got something way over there in the water." The people all looked and said, "It's probably just a log or something like that." They were going to motor on. And I said, "Oh no, let's go over and have a look at it." You always play it safe. Sure enough, there it was.

Wulff: They were really happy to see us, they'd lost so many people. I wasn't sure if they had a harness for lifting us off with the Labrador or not. But on the horizon we could see the Coast Guard coming. I'm not sure if it was the *Racer* or the *Ready*. It was one or the other.

> It was the Coast Guard cutter *Ready*, under Montgomery's command. When Campbell had spotted the skiff from his helicopter, Hansen and Wulff had drifted outside Montgomery's expanded search area—hopelessly beyond the limits of the original search area. "You talk about feeling good after making a decision," Montgomery said recently when reflecting on the *Star Shine* search. "It was one of those times that you're glad to be doing your job."

Wulff: By that time the weather had picked up, and there was a big, big swell running. The Coast Guard cutter came alongside, threw us a line. When the swell picked the skiff up they grabbed Trent. I said, "You go first." He put his arms up and they grabbed his arms. And of course the skiff dropped away by ten or twelve feet; he's dangling there. Luckily the guys on the Coast Guard boat hauled him up.

Then it was my turn. Hanging onto me ... I'm hanging onto the guard rails and a cable, and I got on. They said, "What do you want to do with the skiff?" I said, "Leave it. Let her go. It's too crazy to try to hook on to it." So we just took off.

Montgomery: To get them in to medical attention right away I just cut the skiff adrift. I wasn't going to try to tow it. Later on I got in trouble with their insurance company over it. Another fisherman towed it in and laid a claim on it, and the insurance company was going to lay a claim on me for having abandoned it. The usual garbage.

Wulff: The skiff was found by a fellow from Ladner. He claimed salvage on it. We were fishing for the Canadian Fishing Company at that time, so I just left it up to them. They looked after all that for us; we got it back. I've still got it.

Montgomery: They were in pretty rough shape. Their feet were swollen. They had immersion foot and everything else. Of course they had hypothermia. We took them down, treated them for hypothermia.

Hansen: I had no feeling in my feet. I remember that when they got me on the Coast Guard boat they had to help me down the stairs 'cause I had no feeling from the ankles down. I couldn't feel anything when I stepped.

Those guys on the Coast Guard boat were great. They couldn't do enough for us. They wanted to know what we wanted, if there was anything they could get for us. The first thing I wanted to do was have a hot shower.

They wanted to get us something to eat, but it was funny, I didn't have much of an appetite. I seems to me it was three or four days before I could handle anything you could call a substantial meal.

Wulff: I think we had a shower, a warm shower—not too warm. A guy stood there and made sure we didn't get too much. They gave us warm clothing. They took us to the galley, and I think we had some soup—the best tasting soup. After going that long without they didn't want to give us meat and potatoes. We just rested in the galley on the way in.

We got in to Bamfield. Trent's feet were so screwed up, they carried him up on a stretcher to the Bamfield hospital. Trent had these hiking style boots—something like that. Having them on for that length of time ... his feet got so cold. I found out later, from Trent's doctors, I was actually better off—that he would have been better off without the boots on. They were so wet, and I guess his feet must have swelled in there, caused damage.

Hansen: I was on crutches for about three weeks after that. I still have trouble with my feet. It's only my left foot. My right foot seems to be fine.

Master Cpl. R.J. (Soup) Campbell: "That weekend was a pretty rough one—boats sinking all over the place."
Photo courtesy R.J. Campbell.

Wulff: It's a great hospital in Bamfield, run by the women's auxiliary there. They were so nice—such nice ladies. They put us into bed. The RCMP came and spoke with us for a while.

After we were in the hospital for a while the Labrador came in—landed at the Coast Guard station. They transported us to Victoria General Hospital.

There was a guy from CBC on the helicopter. He asked lots of questions, then he left us alone. When we got to the heliport at the hospital in Victoria, they had an ambulance there and there was lots of press there then. Lots of cameras. They were asking, "Are you going to go fishing again?" All that kind of stuff.

The Coast Guard cutter *Ready*, where Harold Wulff and Trent Hansen were treated to hot soup and a warm shower after being rescued.
Photo courtesy Monty Montgomery.

I just said, "Yes." That evening we were on the national news. I remember watching myself on TV being interviewed. That seemed so unreal.

Hansen: I think what we were most worried about was our families—what our families were thinking. Our parents came over and picked us up from the hospital in Victoria. I remember riding back on the ferry and Nellie, Harold's mom, saying she hadn't slept a wink for two nights straight. She just walked the floor all night. My parents the same. That was the worst for me.

Wulff: When we were out there we could imagine what everybody was going through. But my brother and my dad said they didn't believe that we were gone. 'Cause when they found the *Star Shine* the next morning they stated that there was no skiff. But a lot of people felt that we were gone.

The *Star Shine* was towed in by one of the Coast Guard lifeboats to Bamfield. They didn't know at the time if our bodies were inside. They towed it in to Ostroms'.

The Coast Guard sent divers down, and of course we weren't in there. That was good news—they reported that to my parents and my brother. They got the boat up, pumped it all out. Ostroms secured the boat, nailed plywood over the windows. We went about two weeks later to pick it up. We wanted to settle up with them. They wouldn't take any money at all. No charge whatsoever. Such fine people.

Today Captain Monty Montgomery is retired and living in Qualicum Beach. Montgomery began his Coast Guard career in 1956 as a mess boy on the lighthouse tender *Estevan*, served on all three R-class cutters and retired off the *George E. Darby* in 1991. One of his last major assignments on the *Darby* saw him escorting the oil tanker *Exxon Valdez* through the Canadian economic zone as it limped south for repairs after spilling its cargo of Alaskan crude into Prince William Sound.

Master Cpl. R.J. (Soup) Campbell, now retired from military service, lives in Sidney, BC.

Harold Wulff fishes herring and salmon from the 33-foot gillnetter *Joanie*, and fishes shrimp from the 32-foot *Little Ocean*, which he owns with a partner. He lives in Gibsons. Trent Hansen chose never to make a second commercial fishing trip. He lives in the Lower Mainland, where he works as a grocery clerk.

Hansen: I don't know how many guys I've talked to who have this romantic attitude about fishing. I imagine it can be like that. I talk to people, and they go up north fishing, and they say, "Well geez, Trent, it's so nice." But by God, if you get caught in some dirty weather ... it doesn't become so romantic then. It's a matter of life and death. And then it's not fun at all. Not fun at all.

He is
Her
Sunshine
(And
Vice
Versa)

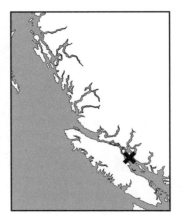

He is Her Sunshine
(And Vice Versa)

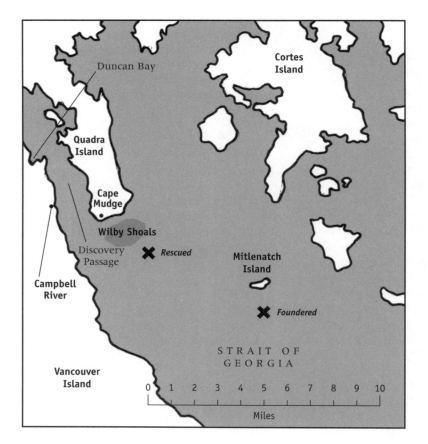

BRENT MELAN AND HIS BROTHERS
SEEM TO HAVE developed an uneasy relationship with
the waters around Campbell River. It began when
Brent's brothers ran aground there in their father's boat,
the *Lennie Jane*. It ended, at least for the time being, in
September of 1996 when Melan's older brother Frank
had a loaded halibut boat, the *Chelsey Dawn*, sink out
from under him within ten minutes of hearing the bilge
alarm sound. Those two events bracketed Brent Melan's
own misadventure, which took place on April 25, 1990,
a stone's throw from the spot where the *Chelsey Dawn*
was lost, as he made a night run in deteriorating weather from Westview (Powell River) across the northern
Strait of Georgia.

Brent Melan: My brothers had had the *Lennie Jane* to use as a
live-aboard during the roe herring fishery. They'd run aground
close to Campbell River, and the boat had been in Vancouver for
repairs. My dad was sick, so I offered to take the boat home for
him.

I left from Vancouver in the afternoon, and I run as far as
Westview. I was going to visit my uncle and aunt, Les and Cindy
Melan. I had a nice dinner with them—spent the evening with
them, then I went back down to the boat and listened to the
weather forecast. It was forecast to come up to about 25 southeast, which to me is not a bad wind. They had storm warnings
out for the north end of Vancouver Island, but the Strait of
Georgia was a small craft warning, which is no problem.

I went to leave for Campbell River, but I had a problem with
the hydraulics, and I fixed that up. I must have left Westview
about ten-thirty, eleven at night. Everything was fine, then the
weather started to pick up. I didn't realize it was blowing that
hard. I was in the wheelhouse and travelling with the wind, and
it got rougher and rougher—a following sea. I just started running slower. It felt almost like you were riding on a surfboard.
One wave caught the boat, picked the stern up, and she started

to lay down. She broached—lay down on her starboard side. That's the side of the cabin that the door's on. I had the bottom half of the door closed. The top half was open three or four inches. I could see water was starting to come in there, so I was trying to close this door to keep the water out. There were ropes hanging in, jamming it, but I got the door closed.

Also on that side of the cabin there's a vent that goes through the side of the cabin up close to the ceiling—for the stove. Water started coming in through there. I could see I was in trouble. I gave a Mayday call on Channel 16, Channel 78. The boat was completely on its side by this time. I was trying to look into the radar to see where I was. I couldn't see much. I knew I was a mile or so from Mitlenatch.

We'd really put that boat through its paces, all up and down the coast. It'd been on its side before—but it had always come back. That time, when it was on its side, I had deep faith that the boat was coming back. But after that first wave hit it and knocked it down in the water, another big one came along and just buried it.

I had time to more or less climb up the cabin, out through the window, and walk around the hull. The boat just kept going over. Finally she was upside down. The lights came on—all the deck lights. You could see the glow underwater. The salt water had completed the circuits. The engine was still idling, but it quit soon after that. I said to myself, You're in quite a mess here. You've really done it this time.

At approximately one in the morning, Comox Coast Guard Radio picked up a faint and incomplete VHF radio signal. Though uncertain of the transmitting vessel's name, and unable to fix its precise location, the Rescue Coordination Centre (RCC) in Victoria initiated a needle-in-the-haystack search which featured Melan as the needle in a haystack that encompassed much of British Columbia's south coast.

The task of finding the source of the Mayday was sufficiently challenging that the RCC has developed a training exercise in which new personnel attempt to solve the mystery that their colleagues struggled to unravel that stormy spring night.

While Melan balanced precariously on the *Lennie Jane*'s overturned and wave-rocked hull, Captain Dyke

Brent Melan awaiting rescue: "I stood up all night, dancing around."
Painting by Graham Wragg.

Noel and his crew waited aboard the tug *Comox Crown* while the barge they were about to take under tow was loaded at Fletcher Challenge's Duncan Bay pulp mill. Noel heard and responded to the RCC's request for assistance, and soon had the 65-foot tug southbound toward Cape Mudge, the spot that he considers the most treacherous of BC's inside waters. Noel, who has since gone on to become a BC coast pilot, began his marine career as a Coast Guard deckhand.

Noel: It was quite an ugly night out that night. They reported the boat rolling over right at Cape Mudge light. I gather that he got a Mayday call out as the boat was rolling over—he was going out the wheelhouse door with the mike in his hand.

The *Lennie Jane*.
Photo courtesy Brent Melan.

We're quite familiar with the tides around that area. There's a huge back eddy at Cape Mudge. They said it would be a while before they could get the Coast Guard crew down to the rescue boat, so we just took off and headed out there.

We worked the tideline. We figured he'd be along there somewhere. We zigzagged back and forth. I thought he might have gone in to the shallow water, so we went in there with the depth sounder on, going back and forth over Wilby Shoals.

We knew where he said he went over, but it was very poor visibility; I think it was a quarter of a mile or less ... heavy rain and mist. Dirty weather.

Melan: I had a pair of blue jeans on, a long-sleeved shirt and one of those fibre-filled vests. And running shoes. It was blowing quite hard, and waves were slapping against the hull.

On the stern of the boat there's a four- or six-man Beaufort life raft. I'm a good swimmer—I was in competitive swimming, so I'm quite comfortable in the water. I stripped all my clothes off, put them on the keel of the boat, and tried to dive down to this life raft. By that time it would be about ten, twelve feet down under water, and I couldn't get down to it. Plus I got worried about getting tangled up in lines. I could see I couldn't get it. I climbed back up, put my clothes back on. And my keys fell out of my pocket, started skittering across the hull. I grabbed them. I said, "I'm going to need these."

The boat started settling down more and more in the water. It was amazing how peaceful it was out there. The wind was blowing and it was raining, but it was quiet. And you could hear the birds—it was amazing how much bird life there is out there.

I could see Campbell River, the Cape Mudge lighthouse—all

that kind of stuff. And after a while I could see a helicopter searching.

First they'd phoned my dad's house. They thought they'd heard a Mayday from the *Lennie Jane*, so they'd wanted to know my destination, what time I'd left—all that. I guess they talked to my Uncle Les in Westview. They contacted another uncle of mine. He told them to draw a line from Westview to Campbell River and search north of that line. I was watching them search, and they were searching to the south of that line, more to the Campbell River side. It was kind of frustrating to watch. I didn't have no flares or nothing. There were survival suits on the boat. I didn't have time for that kind of thing—it went over that fast. If I would have been fumbling around for that kind of stuff I guess I would have been fighting my way out of the boat upside down.

It was blowing so hard you couldn't look straight into the wind with the rain. It stung your eyes. I more or less just kept one side to the wind—let one side get cold. All that time the boat's heaving, dipping around; I was performing a balancing act. It was hard. I stood up all night, dancing around.

One brother who lives in Black Creek—they tried to come out on a 50-foot fibreglass packer called the *Pacific Baron*, belongs to another friend of ours, but it was blowing so hard they couldn't get across the Comox Bar.

My younger brother and another friend, they had it all arranged. In the morning they were going to come and look with airplanes. I guess they were prepared for the eventuality that I was drowned, but they weren't going to give up on me just yet.

We have a song, Shelley and I: "You Are My Sunshine." I sang that. It was mind over matter. I wasn't giving up without a fight. Shelley and I had just gotten together, and I said, "I can't do this to her."

Shelley Brown: It was around one o'clock in the morning, one-thirty. The phone rang. It was Brent's sister, saying that she'd received a phone call saying that they'd had a Mayday from a boat and it sounded like the *Lennie Jane*. It was just five hours previous that Brent had phoned me, and he had been in Powell River and had dinner with his aunt and uncle. I said, "Where are you?" He said, "On the boat." I said, "Are you going to stay there for the night?" And he said, "Yeah, I think I will. Otherwise I'll press on to Campbell River."

Capt. Dyke Noel aboard the tug *Comox Crown*: "quite an ugly night out."
Photo courtesy Dyke Noel.

It was already rainy and windy and stormy here, so I was hoping that he'd stay put. So when I got this phone call and she said it was a boat that sounded like the *Lennie Jane*, I just threw up my hands and said, "If they got a call from a boat that sounded like the *Lennie Jane*, it's got to be him because he's the only one out there that would be travelling in this kind of weather."

I was here by myself. The house was dark and the night was very stormy. The first place I came was here to the sunroom, and looked out the back, and could see what the conditions were. Then I went right to the stereo and put on our favourite piece of music, which is "You Are My Sunshine."

Melan: I believe in religion. I don't go to church and all that. I prayed—called on some dead people to help me. I didn't want to die, and I knew I was close. I looked around for a piece of line to tie myself to the boat so at least they would have a body to bury.

Brown: Brent's aunt went to her window when she got her phone call in the middle of the night. She looked out and saw the weather and said to Brent's mother [Lennie Jane], who has been deceased for eighteen years now, "Jane, you put him back. Put him back right now!"

Melan: Daylight come, and one boat went by right close—it must have been fifty yards away. I was waving and hopping up and down. If I'd had rocks I would have thrown them at it. Anyway, they weren't paying attention.

It was about half an hour later, the tug, the *Comox Crown*, come right by and found me.

Noel: We spent the whole night searching. We had the crew up and two searchlights going for just about six hours before we found him. We were just about ready to give up hope. We were getting pretty tired by that point. We'd figured we'd lost him. I think Comox [Coast Guard Radio] actually told us to stand down about six-thirty in the morning. We found him over by the can buoy off Wilby Shoal. He was standing there on top of the keel, just the bottom of the boat showing. It was actually pretty hard to see it. It was just turning daylight. Coast Guard was quite upset that we got there before them.

Melan: It was still too rough for them to come alongside. They backed the stern up to the *Lennie Jane* and I jumped across onto the tug. One of the crew said to me, "How long have you been there?" I said, "What time is it?" He said, "It's six o'clock in the morn-

Brent Melan's unstable platform—the overturned *Lennie Jane*.
Photo by the crew of the *Comox Crown*, courtesy Dyke Noel.

ing." I said, "About five hours." He said, "Jeez, are you ever a tough bastard. I'd hate to get in a fight with you."

I got a shower—just a tepid shower. I know you're not supposed to jump straight into a hot shower like that. I got warmed up, and they found some dry clothes for me. I went up to the wheelhouse while we were running into Campbell River, drinking coffee and telling jokes with the captain.

Noel: When we picked him up we figured he'd be pretty cold. He goes, "Oh no, I'm fine." I said, "You'd better get into the shower there and get warmed up." He came out of that shower about forty-five minutes later, just about the time we got into the fuel dock to drop him off.

Brent Melan and Shelley Brown beside the seiner
Star Pacific, owned by Brent and his brother Bruce.
Photo courtesy Brent Melan.

Melan: When we got into the dock the Coast Guard showed
up, and a couple of my brothers were there. The Coast Guard
asked me to go to the hospital. I said, "No, I'm not going to the
hospital. I'm hungry—I haven't had breakfast."

> The *Lennie Jane* was recovered, pumped out and
> repaired. Brent Melan bought the boat from his father
> and leased it out for several seasons before selling it to
> his brother John. In addition to running the 70-foot
> seiner *Bernice C.*, named after his grandmother, Bernice
> Cadwallader, Melan is a partner with his brother Bruce
> in the seiner *Star Pacific*. In partnership with two broth-
> ers and an uncle, he is preparing the boat *Vicious Fisher*
> for tuna fishing and for the experimental offshore squid
> fishery. He lives in Burnaby with his partner Shelley
> Brown and their two young sons.
>   For the four-man crew of the *Comox Crown*, Melan's
> rescue marked the first of two bizarre nights on what
> should have been a routine run to the Lower Mainland

from Fletcher Challenge's paper mill north of Campbell River. Having delivered Melan to dry land and returned for the barge, Captain Dyke Noel crossed the strait in an effort to find some lee from the continuing heavy weather, then steered south along the mainland coast. He had guided the tug and tow to a point not far south of Westview—Melan's departure point the night before—when a twin-engine plane, also southbound, passed overhead. Noel, who is also an airplane pilot, remarked to a deckhand that it was a hell of a night for someone to be out flying. He had barely uttered the words when the plane dove into Malaspina Strait just ahead of the *Comox Crown*.

This time it was Noel's turn to radio the Coast Guard about an unfolding emergency. To his dismay, his report wasn't taken seriously until one of his crew found the plane's log among other debris illuminated by the tug's spotlight—a point at which, Noel recalls, "the shit hit the fan." The search that ensued proved futile. All three people aboard the plane—three flight instructors en route to Boundary Bay—had perished. One of them was the person who had recently purchased Noel's own plane.

Fortunately, Dan Just Kept Hopping

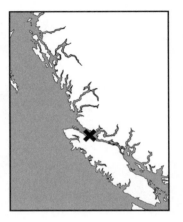

Fortunately, Dan
Just Kept Hopping

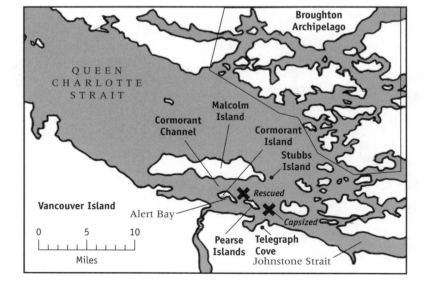

THE POPULARITY OF BOTH SEA
KAYAKING AND WHALE watching have in recent years
inspired something of a renaissance in the tiny commu-
nity of Telegraph Cove on Vancouver Island's northeast
coast. This isolated pocket, once a hub of lumber-related
activity, was on the verge of falling silent in 1979 when
the Wastell family, for decades the operators of
Telegraph Cove Sawmills, closed their antiquated operation. Taking an entrepreneurial leap of faith, employees
Bill Mackay and Jim Borrowman teamed up to launch a
venture called Stubbs Island Charters.

In addition to hauling freight and running dive charters, the pair intended to take the paying public into
Johnstone Strait to show them the killer whales for
which the area has since become world famous.
Telegraph Cove pioneer Fred Wastell, who had spent
much of his life towing logs and hauling lumber in and
around Johnstone Strait, told Mackay and Borrowman
bluntly: "Nobody's going to pay to look at those darned
blackfish." He did, however, offer to lease them his pride
and joy, the 60-foot *Gikumi*. From those humble begin-
nings Borrowman and Mackay and "those darned blackfish" have made Stubbs Island Charters a major coastal
eco-tourism attraction.

Kayakers by the thousands make pilgrimages to
Johnstone Strait to paddle among killer whales and to
explore the adjacent Broughton Archipelago, many
arriving unprepared for the rigorous conditions they're
liable to encounter. As a result, Borrowman and Mackay
have over the years delivered many exhausted, wet,
humbled kayakers to safety on the *Gikumi* and its new
sister vessel, the *Lukwa*. For sheer drama, however,
none of their rescues matches the one they performed
on the first day of spring, 1988, with the assistance of
Dan Mooney, a logger and fellow Telegraph Cove resi-
dent.

Mooney: I was working as a faller and it was very windy—we'd been blown out for the day. It was around nine or ten in the morning. I was living at Telegraph Cove at the time and had come down from Kokish, which is right up the road. At that time you could, if you lived there, drive your car right down the boardwalk. I thought I'd just drive down and have a look at the waves—I had nothing else planned for the day. I parked facing the water, got out of my car and noticed how big the waves were. It was blowing at a steady 40 knots at least. There was pretty big surf out there.

Dan Mooney: "When you see a flare under those conditions ..."
Photo courtesy Dan Mooney.

I was looking out at the horizon across Johnstone Strait. It would be almost due north as you're looking out of the cove. About three to five miles out I saw a big, arcing flare. It was quite brilliant, you could see it drifting in the wind. It went across the horizon in a fairly wide arc and it stayed visible for somewhere between thirty seconds and a minute. Just the one. When you see a flare under those conditions ... I thought, I wonder if someone's in trouble out there.

I turned around and from where I was standing I could see Bill standing in the sitting room on his balcony. I knew he couldn't hear me, so I mouthed the words, "Did you see that?" He kinda gave me a blank look.

Mackay: Dan kind of motioned up to me, and I went, "Yeah, that's right—it's coffee time, Dan." So he comes up—bolting up the stairs—and he says, "Did you see that out there?" And I said, "Yeah, right, Dan, it's real windy out there. Sit down and have a coffee." But he said, "No, no, did you see that? I saw a flare, I'm sure I saw a flare." We said, "Who the heck would be out there? Forget it." He was insistent. He just couldn't sit still. And he kept staring—see if he could see it again.

He was saying, "Please, do something," so I phoned the Coast Guard. At the time it was in Alert Bay, and I explained to them that a friend of ours thinks he's seen a flare out near Cormorant Island. Somewhere in there—the Stubbs Island area.

The Coast Guard person immediately said, "Did you see it?"

"No, I never saw it."

"Did anyone else observe it?"

"No, just Dan."

"How reliable is he?"

I said, "Dan's cool. He's a pretty bright guy."

So they said, "Okay, we'll phone Rescue Centre [RCC]."

They phoned Rescue Centre. Rescue Centre phones us back and says, "How reliable is he?" The whole thing, the same thing. And I say, "Dan's straight, he's not a wacko." And they said, "It's at your discretion, if you want to go, but we're out of it. Just let us know what you do."

So we sat back down and continued our coffee, and Dan just kept hopping. He kept saying, "We gotta go," so I phoned Rescue Centre back and said, "Look this guy's pretty sure he saw something." About forty minutes had elapsed by this point.

We went down and fired up the *Gikumi*, and we've got a 28-, 30-foot skiff as well. We towed the skiff. What we normally do when we set something like this up is, the bigger boat will go and handle the rougher water, and the smaller vessel will do in amongst the islands, going in and checking with people, see if they've seen anything—the shore search stuff.

So away we went. And boy, it was rough. We were taking a beating. The wind's picking up and we're up to about 60, 65 knots when you get out there—really blowing—and a big ebb tide: the ocean's flying out of here heading for Japan, about 7 knots. Dan's really on point, we're all on point, but sort of yawning at the same time, like, "Why are we here? This is really absurd."

As we're cruising down the backside of Pearse Island, I see what appears to be a flour bag, a yellow Robin Hood flour bag. And I think, That's pretty dumb, people throwing their garbage out. So I jumped in the skiff to check that out. I recognized that it was kayak stuff. I undid the Velcro and it's got women's stuff in it and a little camera. And it's all dry as a bone. Well, my heart stopped. I just knew there was something serious going on. And we weren't that far off the mark.

I went back to the *Gikumi* right away to tell Jim. I threw the bag at them, and Dan just started rejoicing. He couldn't believe it: there was really something going on. They went through the rest of the bag to see if there was any name or anything on it— anything identifiable. And there was nothing.

Mooney: When we found that, it confirmed that someone was in trouble out there. That was when we really started to peel our eyes. Up until that point we were thinking maybe it was a false alarm. We didn't have anything concrete to prove that there was anybody in trouble.

Then, when Jim radioed Coast Guard that we'd found the bag, the skipper on the Alert Bay ferry run interjected in the transmission with something to the effect that, "Yah, I saw a couple of kayakers going over about two days ago and they haven't come back on the ferry yet."

Borrowman: Bill went off to the southeast corner of the Pearse Islands and started searching in that area. The reason he went in the skiff up there is that there are small, tight little channels, and it's really difficult to get a big boat in there. And that's where the 50-knot winds were smashing against; it was quite a rough area right in there. I just couldn't get in very close because of the reefs and things.

So we carried on west down the side of the Pearse Islands. We went right down the full length of them. We went into a channel inside the Pearse Islands and did a circuit in there, but there was nothing, so we came back out and were going to go a parallel route east back up Cormorant Channel. We got up not very far and Dan says, "I think I saw something."

Mooney: I finally spotted a tiny black dot on the horizon. It was very, very small. I'd say they were probably a mile to a mile and a half away. I said, "What's that, Jim?" He had the binoculars. As soon as he confirmed that it was moving, we beelined it over there. It was just shithouse luck that we saw them. She was in the front and her partner was in the back. The kayak was half submerged and every swell was going right over top of her head. They were desperate.

The couple that Mooney and Borrowman found were Debra LeClair (then Kuykendall), a student at Oregon State University, and her boyfriend Kevin Johnson, a geologist. The pair had driven north on holiday and somewhat spontaneously had rented a two-person sea kayak on their way.

Johnson: I'd tried kayaking, not necessarily sea kayaking, but kayaking somewhere, and read something in *Outside* magazine about it. I've always liked Canada and thought it would be a great opportunity to go out there and give it a try.

We drove up to Port Angeles, took the ferry over to Victoria and stopped at a place there that rented us a sea kayak. They gave us some advice for some nice areas where you could kinda go around a bit—nice protected areas, that kind of stuff. Being totally unfamiliar with the water conditions up there, I thought, Hell, let's just drive up the island, look for another spot, maybe we can find a little island to camp out on. All this kind of thing. That's pretty much what we did. We drove up the island and ended up in Alert Bay.

I was a little more enthusiastic about it than Deb was. I think she was a little more cautious and I was a little more of a risk-taker at the time. We got out there and the weather was a little rainy and a little cool, but nothing unexpected for March. We put in and the water was beautiful, nice and calm, and we went out maybe a mile to an island, got some of our stuff out, set up a camp. There were several little islands there in the area and there were eagles around and the water was crystal clear. We were just stunned at how beautiful it was.

Debra LeClair paddling in the Pearse Islands the day before it all went bad.
Kevin Johnson photo.

We got up the next day and the wind had picked up and things were a little more active. Deb was kind of relying on me to be the team leader, and unfortunately I was out of my realm. I didn't have a good grip on what the conditions were out there. I could see the weather was getting a little snotty, but we didn't have any water there on the island and I was getting a little nervous about staying out there any more than a day. I wanted to go for it, try and make it back to where our car was parked. We were both pretty nervous about it.

LeClair: Things looked pretty choppy. I got that real bad feeling in my gut, looking out and seeing it get progressively worse. Both of our thoughts were, not knowing the weather patterns up there at all, that it could get really bad. We might be stuck here on this island for days. We didn't have food or water for days.

I didn't feel good about it at all, but Kevin kept reassuring me: "Ah, you know, we grew up on the Oregon coast. This isn't any worse. It's no big deal." Trying to convince me of that. Now when he looks back on it he knows it was a really wrong choice. I remember at one point almost being in tears about going. Just that feeling of, No, this isn't okay, and, Wait, I have to go to the bathroom one more time.

By the time we broke down camp there were definitely whitecaps. That made me real nervous. The other thing was that the chart and the tide book we had didn't seem to correspond, so we couldn't even tell the tides for where we were. That was really stupid, because they were against us.

Johnson: We got through a little bit of rough water and that wasn't too bad. The tide currents up there are really something, extremely fierce. There was some pretty big water for what the day before had been smooth as glass. Not understanding the tides up there I didn't realize that if we'd just held tight for a few hours it probably would have eased up quite a bit and we would have had a much easier time of it. We got within probably thirty yards of an island big enough to put in to and get all our stuff up on. It had some trees on it and was somewhat protected. At the time I was aiming at that thing. But we were dealing with something that neither one of us could handle. It was beyond our experience.

LeClair: The person in the back controls the rudder, and at that point I remember very well asking Kevin why we kept shifting. We had a plan to head straight for this little island, but out a little bit, then cut in and ride the current into it. I kept saying, "Why do you keep changing our course?" He didn't say anything for a while, and I said, "Why?!" I was getting really tense then. He finally said, "I'm not. I've got the rudder all the way the other way." That's when I knew that we were in trouble.

We were almost to this rocky little island and I remember looking at a log resting on the bank and watching to see if we were making progress. I saw that we were drifting back, the current had taken over. That's what drew us into this point where apparently the water is coming from one side and the other— there are about three currents pushing together. It was just this great big whitewater mess. That's where we dumped.

Johnson: We came up on a standing wave. We got into it crossways and it just rolled us over. Out we went. I told Deb to hang on to the kayak. We gathered up a little bit of our stuff, which took quite a while, ten or fifteen minutes to get up into the kayak. We shot off one flare, probably the best $12.95 I ever spent. The current was picking us up and we went just zooming by the island. She was saying something about trying to swim for it, and I told her, "No way, stick with the boat."

LeClair: It took us probably twenty minutes to get our act together, and it wasn't much of an act. Once we did get back in we were pointed straight into the waves. Every wave went up over me. I had this incredible bruise from the back of the cockpit, from each wave wrenching me back. Some of the time I couldn't even get my breath.

I was able to get my spray skirt on tight, but Kevin couldn't ever get his on. That was a pretty critical thing. I think we might have been able to recover if he'd have gotten his spray skirt on, because I had a bilge pump and we had an extra paddle—we'd lost both of our other paddles when we went over. But by the time we got into the boat his hands wouldn't work. The other thing was that our life jackets kept coming unzipped—both of them. I remember trying to get it zipped up to a certain point, and using my teeth because my hands didn't work, and every time I looked down it was just kind of floating around me.

Johnson: We were going farther and farther out into Johnstone Strait, and there again we're hitting these standing waves which are several feet high and they're breaking over Deb and coming up on me and going into where I'm sitting. The kayak had bulkheads but the front one blew out.

So we were going along and trying to encourage each other but not doing a very good job of it. We were both real scared. We'd managed to salvage the spare paddle, and we were passing it back and forth, but once when Deb was handing it to me, she was holding the end of the blade and a gust of wind caught it, and it was ten feet out. It could just as well been miles.

We tried paddling with our hands, but the damn thing was so heavy by now that we weren't really doing anything except keeping ourselves warm a little bit. We could see a house, and I'm thinking, I'm going to die out here within sight of a house. A sense of impending doom was definitely on me. I was starting to think about my funeral and this kind of stuff. I just didn't see how we were going to get out of it. I was getting real weak by this time. Deb was in better shape but not able to do anything without me.

LeClair: The wind caught the first flare and it didn't really go up into the air. I think it was Kevin's. I had a flare in my vest, and it was like having a candy bar when everyone's starving, holding onto it and going, "I can't let this go. I have to wait for just the right moment." I don't really know why we didn't shoot it off sooner. Probably because we were fighting so hard just to keep going. Everything was a struggle. Then, at some point—we were well out into Johnstone Strait by then—we shot off the second one.

Johnson: It seemed like it wasn't too long after that that we saw a boat, which was the *Gikumi*.

Borrowman: The first thing I saw was the guy's head. You couldn't even see the kayak in the waves, and the girl was lower because the bow of the kayak was sunk. The girl was sitting in the forward compartment and he was in the rear compartment. She was in the water completely. They'd been dumped out of the kayak, but they'd gotten back in. This is another reason they lived. If they hadn't gotten in they would have lost their strength, they would have gotten even colder—which is hard to believe—and of course they would have simply drowned.

The bottom line was that the bow was considerably under water with her in it, and the guy was sitting up quite a bit higher. He was almost dead at the time. He was basically unconscious. His eyes were almost closed and he was sort of like a rag doll in there, hanging on. Every wave was washing completely over top of them.

LeClair: I looked around and I sure enough saw this boat coming around the island. I got all excited and pointed it out to Kevin, and he couldn't see it. It really scared me because I thought maybe I was hallucinating. Our eyes were really shot from the wind and the salt water, plus he had lost his glasses. I was certain I'd seen their boat, but it went out of sight, and I just thought, Okay, that's it. That is really it. We're toast.

Then, about ten minutes later, there was the boat again, in the same spot. Again I thought I was hallucinating because it was the same spot. It didn't occur to me that they could have been looking for us. I had thought they were just cruising along. I was crying and screaming and carrying on: "Please, help us." Of course they couldn't hear us. And then that boat just turned its course and headed straight for us. At that point, as it approached, I started getting worried that they were going to hit us because they didn't see us. Before my hands froze I had found a red bandana and tied it around my bilge pump, thinking I could flag somebody down, and I'm waving this thing around. Dan says he doesn't know what caught his eye, but something made him look.

They needed to signal to Bill, so they went past us a little ways to shoot their flare gun. I remember them looking right out and waving to me and I kept screaming at them, "Save us, save us!" I thought that they thought that we were just out there paddling around. I was so mad. I was yelling, "Come back here, come back here! Help us!" Then I saw them shooting off their gun and I knew, Okay, okay, we're somewhere here now.

Mackay: I'd been continuing my search in the skiff. I looked back, and out of my peripheral vision I see red flares going off—a bunch of them. Holy shit! And it's the *Gikumi*. Jim's trying to catch my attention. The radio had flooded—it was so rough I was taking ocean over the side, so we had no communication. But the flares sure caught my attention. I thought, Oh, no: bodies. I roared down there, and there they were, in

Debra LeClair signals frantically to the *Gikumi*.
Painting by Graham Wragg.

the middle of six-, seven-foot swells, stuff breaking over the boat, and they had one person on the deck.

LeClair: They turned around and came in, but it was too close and made us roll over. At that point it was about the last blow. The boat hit me in the face and I got a big fat lip and black eye. When I came up and looked over, Kevin was just sort of floating face down in the water, bobbing. Dan threw a life ring but didn't hold on to the other end. The second one they threw out came to me and I grabbed onto it and I wasn't going to let go. But they said, "Give it to him, give it to him." I sort of paddled over and handed this thing to Kevin. He looked up—it was the first time I'd really seen him during this episode—and he was just whitish grey and he really looked like death. That was probably the scariest thing for me of the whole thing.

Borrowman: I was afraid this guy wasn't going to make it, so I figured we had to make a move here. This is when I came down with my stern to the wind. As I came up to them I put it into reverse several times and gave it a little shot in reverse to stop my movement—I was drifting quite quickly. What happened was, when I hit reverse one time, the wash of the prop came up just enough that it helped to tip them over. The next thing, they were both in the water. That wasn't what we wanted.

While this was happening, Dan was throwing our heaving lines. For passenger carrying we're supposed to have two fifty-foot lines plus life buoys. Dan must have been a little excited, because he threw a life buoy out but didn't hold onto the line. Debbie missed the life buoy and away it went. So we were down to the last one—one proper line for heaving left on deck. Dan threw that and Debbie got ahold of it, and that was how we were able to get her over to the side of the boat. In those waves we were going literally from gunwale to gunwale on the back deck. We had to time the roll of the boat such that as it came right down, Dan and I each grabbed one of her shoulders and we basically flopped her up on the deck like a big halibut.

LeClair: I had bruises—fingerprints from these guys' hands—for about two weeks. I was bruised from just about my head to my toes, black and blue.

Borrowman: Bill showed up and grabbed ahold of Kevin. He was almost face-down, basically unconscious. There was very little happening there and I think he would have drowned in a very short time. If Bill hadn't seen us and gotten over when he did, I'm not sure what we would have done. It wouldn't have been very smart for us to jump in the water. I might have taken a pike pole and grabbed his collar. I don't know. Luckily Bill showed up and slid this guy into the skiff.

Johnson: I was in pretty sad shape. I couldn't move. While we were still in the kayak I knew things had been getting bad because my field of vision had narrowed down so it was like looking through a tunnel. Bill threw a blanket over me and man, he just roared right into Alert Bay, into the dock right in front of the hospital. It went from almost certain death to, I've got a life again.

Mackay: I had asked Jim to phone ahead, get the ambulance crew there—this guy's in pretty serious condition. I checked for pulse: guy's frozen. I couldn't feel anything, I was getting bounced around so bad. I thought, Oh, God, this guy's dead. Jim's got the gal on board. She's conscious—she's fine. She's just screaming for this guy—she doesn't want him to die.

I finally got to calm water and I rolled this guy over. His eyes opened up, and I'm thinking, Okay, okay, this is good. I get to the dock and there's not a soul. Alert Bay's just abandoned—there's nobody around. I waited for about five minutes and I figured this was pretty absurd, so I put the guy over my shoulder—and this is a skookum guy, not fat but all muscle—and I walked him up the street on my shoulder. We're both soaking wet and I'm staggering down the middle of the main drag, walking for the hospital, and each car that goes by is going, "Ah, you drunk, get off the road." I'm out of breath; I can hardly speak.

Johnson: The hospital—that was kind of a blur. I can just remember they got my clothes off and I was standing there shivering. They got us into tubs—Deb was in another room, I believe—and brought our temperatures up really slowly. I can remember getting in the water, and I'm sure it was just tepid at the most, and God, it just burned. I believe they told me my body temperature was below 85.

LeClair: I've got to say that that was probably one of the best experiences of my life, being in that hospital. All the people there were so wonderful. For a little hospital ... I don't know about their technology, but their compassion was enough for me. There was a doctor, Dr. Pickup. He was a great old guy.

Johnson: For all that they did for us in the hospital it cost us 44 dollars. I was stunned to think that Canada had such a good medical system that they could do that. I was really impressed.

LeClair: That was about the doom of our relationship. I don't know why, but it was. We were still together for about six months after that. It was interesting seeing our responses, how we dealt with it when we got back. Kevin didn't want to discuss it at all. I wanted to talk about it a lot. I was very depressed. It started my search for the meaning of life, and he didn't want to talk about it—it just made me furious. I think there was a lot of guilt involved for him. I've tried to make it clear that I don't hold him responsible. He's forgiven. But it was his idea, his call. I just sort of went along: "Okay, I'll do this."

Debra LeClair and Kevin Johnson spent the night following their rescue at Telegraph Cove. The next morning, as they prepared to return to Oregon, they found this poem in a plastic bag on the windshield of their van.

The Rescue

Gale winds blowing white caps abound
Slanting rain grey sky a storming
Looking to sea, red flare glowing
Someone in danger, a boat foundering
Sound the alarm, lives may need saving
Across Johnstone Strait, waves pounding
Make speed, hold on, someone praying
Stinging salt spray storm winds howling
Straining eyes searching, not finding
Someone in peril, someone slipping
Look there, bright yellow flotsam
Alas a clue, we search and scan
Someone calling, young woman crying
Searching searching still not finding
Wind whistles through wires on mast
Hope fading, life will not last
Eyes strain across sea and foam
Somebody praying, God take me home
Luck or will guides the eye of a man
Some distant bobbing far from land
Full speed ahead, people in numbing water
Help us please, can't last longer
Rolling seas, life lines thrown out
From death's icy grip two people break out.

Dan Mooney
23/03/88

Debra LeClair lives near Spokane, Washington. Kevin Johnson still lives in Oregon. Dan Mooney makes his home in the Comox Valley, having left the logging industry after being seriously injured in a job-related accident.

In the spring of 1997, Bill Mackay sold his share of Stubbs Island Charters to Jim Borrowman, who continues to run the eco-tourism operation using the *Gikumi* and the *Lukwa*.

Meteor
Fire

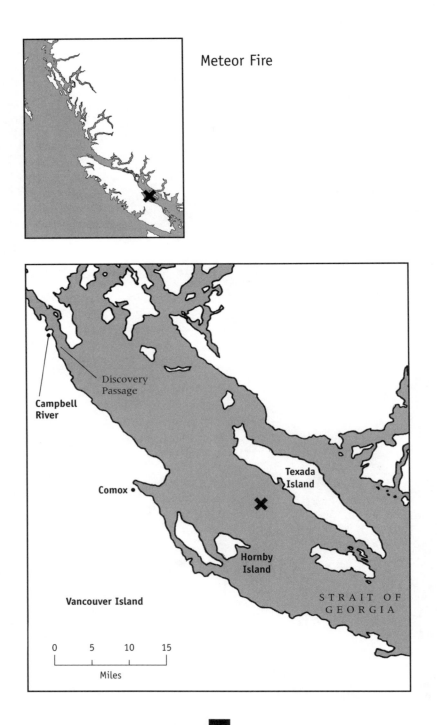

Meteor Fire

BARRY HASTINGS WAS A WATCH-
KEEPER WORKING AT VANCOUVER Coast Guard Radio's
Sea Island station in the early morning hours of May 22,
1971 when he and the other communications specialists
on shift picked up an unusual message.

It came in just after 2:30 a.m. on the international
distress frequency for Morse code. The signal read,
"meteor fire." Hastings remembers his and his co-
workers' immediate response. "There were looks on our
faces like, What the hell does that mean?"

Hastings, now a standards and communications officer with the Coast Guard's marine communications section, remembers the minutes that followed.

Hastings: Somebody said, "This sounds like someone's
observing a meteor shower." One of the guys stepped out the
door and looked up at the night sky and said, "There's nothing
really going on here." Again, because it's our trade, we said,
"Don't we have a ship—a cruise ship—out there, the *Meteor*?"
Someone said, "Yup," so we said, "Let's start checking our messages and traffic." See where the ship was. Was it in our area?

Hastings and his crew soon discovered that there was
indeed a cruise ship named the *Meteor* in their area. It was
located in the northern Strait of Georgia, between Texada
and Hornby islands. And it was on fire: Meteor fire.

Hastings learned years later that the cruise ship's
radio operator, ordered to send out a Mayday, may have
accidentally abbreviated the intended message, which
was later correctly received: "Meteor on fire."

In fact, a major tragedy was unfolding on the
Norwegian ship, southbound on the last leg of an eight-
day Alaskan cruise. Aboard the vessel were sixty-seven
passengers and a crew of ninety-one. Among the latter
was the *Meteor*'s master, Captain Alf Mørner, who had
recently retired for the night.

Mørner: I was on the bridge until we were past Discovery Passage, a very narrow sound running between the east coast of Vancouver Island and a group of nearby islands. I went to bed at something like quarter to one in the morning. A little bit more than an hour later they called me and told me what was going on.

I put on my uniform and rushed to the bridge. We could clearly see flames coming up the stairways. I had two very good pilots on board. They both came to the bridge, and I felt that navigation was safe, so we stopped the ship and turned it away from the wind, so the wind shouldn't rush up the fire.

With the wind on the stern I left the bridge and went down to where the fire really was happening. Not so many people were able to go in, but I went in with them.

> Below decks, a rapidly spreading conflagration had trapped many crew members, most of them under thirty, in their cabins and in passageways. Mørner and the other rescuers encountered many grim scenes as they fought their way into the ship's interior. Several crew members had died in a pile-up behind a watertight door they were unable to open. Another, trapped by advancing flames, got stuck while attempting to escape through a porthole.

Mørner: The alarm went on, of course, but many people were closed in. We took out who we could—alive or dead, we took them out.

We had smoke-diving equipment, but only two pieces, for two people. You have a flask—a bottle—and they don't last very long. So most of the time we were without any protection. The smoke was thick and it was poisonous. At the time we didn't actually know how dangerous it was. It was the chemical reaction between the fire and the paint on the walls.

When we went in, we went in creeping on the floor, where the oxygen is. The higher you go, the worse the gas is. I was a scuba diver for years, and the people who came in with us fire fighting were also scuba divers. They are trained to work in dark and work alone. It gives you strength to believe "I can do it."

We took out people alive who refused to go back. We took them from cabins where they were locked in and we tried to get

The *Meteor* in happier days, cruising the Caribbean Sea.

them to fight the fire—to get more men out—but a few of them just refused to go in. It is not a normal situation and of course people don't act normal. They were in shock.

I was involved in fighting the fire the whole day, until the last minute. I must have been in for more than twenty-four hours. From one day to the second day, I was not out of my clothes for thirty-six hours.

> In the lexicon of the cruise ship industry, a person who returns to sail upon a particular vessel is known as a "repeater." Robert Scott Jr. is an American expatriate who has lived in Switzerland for the past nine years, and he is a repeater of perhaps record-holding proportions. Financial independence has allowed him to spend "a great deal" of his life cruising the world's oceans. This trip was the last of thirty-six voyages he made on the *Meteor*. Many of those trips were consecutive, as he would go aboard in March and stay until June. As a result, he knew many of the crew who died in the *Meteor* fire.

Scott: I do not remember the exact time when I was called by my steward, but I was awakened with the closing of the fire door just outside my cabin. There was no smoke in that area then. I quickly dressed as I had clothes laid out for the next morning's arrival in Vancouver.

With my life jacket on I went directly up to my lifeboat. It was very cold and there was drifting smoke. We were then asked to go to the dining room, one deck below. We weren't really told anything. They came in and asked if anybody was a nurse or a doctor. There was a shipboard doctor, but they needed more people because there were so many they were bringing out. The laundry lady had some nurse's training, so she went off. Otherwise it was very quiet. It was just the pianist there playing the piano, and everybody sitting drinking coffee. It was very, very quiet, except for when the ship heeled a bit. Then people started getting a little more nervous.

Martha Auten, of New York, also a repeater of some standing, recorded her memory of the *Meteor* fire in writing a month after being rescued.

Auten: Stewards and stewardesses were on hand to reassure us. Off and on an officer would appear with instructions about the fire, which they hoped to get under control momentarily. After about a half an hour they told us that tea and sandwiches would be served in the dining salon if we were interested. I wasn't, but most passengers were.

Shortly after I could hear [cruise director] Ole Hadland playing "The Darktown Strutters' Ball" on the piano for good cheer.

At one point Mrs. Mørner, Captain Alf's charming and popular wife, brought me some warm underpants and a tweed skirt to go under my nightgown.

Scott: Some two hours later, with the ship beginning to list, we were asked to prepare to disembark. By then the lifeboats had been launched as there were not enough crew members available to load and launch from the boat deck.

I was asked to stand by the door to the lower deck and allow people through only in small groups as they could man only one boat at a time. This was hard for me as the bodies of the dead were being brought to that deck and covered.

There was no panic or trouble whatsoever with the passengers who went down a short pilot ladder into the lifeboats, which were transferring people to the ship standing by. The senior bartender, the purser and the second steward were helping the passengers.

We went across to an Alaskan car ferry where we had to transfer into one of their lifeboats to be hauled up; it was a high-sided ferry with no lower doors. It was a bit wet and very noisy getting into the lifeboat and crossing as a helicopter was not high above, sending spray all over. I could see one body partway out of a porthole in the forward crew quarters. As soon as the last of us (I was in the last boat) went aboard the car ferry, it departed for Vancouver.

Auten: As the lifeboats took off we could see flames spurting out of the portholes. We all wept to see the *Meteor* alone, afire and alist with the remaining crew and officers still on board. I will never forget how magnificently the crew, officers and staff behaved during the evacuation.

> The Coast Guard cutter *Racer* had been tied up at Gibson's Landing when it was tasked to proceed to the *Meteor*'s assistance. On the way, Captain Ken Clapp learned that he had been designated on-scene commander for the massive operation, a task which would have been daunting for the most experienced mariner. Ironically, Clapp had little experience to draw on: he was putting in his first shift as captain, having just received that promotion. He had previously spent one year on the R-class cutters after spending four years on Coast Guard buoy tending ships. He did not consider himself a search and rescue professional, having never received training in either search or rescue. He had never even seen anyone act as on-scene commander. Nonetheless, he spent the next twenty-two hours manoeuvring his ship and maintaining lines of communication from ship to plane, ship to shore and ship to ship, in addition to commanding his own crew.
>
> Upon arrival at the now listing and smoke-wreathed *Meteor*, Clapp reluctantly sent aboard four crew members under the direction of Chief Officer Norm Scott, to assist in the fire-fighting. Helicopters from nearby Canadian Forces Base Comox shuttled oxygen and air

The Coast Guard cutters *Racer* and *Ready* pour water on the bow of the listing *Meteor*.
Photo courtesy Jack McNaught.

bottles to the *Meteor*. The Coast Guard cutter *Ready* arrived on scene approximately two hours after the *Racer*, and both vessels pumped massive amounts of cooling water onto the cruise ship's forward section as well as extinguishing the fire on A deck by pouring water through portholes.

Clapp: All the trauma had taken place before our arrival. Everything was done, including the removal of the bodies from the watertight door. The bodies were laid out under a tarpaulin on the afterdeck of one of the Seaspan tugs [the *Le Beau*, which had arrived before the *Racer*].

The fire had been contained, and this was the problem. The scene of the fire was down two or three decks. The fire was contained because of the watertight door, and it wasn't going to go any farther. We were patched through to the Rescue

Coordination Centre (RCC) in Victoria. They kept saying, "Is the fire contained?" And of course it was. It was still burning in between decks, even though it wasn't going to go anywhere. I asked for professional assistance in fighting the fire—we had no trained personnel. They said, "Is the fire contained?" I said, "Yes." They said, "Well, that's all we have to do, because we've got this Seaspan tug, the *Sudbury II*, coming up with all this foam generating equipment, and they'll take care of the fire."

Norm Scott, in talking with Captain Mørner, felt that we should be doing something. I didn't feel that we should be doing anything more than what we'd decided to do: use our monitors to cool the outside of the ship—just keep it cool. We had fire monitors throwing about 500 gallons a minute.

Norm kept trying to get me to send him in there. He just felt that rather than sitting around doing nothing, he could probably put the fire out. It was against my better judgment, but I let him go. If I had to do it over again I would never agree to him going in.

As water was pumped into the burning vessel, its list increased to 15 degrees. Holes cut through the hull allowed the tugs *Le Beau* and *La Garde* to pump out some of the accumulation. It was early evening by the time the salvage tug *Sudbury II* arrived and pumped fire-suppressing foam into the lower decks, a tactic it would repeat in the early morning hours when a resupply of foam was delivered. Shortly before midnight, twenty-two hours after the fire was first discovered, the *La Garde* departed for Vancouver carrying forty-seven of the ship's crew and fourteen bodies. A handful of crew members remained aboard the *Meteor* to fight the persistent fire. A further eighteen remained missing.

All the passengers survived. Having been transferred to the Alaska state ferry *Malaspina* in the pre-dawn hours, they were transported to Vancouver.

The rescue effort succeeded in saving several people from A deck. On B deck, where the fire was initially discovered, the human loss was almost complete: of twenty-six crew members trapped by flames and suffocating smoke, only three were pulled out alive. In total, thirty-two people died, making the disaster the second worst in BC's marine history.

Mørner: We sailed the ship back to dock in Vancouver—the Burrard dock. When we came in, the police came on board. They wanted somebody to show them where the people—the dead people—were located in the ship. So I went in with them, the first team. That was difficult. Then, of course, we had protection: masks and oxygen.

When I docked the vessel, my wife was waiting at dockside. Everyone on the dock knew that we had lost many people, but they didn't know exactly who. I could see her worried face, so I went out to the bridge and waved to her, so she knew that I was one of the survivors.

When we came in we were taken to a motel, where we slept for the night. I had to get my clothes off after between thirty-six and forty hours. I was black from the smoke.

When we were first married my wife and I went to a cinema to see a film. And my wife wanted to know what I was doing. I said, "I want to know how to get out if something happens and the lights go out: ten steps this way and four steps that way and there you have your door." I always do that in coming in to new places. So the first thing I did when we went to the hotel was to find out how to get out in case something happened. Then, in the night, the alarm went—the fire alarm went. I had taken some drugs to sleep because I couldn't sleep. So I was half conscious. I went in to the toilet, sat on the toilet and fell fast asleep there. What had happened was, there had been a robbery. Somebody drunk got robbed and somebody pulled the alarm.

The mounted police were there for weeks studying the whole *Meteor* incident. I think they put in twenty-five or thirty men. They sealed up the ship completely. We were in there with them for the investigation the whole time. I was asked by the mounted police—I think I was in three or four investigations, and I was asked to relate in detail what I knew. And I said to the judge that to my knowledge I just can't understand why and how.

I know they had several theories. I don't know why, but they never came out with a complete conclusion. I must say that I have spent more than one night thinking over what happened. I still can't understand.

I still think of it. You never get it out of your mind. I met many of the families here [in Norway], went to their homes, and went to the funerals. That was hard. Very hard.

Captain Alf Mørner and his wife, Inger, photographed at a wedding party two months after the *Meteor* disaster.
Photo courtesy Alf Mørner.

More than two dozen police investigators spent several weeks sifting through the wreckage of the *Meteor* and interviewing crew members. While no conclusive cause was ever established, a coroner's jury in Vancouver determined that the fire may have been started by a cigarette dropped by a drunken crew member—a baker whose corpse showed an elevated blood alcohol reading.

Captain Alf Mørner and the ship's owners were represented at coroner's court by lawyer Garde Gardom, BC's current lieutenant governor. The coroner's jury found, among other things, that "the Captain and Crew and all people involved in fighting this fire acted in the highest traditions of the sea."

When interviewed twenty-five years after the *Meteor* disaster, Mørner continued to take pride in his crew's comportment during those harrowing hours. "I would like to add," he said, "that not even one of the passengers were hurt or pinched a finger."

Mørner had a forty-seven-year career at sea, including service on a gasoline tanker in 1939 at the outset of World War Two. He served on eight passenger vessels, beginning as a second officer on Norwegian coastal mail boats and ending as master on the Royal Viking Line's *Royal Viking Sky* before becoming that company's manager of operations. Mørner had been master of the *Meteor* for eight years when this incident occurred. Now eighty years old, he lives with his wife Inger in Nesttun, Norway. The Mørners remain close friends of Robert Scott Jr.

Captain Ken Clapp was appalled at the Coast Guard crew's lack of fire-fighting expertise going in to the *Meteor* situation. Of twenty-four personnel at the scene of the disaster, only three had any fire-fighting training— all of it experience they brought with them before joining the Coast Guard. Clapp took it upon himself to have rudiments of marine fire-fighting training provided to his crew by a member of Vancouver's fireboat crew who, at the same time, showed them how to use some of the specialized rescue equipment they had been provided with on the *Racer* but had never been trained to operate. Now retired, Clapp lives in the Comox Valley.

The *Meteor* was sold and its interior rebuilt. It continues to cruise the Mediterranean and Red seas under the name *Neptune*.

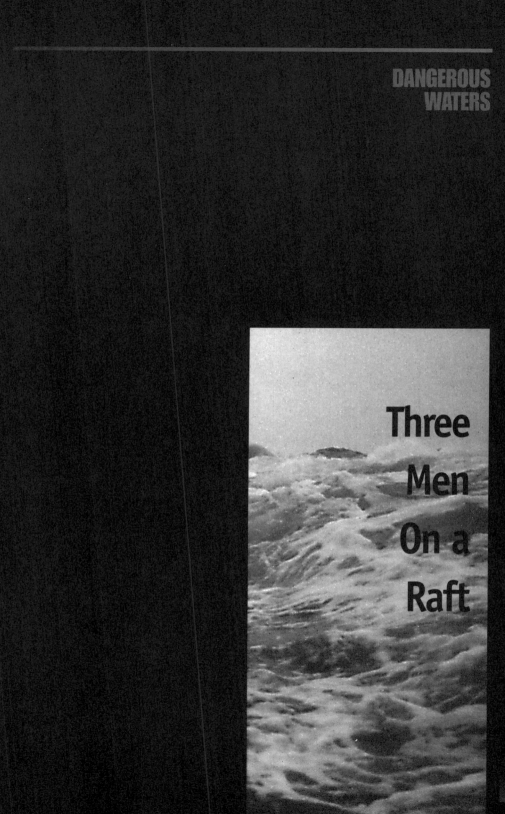

Three
Men
On a
Raft

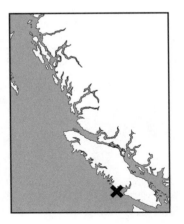

Three Men On a Raft

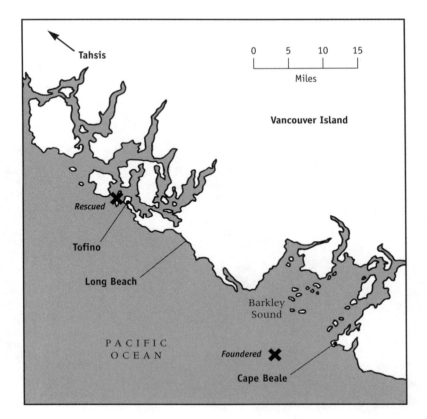

Tahsis

0   5   10   15

Miles

Vancouver Island

Rescued

Tofino

Long Beach

Barkley
Sound

PACIFIC
OCEAN

Foundered

Cape Beale

TOWBOAT SKIPPER PAUL
BOTTOMLEY WAS OUT OF A job in the spring of 1993 when
Mike Daynes offered him a brief stint of work. Daynes
owned a small towing company in Tahsis, and was plan-
ning to take his own tug out of service temporarily for
mechanical work. He had found a replacement vessel,
the *Kitmano*, an aging workhorse owned by Rivtow
Straits Ltd. of Vancouver. Daynes needed someone with
the necessary qualifications to run it from the Fraser
delta, across the Strait of Georgia, and up the west coast
of Vancouver Island. Bottomley accepted. Now Daynes
had to find a deckhand. Enter Kurt Guilbride, a veteran
fisherman who also owned and operated a small tug.

The trio assembled on the afternoon of Friday, April
23, at Annacis Island in Delta, where a Rivtow shore
crew was preparing the *Kitmano* for its two-month Tahsis
charter.

Bottomley: Mike Daynes was there already. Kurt and I
arrived and went down to have a look at this thing, and it was
certainly no prize. I was told that it hadn't worked for about a
year and a half, and it showed it. This boat had really been
knocked around—it had had a tough life.

Daynes: I knew what the boat was before I took off. I knew
basically that it was an old tug that was pretty well taken out of
service. I only needed the boat for sixty days; I didn't need it forever. It still had a current CSI on it—we got an extension on it,
basically. I had talked to the skipper who ran it before, and he
said that the boat was a good boat. When it had come down, it
had towed a barge down from Kitimat. But it had been sitting for
a little while, so they had to go over it. It was no gem. But you
can look around and there is no gems around. You just don't get
them like that. You can't just call up and say, "I need a boat
tomorrow," and get a real good boat. The thing was, we were on
a budget.

Kurt Guilbride: "I wasn't worried at all at first ..."
When not at sea, he's often busy in his private
museum, the Black Nugget, in Ladysmith, BC.
Keith Keller photo.

Bottomley: This steamship inspector saw fit to give it a certificate of seaworthiness. So we went down and we checked this thing over. Mike had brought three survival suits. The radios worked and the radar worked. The radio inspector had certified it all right on the previous Wednesday. The shore crew went home about four-thirty, five o'clock. We went up and got some groceries and swung the compass out in the river. One of the guys—I forget his name—came down and swung the compass. And away we went.

We went down to Steveston and got fuel. The weather wasn't supposed to be bad so away we went. We left about ten or eleven o'clock at night. Went across the gulf, no problems, down through Active Pass. I got as far as Race Rocks. I stayed up all night 'cause the other guys had been up all day. In the morning I went to bed.

Guilbride: We had noticed a list coming down the river. Apparently they had told Mike that it did that quite often. It was just a fuel list.

When I got up, Paul went to bed and Mike and I took over. I went down and had some breakfast. Mike wasn't feeling too good, he was a little bit seasick. I came back up and we were just maybe five miles south of Cape Beale and we noticed there was a little bit of a list again. We weren't too concerned because of the previous night with the fuel list. It had straightened itself right out after we fuelled it up. I don't know whether Mike noticed or I did first, but we commented on it and neither one of us was very concerned.

About the same time there was a deep-sea freighter over-taking us. It was heading in to Barkley Sound, we assumed. We altered course to go around his stern as we were pretty well on a parallel collision course. Which put us another mile or two miles farther away from the shore than we had been running.

The list continued after we ran around the stern of the freighter, so Mike decided he'd go and shut the fuel tank off. Theoretically it should have straightened itself out. He went down and did that and we continued on for ten or fifteen minutes and it wasn't getting any better. If anything it was getting worse. We talked it over and thought there might be some water laying around somewhere, so we kind of zigzagged a bit and laid the opposite way in the trough than we had been to see if that was going to shift the water around any. And it didn't. The list continued getting more and more severe on the port hand side.

Daynes: We thought it was a fuel transfer problem at first. We thought it was returning to one side quicker than the other. First of all we shut off the return to the side it was listing on, so it would only return to the other side. That's pretty normal on a lot of vessels I've been on. Usually it doesn't start to happen until the tanks start getting slack. These tanks were not slack. They were full. They were all full.

She was a level ship right up 'til about eleven-thirty, I guess. Then she started to take a list, so we tried to correct it. Went down, shut the return off to one side. Went up—wasn't up there more than a few minutes, realized that it wasn't quick enough, so we went down and shut down and shut the suction off to the starboard side so that that side would fill up. When I got up top then I realized that something's happening, so I went to the back deck, had a look around, and I seen those pancake vents—I call them pancake vents, I don't know what anybody else calls them—and one was awash on the back deck and the port quarter wasn't coming clear.

Guilbride: Mike said the port stern quarter of the bulwarks was not recovering from the swell. It was underwater, more or less, all the time. We both figured that probably the after lazaret must be taking on some water. He went back down to start the pumps up. I had been on a tug some years before where the after lazaret flooded completely and the stern went right underwater. It was no problem; we just pumped it out and carried on.

He came back up and was concerned. In the time from when he had gone down previously to when he had returned, the stern port deck was now completely underwater and was in the process of sinking. He told me I'd better get Paul up, which I did. I slowed the boat down some and headed into the wind a bit so that we weren't travelling in the trough as we were before, which unfortunately headed us out to sea a little bit.

I went back to help Mike. I had my head in the engine room door and he was laying on his stomach trying to open up sea cocks to prime one of the pumps. He was having a little bit of difficulty so he asked me if it was pumping. I looked over the side and it was pumping so I stuck my head back in the engine room and yelled at him that it was pumping. He continued trying to get the other pump going. All the time it was listing a little bit more.

Bottomley: The skipper's cabin was a little room behind the wheelhouse—it wasn't a very big boat. I guess it was about eleven, eleven-thirty in the morning Kurt Guilbride came in and said, "You'd better get up. The stern is full of water." Now this boat had been built to haul freight around Kitimat, and it had quite a long stern on it. It had a couple of cranes at one time and they used to load the freight right on the stern.

I'm getting up, waking up, getting my pants and shoes on, and while I'm doing this you can feel the boat heeling over to port. I got dressed, got my Floater coat on, thank God, and went into this little wheelhouse. By this time we're right over, and I can see dark green water on the porthole on the port door.

Guilbride: I noticed out of the corner of my eye that Paul was coming out of the wheelhouse. I pulled my head out of the engine room and stood up, and I realized that the boat was over considerably more than it had been previously and that it was going quite rapidly. But because my head was in the engine room I didn't have any point of reference and didn't notice it. As soon as Paul came out of the wheelhouse he said, "We're going over." I realized at the same time that we were.

I stuck my head back in the engine room, which was really the only scary part of the whole deal. Mike was lying on his stomach and because of him not having any point of reference— he didn't know where up or down was because the boat was rolling. He couldn't hear me yelling and I was pretty concerned that he wasn't going to get out.

Finally he heard me, looked around, got his point of reference and realized that it was rolling over. He started to climb up the ladder, and on the last couple of steps he was more or less hanging from the ladder—the boat was on its side before he got out.

Bottomley: After Kurt woke me up, we had gone outside and got the life raft down off the roof and was just in the process of launching this. I think he was just pulling the painter. Mike Daynes had gone down to the engine room to see if he could pump something—to see what the problem was. It turned out that there was no water in the engine room. It was all in this aft compartment.

By this time the boat is awash at the stern and getting worse all the time. We were about four miles off Cape Beale lighthouse. It was a nice, sunny day, an early spring day. It was maybe 15, 18 miles-an-hour southeast, just a chop on the water. And there's always a low southeast swell out there. Nothing unusual.

I went back in. I thought, I have to get some sort of message to somebody. The boat was fitted with one of these hand-held EPIRBs [Emergency Position Indicating Radio Beacon]. It's about the size of a walkie-talkie, and it was on a clip on the inside of the wheelhouse. I got that off the wall. By that time Mike Daynes was coming out of the engine room. In the *Kitmano*, the survival suits were down in the fo'c'sle, 'cause the galley's downstairs. One thing went through my mind: that if I went down there and water started pouring in, there's no way you'd ever get back out—you'd have tons of water coming in on top of you. So I didn't go down there to get anything.

Guilbride: The sun came out and it quit raining. The motor was still going and the boat was going around in circles like a limp turtle. Paul said he hadn't had a chance to put a Mayday out because the boat rolled over so fast. But he did manage to grab the EPIRB. Paul and I went up to the wheelhouse, walking along the housework, and stared in the wheelhouse door, which was now just a ten-foot well—it was like looking into a great big fish bowl. We considered crawling back down there and getting the radio on the far side and trying to make a Mayday call, but we decided that the boat was kind of precarious so we cancelled that idea.

Mike by that time had the raft. Paul was the first one in. He's … got rather a large girth, and when I jumped in he reached over to help me in. Because of his girth and my weight landing on the edge, the raft flipped upside down. In Paul's recollection he doesn't remember that. I know in all three of us the story's a little bit different.

Bottomley: Mike and Kurt got into the raft, and I climbed out the door—again, I guess—and I just stepped off the side of the boat into the water. I stayed in the water, because I was pushing the life raft away from the boat—trying to kick with my feet and push. The *Kitmano* went down by the stern and it hesitated a little while, I guess with the air in the fo'c'sle.

Guilbride: The raft flipped upside down and we were all soaking wet. Mike jumped in to help us put the raft up properly. The boat was continuously sliding down and the boom was coming down on top of us until we got the line cut and the raft away. We pulled Mike in, so now we were all soaking wet and the raft was half full of water. We started to paddle away from the boat a bit, then just sat there and watched it go. It went extremely rapidly. We were maybe eight miles off the Broken Group by that time.

Bottomley: I had the EPIRB, which I gave to them as soon as I got to the raft. It was only a few feet away. I got in the life raft and the *Kitmano* just let out a few big bubbles and down she went. We didn't have a chance to get out a Mayday or anything.

A few duckboards floated off—one-by-fours that you walk on with caulk boots. A life ring or two floated off. There was a big life raft, an eight-man one in a cradle, with one of these hydrostat releases, which is supposed to release when they get down about thirty feet and the water pressure sweats it off. It didn't work. This is one of the things that's supposed to be checked.

So we're in the life raft, the boat's sunk and we can see Cape Beale. By this time it's about noon. We turn this EPIRB on, and the indicator light comes on, so we figured it's working. Give it a couple of hours and the Bamfield Coast Guard will track us down to where this thing is—somebody will come out looking for us, anyway.

Guilbride: It was kind of funny in my perspective. I don't know about the other two guys particularly, but I kept thinking, Well, this is a great adventure. I wasn't worried at all to begin with because we had the EPIRB, and it was working, supposedly, and we were only eight miles off the Broken Group and Cape Beale. We weren't in the middle of nowhere; we were in a major traffic lane. We all laughed and thought we were going to be rescued in a couple of hours, because the Bamfield rescue station is right there. We weren't any of us too concerned, although Mike, being the boss, was a little upset, because he'd just lost a couple-hundred-thousand-dollar boat down the drain. I guess a brand-new one would be a couple of million, but it was in pretty rough shape—it was old. So Mike was upset, but more about the monetary loss than the position we were in. We'd all been working on the coast for years and years, so nobody panicked.

We pulled Mike's cowboy boots off and started bailing out the raft. There was some wreckage starting to float up from the boat at that time. I noticed a life ring pop up and I said to the other two guys, "Maybe I'll try and paddle over there and grab that." They said, "Go ahead," since there was only two boots anyways. So I grabbed a piece of the false decking that was floating by and started paddling, not realizing there was some paddles there underneath some of the stuff in the raft. I paddled over to the life rings and tied them on to the raft, thinking that the more wreckage we had the better visibility we'd have.

We sat there and discussed our situation and laughed. I told Mike it was better off that the boat sank anyway because it was an ugly fucking boat. I didn't want to work on it, it was so ugly. Paul said, "I'm not really too enthused with Westview Towing right now, Mike. I've only been working for you for twelve hours and I'm already floating around in a raft. I think I quit."

We were all still very confident that we were going to be rescued within a couple of hours. I had a permanent grin on my face at the time 'cause I just thought, Oh well, this is going to be a good story to tell everybody. No big deal. I had my sunglasses on.

After we finished joking and kidding around and bailing out the raft and looking to see what we had in the raft for supplies we discovered two small paddles slightly bigger than Ping-Pong bats, and a flashlight and a knife. That was about it. There wasn't any food. Then we kind of discussed the situation we were in. Paul was worried about how long we were going to be drifting there—whether we were going to starve to death or die of thirst or something.

Daynes: Paul was a little bit more distressed than everybody else. Kurt thought it was an adventure. I was more concerned about when I got back: how I was going to handle it on the insurance end and all that kind of stuff. I figured my wife would eventually figure it out and she'd send a search party. I wasn't really concerned about that. We keep in fairly regular contact. The only reason that she didn't is 'cause she was on the road and I had called her just before this happened and said everything was fine—we'd be there in the morning. We didn't show up at eight and she started getting a little concerned so she figured she'd wait 'til noon. Because I'm always telling her, "Don't worry about us—we'll make it." That kind of stuff.

Paul's at an older age. He's looking forward to retirement, he's got his family, all that kind of stuff. He'd just got on the boat. It would be pretty trying for the guy. Whereas Kurt would look at it as an adventure—no big deal.

Guilbride: I suggested that we start paddling toward the Broken Group. We had actually drifted a little bit closer. I thought we might just as well do something while we were waiting to be rescued. If they don't get here immediately maybe we can at least get to the Broken Group. We started paddling, Paul and I, because Mike didn't have as much clothes as either Paul or myself. So we took the Ping-Pong paddles and paddled away for about five hours straight. We paddled for a couple of hours and realized that maybe we weren't going to be rescued right away, so then we had a little rest and continued on for another three or three and a half hours.

In retrospect it was a lucky fluke that we had decided to paddle, because the tide was ebbing out of Barkley Sound, and if we hadn't paddled, the tide would have pushed us out beyond the coastal tide rip. So we managed to get to within about three miles of the Broken Islands. That was about as close as we could get; we more or less came to a stall.

By that time it was about six hours after we'd sunk. It was starting to get dark and we realized that we weren't going to get rescued within a couple of hours and it was going to be dark soon and it was forecast to go up to 40 during the night, so it was beginning to get a little more serious. I still don't think anybody was too concerned. Mike, unfortunately, was suffering from seasickness and he didn't have as many clothes on so he was extremely cold. We were all getting kind of cold by then because we were all soaking wet. Paul was the only one who managed to get a coat on, which was a Mustang with one of those beaver tails. He had lots of girth anyways—he was in the best position of any of us. I was probably the lightest and the most susceptible.

Bottomley: I was all right. I'm fairly fat, and I had a Floater coat on. So you're wet but you're still reasonably warm. Mike Daynes got sick early on, throwing up and stuff. And of course the wind is increasing by this time and it's starting to rain. We tried paddling for a while, but these little rubber boats are just a waste of time. You just cannot get anywhere, and they give you a little plastic paddle like a kid's paddle.

All that night it just got worse and worse. I guess it was blowing 30, 35, maybe even 40 southeast. Then of course the big swell starts with it. We're really being tossed around. I'm surprised it didn't flip over. But you can hear these big breakers, and after dark you don't know if you're getting close to the beach. And we're thinking that if we hit the beach in the dark there are going to be major injuries.

So we spent a horrible night out there. I don't know what the other fellows were thinking, but I was thinking that I'm not going to make it. You think of grandchildren and all kinds of things: the things you could have done, the things you were going to do. The rain is just coming down like bullets. You can hear it pounding down on the cover of this life raft. And it leaks. It's a brand new life raft that Mike had purchased, and the thing still leaks.

Capt. Paul Bottomley: "You think of grandchildren and all kinds of things: the things you could have done, the things you were going to do."
Nadi Bottomley photo.

Mike had on a pair of boots, we used to call them engineer's boots years ago. Similar to a cowboy boot-type heel. And he tore half the heel off climbing out of the engine room or something, and he had about half a dozen nail heads sticking out of this boot. And all I can think of is, every time he moved I would see where his boot was going, because I didn't want him poking a hole in this life raft. When you're a kid they always tell you not to get on inner tubes. And Mike was incoherent by this time. He was so sick, he didn't care where his boot was. But I certainly cared.

Nobody talked very much. We didn't talk hardly at all. Everybody would have their own thoughts, I would think.

Guilbride:　We just resigned ourselves to the fact that we were going to have to just shut down for the night, and in the morning somebody would find us or maybe we'd wash ashore. We spent rather a restless night, although Paul snored off and on during the night. Mike and I looked at each other a couple of times and shook our heads 'cause our teeth were chattering. I was bundled up in a little fetal position trying to keep as much heat as I could in. I'm very familiar with hypothermia, being a commercial diver. I've taken some courses on it and I know the best ways to counteract it and all the signs for it. I was very concerned about that. So most of the night was spent just kind of sitting there shaking and listening to Paul snore. Mike and I chuckled a couple of times. We couldn't believe it. Here we are, drifting around, and the wind's coming up—in the middle of the night it was blowing around 40 and the raft was really getting kicked quite a bit.

In the middle of the night Paul woke up when Mike relieved himself over the side. He asked me to take a look through my little porthole to see if I could see any lights, because we were right in between Cape Beale and Amphitrite. I couldn't see anything, no lights at all. And I thought, No use telling these guys I can't see any lights, so I just came back and said, "Oh yah, I can see some lights. We're still in sight of the lighthouses." So they said, "Oh, that's good."

We just rocked and rolled all night long. The waves were starting to break right over the raft. It got a little bouncy there. I can see why Mike wasn't feeling well.

Daynes:　I was just a little bit seasick. Well, I guess I was quite a bit seasick. But not incapacitated. I was a little bit down and out because here I am: what am I going to do when I get back? I've got to get another boat. Just business stuff. I wasn't really concerned about our lives. In the beginning, yah, because the waves were breaking and the raft was filling up every once in a while. We'd take a big green one over it and it would pretty well fill it up and we'd have to bail it out.

Guilbride: Daylight came along. Paul woke up and opened his hatchway. I was expecting him to say, "Well, I can't see any land at all," 'cause I hadn't seen any lights the night before. And he said, "Oh, we're just off Long Beach." I said, "How far?" He said, "We're really close." So I looked, and to my relief we weren't very far off. Maybe two miles. So we were being pushed up the coast at a fairly good clip. Paul undid his coat and was looking out the window, looking around. Mike and I were shivering away, and we said, "Paul, do you think maybe you could shut the hatch just a little bit there 'cause we're a little cold here." He said, "Oh, right, okay," so he shut it a little bit. But he said, "I want to keep my eyes open in case I see a boat or something." We said, "Okay, but try to keep it closed as much as possible," 'cause we were really getting cold.

Bottomley: We were still about the same distance offshore— about four to five miles. We were in swells that must have been a good twenty feet or more. With daylight I thought the whale watchers would be out. It was the time of year for them to be out there. Of course it was too rough for the whale watchers—they didn't take anybody out.

We went by a survey buoy that's moored to the bottom. I guess it sends tide data or wave data to the weather people. We went by this thing but we weren't close enough that we could paddle to it so we could get ahold of it and break the aerial or do something. I estimated the speed that we went by it. I guess we were making probably a knot and a half.

The southeast kind of blew itself out in the morning, and it swung around into the southwest, which is what usually happens. And as we were being carried along, the southwest wind started to carry us in to the beach. We could see that we were angling in. A plane flew down the coast and I peeled a flare off, but as I say, they were just the kind that you hold, not the parachute exploding type, and this guy was two or three miles away. And we were just a speck.

We could see that we were coming up on this place called Templar Channel, which is Lennard Island. And this is roughly where we're going to hit—the Lennard Island lighthouse. Mike Daynes is so sick he doesn't care about anything. He's got hypothermia, he's shaking.

Kurt was okay and I was still okay, so we figured we're going to have to start trying to paddle, no matter how silly it seems, or fruitless. So we started paddling. We can see the lighthouse and we're getting closer.

Guilbride: We got closer and he said that maybe we should start paddling again to get into the bay before Lennard Island— Cox Bay, I think it is. I said, "Well, I've only got one paddle left in me." The one the day before just about completely exhausted me. Hypothermia was starting to set in, and one more paddle and I'm toast. I said, "You'd better wait 'til the last minute, when you figure we've got to do it, 'cause otherwise that's it."

We got closer and closer, and Paul said, "I don't think we're going to get into Cox Bay. We're going to have to start paddling." So Paul and I grabbed our little Ping-Pong bats and tried to steer ourselves into Cox Bay, but the tide was pushing us too fast, toward Lennard Island. I was on the side that could see what was going on, so I yelled over to him, "We're not going to make it. We're going to have to try to go in between the rocks at Lennard Island."

Bottomley: We can see that we're going to hit these reefs just off the Lennard Island lighthouse. The water shallows off of Templar Channel, and of course you've got the big swells left over from the night before, so the seas are getting bigger and they're breaking. They're all breaking now.

Guilbride: There were only really two reefs that were of concern to us. We paddled like crazy trying to get around. It was starting to get rough again and the waves were starting to break and filled up the raft again full of water. We started running in toward one of the reefs that was covered with those great big, three-inch-long mussels that they have on the west coast. One minute you could see those mussels sticking up about ten feet in the air and the next minute all you could see was white water.

Witnessing this unfolding drama were the keepers of the Lennard Island light station: principal keeper Tony Holland, his wife Margaret, and assistant keeper Gerry Warmenhoven. Warmenhoven had noticed an orange object being tossed in heavy seas south of Lennard Island while giving a weather report. Unable to launch their own boat in the prevailing conditions, the light-keepers could only report their sighting to the Tofino Coast Guard radio station and then watch while the fragile raft surged, out of control, toward the line of reefs that guards Lennard's southern approach.

Margaret Holland: The scene was heart-stopping. The raft was driven by the wind and hurled about by the force of the heavy surf. We feared that at any moment it would be dashed upon the rocks. The hope and chance of it being safely carried through the narrow, rock-strewn entrance to the slightly calmer waters of the gap between Lennard Island and the outer reef was extremely thin.

Bottomley: We can see that if we hit these reefs we're going to have serious injuries. A lot of broken bones. Because these bloody big seas are crashing on them. But there's this gap between these two reefs, and we figure if we can get through this gap it'll be a hell of a lot better behind the reefs than it is out in front of them. So Kurt and I paddled with these flimsy little plastic paddles as best we could. We ended up going through a hole in the reef that was maybe twenty, twenty-five feet wide.

Tony and Margaret Holland atop the light tower on Lennard Island, their home for twenty-two years.
Photo courtesy the Hollands.

The reef line which the *Kitmano* crew narrowly escaped.
Photo courtesy the Hollands.

Guilbride: About this time we were roaring in toward another reef, and I looked up and there was the entire group of lighthouse keepers standing on their porch watching us. We'd discussed it the night before and thought that there wasn't anybody left on Lennard Island, that it was already de-manned.

About ten minutes later … we'd gotten around all the rocks, missed them all, but just by chance we were in the lee of everything and only sixty to a hundred feet from Lennard Island and safe then. A Zodiac—the Coast Guard—came roaring around Lennard Island, and I yelled at Mike and Paul again, 'cause they were still on the other side, that I could see this Zodiac coming.

They came roaring up to us. They were on my side of the raft first. I jumped in, or tried to jump in. I was so cold that my legs weren't moving any more. So they dragged me in, more or less, then propped me up. Then they ran around the other side and grabbed Paul and Mike. Just then another big wave came roaring in and hit one of the reefs and splashed on the rescue boat and killed both motors. So then we were drifting around with the Coast Guard in the Zodiac with no power. They were trying to get it going and it wouldn't go.

Finally another Coast Guard Zodiac came roaring around the corner, and just then the boat we were in got their engines going, so they took us in to Tofino, helped us up the dock. I could hardly walk by then. I was a mess, shaking and shivering and my teeth were chattering. I could hardly talk. Mike was not as bad as me. He was pretty cold and shaking. Paul didn't seem to be affected by the cold, although it must have hit him that we were in kind of a tight situation 'cause he was really, really quiet.

Bottomley: They took us right in to the Tofino dock. There was an ambulance waiting there for us, and they just bundled us right up into the Tofino hospital and stripped us down and into the showers. The doctor and nurses were there taking thermometer readings up your rectum—they want to find out how bad the hypothermia is. Standing in the shower … I don't know if it was straight hot water, but it didn't make any difference. It was great. Then we had some hot tea and then into bed. Then some soup.

Guilbride: They took us to the hospital and everybody in the hospital was great. They really looked after us, gave us some warm soup and tea and hot blankets, checked us all out. Hypothermia was just starting to set in. Paul was fine. Mike was down a little bit, and I think my core temperature was down a degree and a half or two degrees. It came back up right away.

> The three survivors, having drifted 50 kilometres north along Vancouver Island's rugged west coast, were taken from the life raft and rushed to hospital in a fast response boat operated by Bill George of the Tofino Coast Guard. While still in hospital they learned that contrary to their expectations, no one had been looking for them up to that point: the EPIRB didn't work. An examination proved that the device, though advertised as waterproof, and having been officially inspected only days earlier, malfunctioned as a result of saltwater corrosion. The

Mike Daynes aboard his tug, the
Squamish Chief.
Photo courtesy Mike Daynes.

cause of the *Kitmano*'s sinking was never determined.

Paul Bottomley, Kurt Guilbride and Mike Daynes continue to work in the towboat industry.

Tony and Margaret Holland retired from the Canadian Coast Guard almost exactly a year after the *Kitmano* incident, having served on light stations for thirty-one years—the last twenty-two years on Lennard Island.

Making
History
with the
Velcro
Grip

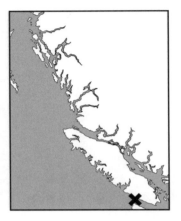

Making History with the Velcro Grip

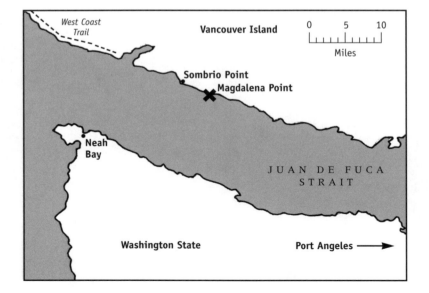

ON THE NIGHT OF OCTOBER 21, 1995, THE US Coast Guard air station at Port Angeles, Washington, responded to a report that a sailboat on the American side of Juan de Fuca Strait had spotted a flare near Sombrio Point on the west coast of Vancouver Island. A letter of agreement between Canada and the US permits both countries to respond to incidents in each other's waters, on the basis of fastest and most appropriate response.

The helicopter crew studied charts of the area, updated themselves on weather conditions, and tried to determine whether the sighting, situated near the popular West Coast Trail, could have been something other than a flare. While this preliminary investigation was underway, a second flare was reported. Within ten minutes, an HH65 Dolphin helicopter was making the sixty-kilometre transit to Vancouver Island. As the helicopter's co-pilot, Lieutenant Larry Littrell, later commented, "Once you get more than one red flare reported in an area, the adrenaline starts going and the reality sets in that this is probably something going down and not just fireworks or somebody seeing a star." A 41-foot rescue boat from the US Coast Guard's Neah Bay base was diverted from a training exercise to provide assistance.

Littrell: We'd set our course so that a direct pass would set us right at the coastline in the area of the flares, which was near Magdalena Point. While we were en route I was using night vision goggles, the aircraft commander was using the aircraft radar, one of the crewmen in the back, Petty Officer Manes, was also using night vision goggles, and the rescue swimmer was using the locator light just so we could see where we were going. We were flying about five hundred feet above the water.

The weather at the time was extremely dark, a heavy overcast with no moon, no stars, hard driving rain, and when we got on scene we also encountered a lot of patchy fog and winds pretty strong out of the west. Nobody seems to get lost when it's real nice out. What we could see was some pretty heavy surf, good swells. That's how we finally ended up finding the shoreline and following it up to where the vessel was on the rocks: by following the breaking surf.

While we were en route we noticed another aircraft in the area that seemed like he was going the same direction. He was at the same altitude, on a slightly converging course. I couldn't get the Rescue Coordination Centre [in Victoria] to identify him. Nobody else reported an aircraft responding to the scene. We made some calls on Coast Guard frequency and we managed to raise him. It turned out to be a Canadian navy helicopter. They just happened to be transiting the area out to their ship. We told them what was going on, asked them if they wanted to help, and they said, "Yah, great, tell us what you want."

The second aircraft on scene turned out to be a Sea King helicopter en route to the HMCS *Annapolis*, located off Cape Beale.

Littrell: We set up with them to start a search in one area and we were going to go on to the point. They thought they'd seen another flare so they diverted to investigate that and we continued toward the reported flare.

When we got to Magdalena Point we didn't see any flares or anything. That's what we hope to do: draw a flare when we get on scene so we can pinpoint the location. Our helicopter carries about a 300-million candlepower spotlight, and even with that light and the night vision goggles, we could pick up the shoreline but there wasn't enough illumination with the driving rain to actually see anything.

The crewman on night vision goggles saw what he thought was a flashlight along the shoreline. The original reporting point put the source at Sombrio Point, which was about another five miles to go from Magdalena. With the fact that there are a lot of campers along the Pacific Trail we associated the flashlight with somebody camping walking down the trail, so we continued toward the scene.

At that point the 41-foot boat had gotten pretty much on scene and they said, "The report of the flares is right off our bow and we see a flashlight." So we looked back, and the way he was

Rescue swimmer Tony Dicataldo (left) and pilot Lt. Larry Littrell: five feet of clearance from rotor to cliff.
US Coast Guard photo.

pointing was right at the flashlight. So we turned around and made our first pass from the west to east along the shoreline about a quarter mile out, maybe closer to a half mile out, at 500 feet, 70 knots, using the night vision goggles. As we passed over the point I could see something on the rocks but there wasn't enough light to give it any definition.

We made another turn, kind of an elliptical circle, back to west and came in closer to the shoreline on the next pass, a little bit lower—probably about 400 feet. Again we couldn't get any definition other than that there was something large on the rocks, and it wasn't a rock. We were getting ready to set up for a third pass. The 41-foot boat was getting ready to launch a flare so they could see. The Canadian helicopter said, "Hey, we've got night vision goggles, we're lined up to make a pass into the wind." We said, "Okay: Canadian aircraft, Canadian soil. Let's let them have at it."

The Sea King helicopter made a low, slow pass along the shore and was able to locate a boat on the rocks.

Efforts to establish a hover over the stricken vessel were frustrated by weather conditions, the helicopter's size and its lack of external lighting. Before pulling out and turning the mission back over to Littrell and crew, the Canadians were able to also identify a life raft on the nearby cliff-fronted shoreline.

Littrell: At that point we co-ordinated with the 41-footer to fire off a parachute flare as we flew over the target. With the parachute flare and the night vision goggles it was like daylight as we made the third pass. At that point we went about two miles to the east, because the wind was out of the west, set up an approach so that we arrived at the breaking surf at about fifty feet and 30 knots, almost parallel to the cliff line. Once we could fly safely and we knew we weren't going to fly into the cliff, we started creeping along the shoreline, following the surf line up. We coordinated with the 41-foot boat to launch flares over our head so that we could see. It took seven more flares for us to move probably a mile.

Once we got to the point where we could see the boat, we had enough of our own light so we could see the cliffs and maintain a hover. The boat was laying up on its side with the stern awash, on the rocks, and the surf was pounding on it pretty good. While we were in the hover for about three to five minutes we watched the boat go from a fishing boat to basically splinters. It was really impressive to watch.

The vessel being impressively reduced to splinters turned out to be the *Georgia Saga*, a small wooden commercial fishing boat owned by Kenneth Rivard of Nanaimo. It is unclear whether Rivard was aboard the *Georgia Saga* that night. Whoever was at the wheel was making a solo transit of the aptly named Graveyard of the Pacific when the boat apparently struck a log and foundered, drifting onto the nearby shore.

Littrell: The 41-footer was also using flares to evaluate the scene and see if they could get in closer to where the boat was on the rocks. What they saw was the same thing: breaking surf and a lot of rocks. The conditions were beyond that boat's capability—probably beyond any boat's capability—to get in there. We could see the raft but we couldn't see anybody in it, and it was being washed up against the base of the cliff. From our point of view we couldn't see the tops of the cliffs. All we could see was a few feet above our helicopter. My understanding is that they're from about 110- to 130-foot cliffs.

At that point a hand popped around part of the cliff, an outcropping, waving a flashlight. This outcropping was probably 110 feet high and had a pretty large tree at the top of it. It formed kind of a cove where the gentleman was sitting. We had to move the helicopter into this cove, up against the outcropping. At that point we had about five feet of clearance between the tips of our blades and the rock.

> Before moving in against the cliff the helicopter's entire crew had discussed how the rescue attempt could proceed. The best bet, they felt, was to do a direct deployment of their rescue swimmer, Aviation Survivalman First Class Tony Dicataldo. Dicataldo would be lowered by cable and, if able to make contact with the shipwrecked fisherman, would strap him to the cable, at which point both would be hoisted to safety.

Dicataldo: The tide was incoming, bringing the surf closer to where he was. It was either take him out now or wait for him to float out later. We discussed that there was no other way to get him out of there. We discussed the different ways that we could do this. Everyone, including myself, was a little bit uneasy about just putting me in the water and letting me swim in because I'm not familiar with the area and it was really hard to keep track of where all the underlying rocks were. It would have been a first-time surf entrance to a vertical surface area, which is just not good. So we decided to go with the direct deployment.

Littrell: We had a small outcropping of rock that we could put the rescue swimmer's feet on, and that's what we'd planned to do. As the safety pilot I'd normally guard the controls and watch all the instruments, to stabilize the aircraft if there's a problem and back it out of the situation. With our proximity to the cliff it was more important for me to actually lean over, almost into the other pilot's lap, to look up through the windows and call clearances from the rotor blades to the cliff. Which was kind of interesting, because I was the only one who could see the gap, or lack thereof, between the blades and the cliff. I remember thinking at that point, I should probably really be scared to death right now. But none of us were. It was strange, there was a kind of calming feeling over the whole crew. Everybody knew exactly what to do, how to do it, and we went in.

Dicataldo: They started lowering me down. The last thing briefed was that if shit starts to go bad—if things start to go wrong, or for some reason they've got to bail—the only thing they were supposed to do with me was cut me loose, basically cut the cable. There was not supposed to be any attempt to recover me if things were to go bad. If the helicopter's going down, that at least leaves somebody in the water to try and continue the rescue via the one person. It also gives me a fighting chance of staying alive, too, if the shit goes bad.

I got about ten feet below the helicopter and the guy started to make his way out on the rocks that we were trying to go to. There was a little pinnacle, a jut of rock that was being periodically swamped by surf. The idea was to put me on the end of that, because that was the farthest point from the vertical surface. They got the blades of the helicopter five feet away from the vertical surface and I was still two feet away from the pinnacle. The flight mech attempted to swing me out toward that. But during my descent on the cable, the guy who was behind the rocks started making his way out across there. I tried to give him hand signals to tell him to stay where he was. He was at a point where it was, I'm out of here, dude. You're coming to get me, I'm going to meet you halfway.

The guy was about six to ten feet from the edge of the pinnacle. He was watching the swells coming in, using the helicopter lights as a source of illumination. He timed it between swells to run across that thing and to jump. He jumped about five, six feet, total, and he did what we call the Velcro grip— that's what we've nicknamed it. As soon as he came in the air, I put one leg between his so I could lock my other one behind him. Basically we both opened up like spiders and that's how we came together. It's just lucky that I was facing directly at him when he jumped.

The pilot was able to back away without us making contact with anything. They got into a safer hover and just hoisted us on in instead of putting us in the water, which is what we've been trained to do—so we can put a quick strop on them, make the guy safe and not have to worry about the basic brute strength it

Dicataldo: "He timed it between swells to run across that thing and jump."
Painting by Graham Wragg.

takes to hold two people together. There was no place to put us down because of the surf and the rocks below us. Nobody was slipping, there was no movement between me and the guy as far as trying to get a better grip, and the flight mech made the judgment call to bring us right in. At that point it was a good judgment call.

All the guy did was hold on and close his eyes and that was it. That was the only thing on both of our minds: don't let go. His raft was floating in the cove up against the rocks, and we could see reflective tape glowing out from inside the door, so we assumed there was someone else inside. Once we got inside the cabin I asked him how many people were on his crew, and he said, "I'm the only one." I asked him three times, and he answered with the same reply: "I'm the only one on the boat." I turned around to the flight mech and said, "We're done. Let's get out of here."

We had a good tailwind and they had to do some dancing to get the helicopter turned and in a safe position—for us to get forward flight. They had to do some of that pilot shit up there, but it was a good deal.

Dicataldo later discovered that he had performed, in Canada, the first "physical grip" rescue in US Coast Guard history.

Glen
and
Glenn
Go
Overboard

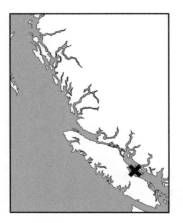

Glen and Glenn
Go Overboard

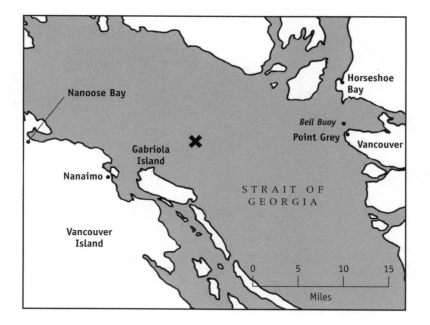

JUNE 5, 1993 WAS A DAY OF SUN-
SHINE and brisk northwesterly winds on the central Strait
of Georgia. Chef Jurgen Schulte of West Vancouver was
at the wheel of his 36-foot sloop *Chesa*, in the lead and
with a good prospect to win his class in the Royal
Maritime Sailing Association's single-handed race across
the strait. The race took place over two days, crossing
from the Point Grey bell buoy at Vancouver to Nanaimo
on Saturday and returning the following day. Schulte
had won his class the previous year and was successfully
maintaining his strategy of completing the entire
Saturday leg on one long, efficient starboard tack. Search
and rescue was very far from the front of his mind.

Search and rescue was also, initially, a distant
thought in the minds of Glen Ringdal, a Vancouver busi-
nessman, and his nephew Glenn Baron. Baron, an engi-
neering technologist from Alberta, was in the Lower
Mainland working on a chemical plant expansion when
the opportunity arose to go fishing with Ringdal. Their
plan was to cross the strait in Ringdal's 21-foot power
boat and spend the day chasing salmon with Ringdal's
son, who lived at Schooner Cove, near Nanoose Bay.
The trip was to be a treat for Baron, who had never been
on salt water.

Ringdal: We took off at about ten in the morning from
Horseshoe Bay. I had never crossed the strait before in this boat.
As we were getting ready—gassing up and whatnot—we ran
into some people that we sort of knew, and they said, "It's a lit-
tle rough out there. But not bad." It was a beautiful, sunny day.
We thought, Well, even if it's a little rough, we'll just go slower.
So off we went.

Having never been before we had to use our compass and
our charts. We were quite amazed at the angle we were going at,
but it was very interesting. Anyway, sure enough, gradually it
started to get rougher and rougher.

I had phoned over to Roberta, my ex-wife, who my son lives with, and said that we were heading over and that she should expect us in a couple of hours. It got to be eleven o'clock, and we were around halfway over, I would think, and it really started to get rough. We couldn't plane any more, so we were down to around eight miles an hour, something like that, getting splashed a lot. The water was coming right over top of the boat— we didn't put any cover on. So we were getting quite wet from the splashing and rocking around. But other than that it was pleasant enough, and we were quite proud of the fact that we were navigating and doing okay.

The weather was fairly warm. I had a sweatshirt on, and shorts. Glenn had his blue jeans and a T-shirt on.

We got halfway, maybe a little more than halfway, and it's eleven o'clock. I phoned Roberta and told her what's happening: We're really going slow and we're going to be a lot longer than I thought. I didn't know how long. It depends on whether this water settles down. Just so she knows, so she's not worried. I think I suggested that we should be there at around one.

I had a kicker motor on the boat at that time. Once before it had already come down. You raise them up on a little latch, and if they fall down they're dragging, and you don't want that. It looked like it was falling down again, so I said, "I'm going to go check this." I just stopped the boat. And as I was climbing over— I had thongs on—I realized I had my wallet in my pocket. I said I'd better take my wallet out, 'cause just two weeks before I'd been at my partner's house and I'd been thrown into the swimming pool with my wallet, and I'd just been through that exercise of drying everything out. So I said, "I'd better take my wallet out in case I fall in the water."

Sure enough, as I stepped down a wave came, I slipped, and boom—over I went. My foot got caught in the kicker motor mount as I went down, so I had to kick to get free.

When I came up I was about ten feet from the boat. Not far. But immediately I realized … I had this big sweatshirt on and it became very, very heavy. And I'm not a good swimmer. I can swim a bit. I can certainly dog paddle around, and I do swim a little in my pool at home. And I realized, "Hey, I can't swim!" And these are big waves.

Glenn was laughing—sure enough, I'd fallen off the thing as predicted. I said, "This isn't funny. You're going to have to save me."

"Oh."

I said, "Get a life jacket. Throw me a life jacket."

Baron: I didn't see any life preserving gear in the rear of the boat, so I went up front to the cabin part, grabbed the first life jacket I came across, went to the back, took my shoes off and jumped in the water. I brought it to him, made sure he put it on, then I started pulling him. He said, "No, no, I'm fine. Don't worry about me. Go back there and get in the boat."

I turned around and it was quite a ways farther away than I thought it would be. It was for sure fifty feet, maybe more. I just put my head down and did the best I could. I never took any swimming lessons as a kid, but I do most other sports naturally. It's more effort than technique. I did go with everything that I had for what seemed like the longest time. I'm sure that it was only a few minutes—not more than five minutes. I gained for a while. I got pretty close, a dozen feet or so, and I was looking at the step I was going to grab and climb up on.

I was taking a big breath, and I had a splash hit me from behind and sucked in over a cupful, I'm sure. There I was, gagging and coughing, and I couldn't do anything. I looked up again and it was probably more than fifty yards away. It was probably closer to seventy.

I thought the only thing I could do … if I caught up to it once I could do it again. So I kept going, it seemed like more than five minutes—it was probably closer to ten minutes. I didn't look for a while. I rested for a second and got to a crest and looked in the distance and it was quite a ways away—more than a hundred fifty, two hundred yards. I knew I wasn't going to get it then.

> There they were, two boaters without a boat, separated from each other by an undetermined distance, their horizons consisting of distant mountains visible across ten kilometres of whitecapped water.

Baron: It was a pretty bad five minutes there. I looked around for Glen, and I yelled for him. I thought I knew which direction he was, but I could have been turned around a little bit. And he naturally would have drifted some, too. But I couldn't see him and he never answered when I yelled. I just felt terrible then. I was very upset.

Ringdal: The water felt fine—I wasn't thinking about the temperature—other than the fact that the waves kept coming over my head. I tried to bob with the waves, but still it would come over my head. I swallowed a fair amount of water.

I started thinking, I wonder what's going on here? What am I going to do? I started thinking about all the logical things, like the boat drifting into the ferry channel, which I knew was just to the south of us. I thought, Somebody'll see it and they'll report a drifting boat, and that means there's somebody out there, and they'll send the Coast Guard, and what is going to happen eventually is I'll see that big helicopter up there and they'll lower that big thing down and lift me out of here. That is what is going to happen. If nobody sees my boat, eventually my ex-wife and son will figure out there's something wrong—he should have been here by now—and report it.

The fact that it was quarter after eleven when I fell off the boat, it's daylight and it's a lovely, warm day—other than the wind—chances are excellent that if I don't drown for some reason, I should be okay. But I had no idea what was happening with Glenn. I was much more worried about him than about me.

Baron: For a while there I thought something would happen right away or it was going to be over for me. I just knew that I had to keep my arms and legs moving. I thought it over and thought it over and looked around and realized that I had to calm my heart down and breathe so that I could swim for a while. I put my head in and floated for a while and slowly got my heart rate down ... swam on my back for a while and decided that my only good chance was to get in closer to one of the big ferries, where they have dozens of people looking out over the sides all the time. That was the only thing that appealed to me. I didn't see any other small craft or anything.

I could see land and I knew that if I could keep going I would get there eventually. It looked like only a few miles, maybe five miles. I'm normally a pretty good judge of distance, because that's what I do for a living, taking measurements in the outdoors. But it was the strait playing tricks on me—I'm so foreign to that environment. It turned out it was at least seven or eight miles either way. I was pretty much in the middle.

I kept going more or less south, toward the island and the ferries. Every half hour or forty-five minutes—whatever it is—one went by. The first two or three were on the south of me so

I kept going. After a while there was one on the north, so I got pretty frustrated—I thought maybe they varied routes whenever the captain felt like it. I thought if they go wherever they please I can't aim for any spot in particular.

A lot of people have asked me about my clothes, my clothes and my watch. The first hour, hour and a half…at the beginning of June it was very nice, very pleasant. I had baggy pants on, some of my work pants, and I had to get rid of them because I couldn't swim very well. So I only kept my T-shirt on and my underwear—ditched my socks and my pants. And all the things I had in my pockets along with them. My watch was in the pocket of my pants, but I had no desire to keep that whatsoever. I thought it would be very disturbing to watch the time go by.

The whole time, from when the incident started, it was five-foot waves or better. It didn't stop. And significant wind. I took in water steady that first hour and a half. It didn't occur to me to keep my eyes on the waves, so I just kept swimming. It turned out to be very unpleasant: the salt water went right through me. I was throwing up and after half an hour I had diarrhea, too. It was incredible.

Ringdal: Gradually I moved to the thought that, Gee, maybe I am going to die here. I thought I might just up and drown because my lungs gradually get too much water in them. I might just slowly drown. Or, after an hour I started to realize I was getting cold. I thought, If I move I keep myself warmer, but if I move too much I'll tire myself out, and I might not be able to hold my head up, and then my head will fall in the water and I'll drown. Or I'll fall asleep if this happens to go an awful lot longer. So I weighed that in my head: how much should I paddle around?

Eventually, at quarter to two, I was bobbing along, facing Vancouver Island, and all of a sudden I wasn't sure if I heard something, but I turned around and boom—here was this boat, just about ready to run over me. It was a sailboat, so of course it wasn't making any noise. All I heard was a splash or something, but it made me turn. He came right by me. He would have missed me by ten feet. Hell, he would have missed me by five feet.

Schulte: The wind was pretty good—I think something like 20 knots, 22 knots over the deck. I was perhaps ten miles out of

Nanaimo, so I had been racing for about three hours at the time. And I saw this red thing bobbing in the water. I couldn't identify it. Normally life jackets are red, and it did look like a life jacket, so my first idea was that somebody had lost his life jacket. I said to myself, "Forget that, put it out of your mind. You are racing. Never mind this thing."

After consideration and soul-searching for a while, I looked again and the thing was still there so I said to myself, Gotta check it out. I fell off, as we call it in sailing, and went toward it.

Ringdal: I started yelling my head off. The guy had already seen me before I saw him. He had thought it was just an empty life jacket lying in the water. Occasionally when you're in a boat you find things in the water. Then when I turned around and he saw my face he was shocked to realize it was a person.

Schulte: When I went toward it this person in a life jacket turned around facing me. And it was Glen Ringdal. It was something else, really. You're racing—you're not expecting anything like that. He was a little bit cool. He was glad to see me, I can say that. I threw him the life ring. I dropped my sails, started the engine, deployed the life ring, circled him and pulled him over to my stern. He actually was able to come up the stern ladder. I said, "Hey, what are you doing?"

> Ringdal briefly summarized the events of the previous three hours. Schulte immediately radioed the Coast Guard, and learned that Ringdal's empty boat had been found near Gabriola Island, thereby activating a search for the missing men. Ringdal and Schulte then turned their attention to the unappealing question of Baron's possible fate.

Ringdal: I asked Jurgen, "Do you think he could still be alive, swimming this long without a life jacket?" And he said, "Well, he *could* still be alive." I didn't like that very much.

Schulte: A person three hours in the water without a life jacket—you tell me who has survived that? There aren't too many. Even if you're in good condition.

Ringdal: Minutes later the Coast Guard arrived. Not in response to Jurgen's call, although they got the location from his call. But my boat had been spotted by the BC Ferry *Queen of Oak Bay*. And apparently by some other sailors as well. And here was the Coast Guard out in the hovercraft.

It had been reported before twelve o'clock, but they couldn't get the motors going on the hovercraft. It took them a couple of hours, they said. They took control and said that they would commence the search for Glenn. A couple of other boats in the vicinity were asked to take part in the search. Once they did that, Jurgen said he had to phone in to the race officials. He had to phone in and officially pull out of the race.

He said, "Do you want to drive while I'm doing this?" I said, "Okay." I got up there, steering with this great big wheel. I'd never been on a sailboat in my life. I said, "I don't think Glenn will be around here." The hovercraft had started to search; they were going back and forth. I said, "He'd be farther south—they were heading that way." He said, "You go wherever the hell you want."

Jurgen Schulte at the wheel of *Chesa*: "That was quite a day."
Photo courtesy Jurgen Schulte.

So away I went, about a kilometre probably from where we'd been. Then the RCMP boat—the big boat, *Sidney*—came along. They wanted me to come onto their boat and give a report. We got together. It was still rough, so it took a little doing. I had to go from one boat to another boat and on to their boat.

Once I was on there, Jurgen put his boat onto automatic pilot, pointed it toward Nanaimo, and sat down to have a smoke and a beer, as he put it. The RCMP connected me to my ex-wife on the phone. She hadn't been told anything. I told her what was going on, that I'd been rescued but we were still looking for Glenn. She went nuts, started screaming. I told her I'd call her back when anything happened.

Baron: I didn't know which way I should go, but I started noticing other vessels around. I was in the midst of that sailboat race to the north. And finally the hovercraft, too. That was kind of a good news/bad news thing 'cause they stopped way too far to the north. I watched them do this grid, and I think about 300 metres is about as close as they got. They didn't see me waving or anything. I thought there was the outside chance that they'd catch me in their binoculars when I was at the crest of one of the waves. Then they went back the other way—they did the grid to the north. That wasn't a very good feeling there.

By that time I was cold in the hands and the feet. Then, some time after that, they were getting really stiff. I started getting really heavy, and a little numbness in the limbs. I guess a little bit of fatigue, too.

Then out of nowhere the sailboat came along. I knew it was going to be close. I swam in short bursts—whatever I had energy for—then rested when I thought I'd got close enough to catch his attention. He was the only craft that had gone straight from when I'd caught sight of them. The rest were on random routes and went in their own directions.

Schulte: We checked for approximately one hour, then I called the Coast Guard back and said, "Look, there's a person in the water, but on the other hand, I'm in a race. I do have to report to the race committee that I'm overdue—something might have happened to me." I had already tried to contact them and I couldn't reach them. There was too much commotion.

The Coast Guard told me there were seventeen boats on the water searching for Glenn Baron, and I may be excused. I said, "Okay, on the way I'll have a look around and see what I see on my way to Nanaimo." Under engine power I continued my way toward Nanaimo.

Now you're in a kind of a shock: you pick someone up off the water, he's shaking, he's a bit hypothermic. So I went down and poured myself a little bit of Scotch. I had the engine going at 1500 RPMs—just going easy. I thought, Just take it easy now, calm down. It's over.

I come up the companionway, sit in the cockpit, and I hear this voice: "Help me. Please help me!" About twenty, twenty-five feet from the boat was Glenn Baron. At first all I could see was the hand. When the wave came down, all of a sudden I could see the head pop up. I said, "God, this is something else!

Single-handed ... by yourself ... the second rescue ... what is going on?"

Baron: He came across on the south side of me, turned the wheel to the right to circle me, and threw the line out the back. I grabbed the rope—I heard later that they were surprised that I'd done that. I grabbed the ladder, climbed up, and wrapped my arms around the top two rungs. I couldn't look up. I was so happy to be out of the water ... I just tried to relax and catch my breath.

Schulte: I had to put the boat onto autopilot again so the boat stayed into the wind with the engine going slightly forward, so the boat stands still. I pulled Glenn Baron slowly toward the boat, with the ladder down. The problem was that I had to stop the engine, because if anything happened, he slips, he can slip into the prop. It's a tricky situation. You cannot be too long in neutral, because the boat can fall off either way and you're going to perhaps run over him. You have to really react fast. He was just hanging on to the life ring. I was down on the ladder. I had put the engine in neutral.

The decision was, if he lets go of the life ring, what am I going to do? Am I going to jump after him and try to save him? His pupils were not showing any more, he could not speak, he could not act. I had to wake him up a bit. I thought, Even if I break a bone in his face or something, to wake him up a little bit ... four hours in the water without a life vest is a tough time. So I slapped him in the face a few times. All of a sudden I saw this reaction—he got angry.

Ringdal: Glenn doesn't swear or anything. But when Jurgen said again, "Come on, come on," Glenn just looked at him and said, "Fuck you." Where that came from I don't know.

Baron: He was very upset with me. He thought that I was going to fall back in the water. I didn't really think about it until after, but it was a very good point. He couldn't very well jump in after me. I was so embarrassed a week later [when the three men met for a celebratory meal], I didn't even look the man in the face.

Schulte: He really got upset with me. That was the point to get him into the boat. He woke up. He was ready.

With my help—you have a lot of strength in that situation—
he got up, just fell into the cockpit. So … there we go again. I
raced down to the VHF, called out another Mayday. Coast Guard
said, "What is your position, *Chesa*?" I said, "I'm a hundred yards
from the search area."

Baron: He sat me down on the back, put a toque on my head
and wrapped a sleeping bag around me. He must have got on the
radio then. He brought me a bit of water to drink. He told me to
get out of the wind until the hovercraft made it over. He wanted to know if I could make it down the stairs—it was very steep
down the stairs into the cabin. I made it—kind of fell the last
one—and kind of fell down on his couch. I think I vomited on
his floor. He told me not to worry about it—a little bit more
water.

The paramedics were pretty concerned. They gave me some
blankets and hot packs. They figured that they shouldn't leave
me in there—that they should get me onto the hovercraft and to
shore. I told them I could make it. I went up on my own power.
It was really strange: they had the hovercraft up beside the sailboat, and I expected them to be a little gentler. I guess they didn't
want to drop me in the water. They threw me across and up onto
the storage bins, and I went banging off the cabin. "Hey," I
yelled. I thought they were trying to kill me.

I went inside, lay down, and they put the heat packs back on
between my arms and between my legs and covered me up. The
ride to shore was so fast for me that I don't even remember it.
And into the ambulance and away. And I was pretty gullible. I
believed the nurses when they told me they were out of beds
and there was no other place for me to be than in intensive care.
I took their word for it. I didn't think I was that ill.

I had to go to the washroom pretty bad but they wouldn't let
me get up until my temperature came up to 35 or 36. I sat there
and sat there and sat there and watched the gauge. I had two IVs
in me. They took some X-rays while I waited for Glen and
showed me the pools in the bottom of my lungs—the dark spots.
They wanted to know why I fell out of a boat. I told them that
wasn't the case—that I'd actually jumped out.

After that the only thing that mattered was that they
wheeled me out so I could see the television and watch the
hockey game. It was during the finals. It was John LeClair scor-
ing in overtime in Los Angeles for Montreal.

Ringdal: They couldn't let him out because the doctor who had done him had now been called away on another emergency. We asked Glenn, "What do you want?" And he said, "I want a White Spot cheeseburger. As a matter of fact I want two of them."

We went back the next morning and got Glenn and we went out fishing. We caught the first-ever fish in that boat.

Baron: I don't remember dwelling on anything. Number one, I only had concentration for the then and now. To be quite honest, I really only paid attention to what was going to happen next—what I needed to do to improve the odds for me. I knew that I needed to swim and float and save energy for as long as I could, to have any hopes. I thought about Glen a lot. I thought if anything bad was to happen, that would be a terrible thing. I knew he didn't swim and I hoped he was floating all right over there. I was very frustrated when I did have a lot of emotions running through my mind. There was no way I was going to let that determine my life.

The hovercraft that sped Glenn Baron to safety.
Graham Wragg photo.

Reunited for a celebratory meal: rescuer Jurgen Schulte (seated at right) with Glenn Baron (standing) and Glen Ringdal.
Photo courtesy Glenn Baron.

Ringdal: The only real big concern I had was about my kids and my mom, just thinking that it's going to be an ugly day. And I thought too—as little as I could, but I couldn't help but think—about my nephew, and his wife, and she's expecting a baby, their first. And I thought, It's just going to be ugly. It's going to be awful. Everybody's going to be upset.

I thought about my own life. People often ask about that: What would you change? It was an interesting revelation in that I was very content with the life I've led, and where I'm going, and my need to change or not change anything. I didn't change anything subsequent to that. I'm a Christian, so I'm content with that part of my life. I thought that what I'd done to, with and for people—it's been okay. I won't regret any of that. I kind of regretted not reaching my fiftieth birthday. I'd just turned forty-nine in April.

I think that the bad thing was my lack of respect for the water—the fact that I didn't feel any fear about falling overboard, and just wasn't smart enough to realize the wind was blowing and what it could do to the boat.

Glenn's bad mistake, theoretically, was jumping in to bring me the life jacket. You should always stay with the boat, they say. The fact is, by the time he'd started the boat and got it pulled around I probably would have drowned. With that heavy sweatshirt on I was having great difficulty keeping my head above the water. I would have tired very, very quickly, and fear would have overtaken me. If he hadn't done what he did, I think I would have panicked and I would have drowned before he ever got the boat around. Whilst it was against all the rules of the sea for him to do what he did, I think it saved my life. It almost cost him his life, but it saved mine.

Schulte: That was quite a day. It was good. It was good to help. I think everybody on the water should keep a lookout all the time, in case you see something unusual. That will be a lesson for me: if there's something unusual in the water, don't even hesitate. Go and check it out. Even if you're in a race. Even if you have to be somewhere at a certain time.

> The incident attracted widespread media coverage both for the nature of the rescue and the fact that Ringdal, well known in Vancouver social and business circles, was at the time vice-president of the Vancouver Canucks. He is currently president of the BC Lions football team.
>
> Baron, soft-spoken and unassuming, was taken aback at being caught up in the ensuing media limelight. "It was," he noted, "a hard way to become famous."

Bright
White,
and
Waves All
Around Me

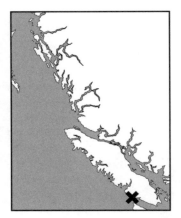

Bright White and
Waves All Around Me

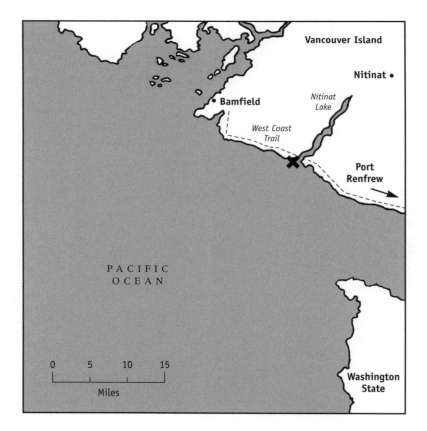

FOR TEN DAYS LEADING UP TO THE
LABOUR Day weekend of 1994, Lauren Holman had
been doing what salmon fishermen like doing least: not
catching salmon. Having been frustrated in the more
sheltered Gold River area, he elected to have one last go
at salvaging the season by detouring while en route to
his Duncan home and tackling the richly productive but
notoriously treacherous waters at Nitinat. This tidal lake
drains through a natural sluice into the open Pacific
between Port Renfrew and Bamfield on Vancouver
Island's west coast. A potentially lethal mix of conditions
occurs at the mouth of the outlet channel when lake
water forced out by a falling tide meets incoming ocean
swells. In native dialect, "Nitinat" means dangerous
rushing water.

Tom Walton, also of Duncan, is a logger and fishing
guide who has been at Nitinat more than once when
risk-takers have paid the ultimate penalty for lack of
appropriate judgment, equipment or local knowledge.
He was there with his friend Ken (Max) MacDowell on
the morning that Holman and his eighteen-year-old son
Jason headed out to turn their fishing season around.

Lauren Holman: I made a couple of mistakes which I normally don't do. Number one, I didn't look at my tide book and number two, I didn't listen to the weather report. Which I always do.
But I didn't because I was fooled by the inside waters at Gold
River. I didn't realize that they'd had a huge storm on the west
coast itself, and I didn't know it because I had been way inland
at Gold River and didn't feel it.

I got up and made breakfast and we went down the lake, my
oldest son and I. It was pitch dark until we were about halfway
down the lake. It was beautiful blue, dead flat like glass. When
you come down the lake it funnels down to a little narrow gap,
fifty feet wide. Long and narrow, about five hundred feet long,
then it empties out into the ocean. So you've got these big waves

coming in and this river roaring down and hitting the waves. I went down through it and looked at the waves and I couldn't believe how big they were—huge, the biggest waves I've seen in my entire life. I turned around right now and got the hell out of there, up into this little bay and sat there. We were tied up to some kelp and just looking at these waves. They were monsters, at least thirty-five feet high—thirty-five to forty-five feet high. Huge.

I saw a couple of boats go down past us and they came back up. We were fishing with someone, and he went down but he never came back up. Jason said, "Dad, they must have got out." I said, "They must have gone out through Canoe Pass." That's an area where you can get through, sneak by all these big waves in behind these rocks.

So I went out, my motor in reverse, and I was pointing downstream, looking at these waves. That was the biggest mistake I made, right there. I should have had my boat turned the other way, pointing upstream so I could go forward.

I happened to just glance to my left—and we were only ten feet away from the shoreline, but it's sheer rock cliff down both sides—and I said, "Holy mackerel, we're moving." And we were doing 10 or 15 knots. I looked up again, and by the time I looked up we were within fifty or seventy-five feet of these waves. There's a grey area in there, they call it the point of no return, and I was in that. And I knew it. And I was in trouble.

I didn't panic. I said, "Geez, we're in trouble." I put the boat in full reverse, but the water came right over the back of the boat, and I was afraid of flooding the motor out. I knew I couldn't go forward and turn around. If I'd turned sideways the current would have just caught me and pushed me into it broadside.

I sat there and sat there. I knew I'd gone too far. I said, "I'll wait for one of these big rollers to lay down in front of me and I'll sneak over the top of it, and I'll wait for the next one to crash down and I'll sneak over it. That's how the guys get out: they time the waves. But I wasn't used to those big waves and I blew it. I went into the first wave not realizing that when they crash down they created such a pile of foam and bubbles—there was so much air in the water—that there was no thrust to my prop. When I gave it full guns to go, the boat just sat there. We're doing 4,000 RPMs, and we're sitting still, the boat's just slowly moving forward. So I'm sinking quickly into these bubbles. All of a sudden it grabs the solid water and it starts to climb this wave. By this time my timing's way out. I'm underneath the crest by this time. The crest is over top of me.

The wave came up and it took the cabin right off the boat. I remember my boy yelling, "We're dead." I just saw a huge blue wall of water in front of me, bluey-green. I looked up but I couldn't even see the top of the wave, it was so high. That's the last thing I remember. It took the cabin right off, took the windshield, took us with it and threw us out of the boat. There was a pile of boats behind us and they said they never saw anything like it in their lives. The boat was right upside down, and the wave threw it through the air about fifty or sixty feet. The wave came down on top of it and just blew it to pieces—nothing left of it.

Walton: A bunch of us were tied up at the West Coast Trail wharf. Max MacDowell and I were going out first thing in the morning because we were having a derby that day. We have an annual derby out there that weekend. I wanted to go down and take a picture of the water from there. I knew it was rough from the storm the day before.

The wharf is just above what they call the River of the Nitinat, the narrow gap where the water boils out to the ocean. There was about thirty-five boats tied up there. Everybody knew it was too rough to get out. I went out there to take a picture and there was two smaller boats that went by me and one of the guys in the first boat yelled at me that someone went down. I didn't really understand what the heck he was saying. I didn't know that anyone had even tried to go out.

The river was boiling out pretty good. It was pushing everybody out toward the ocean, toward the rough water. It's a 150-yard stretch of water that just shoots you out. You can see the big waves coming in, bursting, white water everywhere. There'd been two days of strong southwest wind and the waves were twenty to twenty-five feet consistently.

But we went down and I turned around and faced upriver to stay in one spot so I could take a picture. All of a sudden I spotted three things bobbing out in the water. One was a full gas can, which I found out later. The others were two humans, two guys.

MacDowell: The people who got wrecked were in behind all that white water and we couldn't see them that well. That was the only thing I was a bit leery about: we didn't know one hundred percent that those two black dots were people. The waves were coming in so fast and taking them down to the bottom. You'd see them and then they weren't there for thirty seconds or whatever. They were going to the bottom with every wave.

Lauren Holman: When I woke up I was on the bottom of the ocean, going around and around and around. All I could hear was gravel smacking the side of my head. I didn't know which way was up and which way was down. I didn't have a clue. I had just bought a Mustang jacket the day before and I had all the safety belts on good and tight, but I had big work boots on too. I swam and rowed my arms and kicked like a bugger and all of a sudden I popped to the surface. But again I'd come up into the foam—I had four or five feet of foam above my head so I didn't know where the wave was. I could hear them all around me, but I didn't know whether I was on shore or whether I was out in the middle of the wave. It was just bright white, and waves all around me.

I didn't panic; I actually never panicked once. I was more afraid of dying, of just surviving and getting the hell out of this mess. In the meantime I was thinking, Where's Jason, where's Jason? But he had a full body survival suit on, so I knew he'd be okay.

Jason Holman: I got knocked out on impact. I woke up underneath the water and I started freaking out. I could not get anywhere for about fifteen seconds. I said, "To heck with this," and I stopped struggling, and all of a sudden I popped up to the top. Got a big breath of air and looked in front of me and boom—another wave bashed me down. This happened about five times. Then finally I got out of the waves and I was into the rollers. I looked around and saw the top end of the boat floating up and down. I couldn't see my dad.

Lauren Holman: I could feel myself going up, up, up, up, and I knew a wave was going to hit me, but I didn't know when, so I didn't know when to take a deep breath. Then bang, back down to the bottom again. This happened three or four times. Finally I came up into an area where there was no suds. I'd gone into deeper water—I was three or four waves out by this time. Every time I'd go down to the bottom and get smacked around, the current would push me to the next wave. I turned around and there was a pile of waves on this side of me and a pile of waves on that side of me, so I knew I was going out.

By this time I was pretty beat up. My face was all cut by the glass—when the windshield hit my face. My arms felt like putty because I'd been swimming continuously, trying to stay at the surface. I knew I was in trouble and I knew I was hurt because all the muscles were torn off my neck and I couldn't hold my head up, it was just flopping all over.

Anyways, I knew I had a lot to go yet. I could see the wave coming this time. I held my breath and bang, down I went again. As I was going out farther I was going deeper, too. The last time I went down I remember hitting sand, real soft sand, and then sliding over an edge and going down real deep. I turned around and tried to grab the bank to scramble up. Finally I pushed and swam and I could barely make it to the surface, because I was totally exhausted and I was losing my timing. When I got to the surface, instead of me coming up and taking a breath, the wave was already coming down, so I didn't have time to take a breath. I'd get a real quick gulp, just a little bit of air—half water and half air—before the wave hit. I'd try to cough but I didn't dare cough going down, going down deeper again. The last time I went down it was pitch dark. There were absolutely no light rays at all. It was dead, dead quiet. You could hear a pin drop. Actually it was quite pleasant—really, really quiet and peaceful down there.

When I went down for the last time ... people always ask, "Did your life flash in front of your eyes?" And no, my life did not flash in front of my eyes. I was thinking very clearly. I remember slipping over the edge of the bar and down into the deep. My arms and my head were beat up pretty bad. I couldn't lift my arms—it felt like a ton of weight, from fighting the waves continuously. I remember laying on the bottom, and it was extremely quiet. I sort of said to myself, Geez, it's peaceful down here.

I knew that I'd never have the strength to go to the top. I basically said to myself, "I guess I'm going to die. This is the end." I didn't want it to end like that because I wanted my life to continue. I wanted to see my kids grow up, watch my daughter grow up and be married. All this stuff was going through my head, about my wife and kids. I was feeling how sad they would feel for me, and how sad I would feel for them because I'd died on them. I was really emotionally upset, laying on the bottom down there.

I couldn't even see the surface, it was so bloody far up. I said to myself very clearly, God, I guess I'm yours—better take me now. Please accept me. Something like that. And the instant I said that I was totally engulfed by the brightest light I'd ever seen, all around me. I didn't really know what was going on. And then all of a sudden out of this white light came a voice that said, "You're going to be all right, my son." That was it. The white light disappeared.

And all of a sudden I felt myself being lifted, like someone lifting me under both armpits—a big hand. And I shot straight to the surface. Didn't even move my arms or legs, and all of a sudden I was floating on the surface.

There were still lots of waves in front of me and lots behind me. I could barely move my arms and hypothermia was beginning to set in, when all of a sudden, pop—about sixteen feet away, up pops my son out of the water. He goes, "Dad, Dad." I had lost it, I was all disorientated. I saw a great big boulder out there and I was starting to swim toward it. It would have smashed me to pieces. He screamed and swam out toward me and said, "Don't go near that boulder, it'll kill ya. We've got to swim out." His face was full of blood and mine was full of blood and he was dragging me.

Jason Holman: He was swimming toward the reef—the shoreline reef—and there were waves crashing on it. I saw that happening right away. I didn't know what he was doing—he was so dazed. I swam after him as fast as I could. I had a Floater jacket on so I could swim like a bat out of hell. I rode the waves—the rollers—in there.

I grabbed him and I tried to swim out. We were going on top of the rollers, down to the bottom, back up again, and then back down. I tried to swim out. I knew if we went in toward shore we would have been squashed in The Gap, because it was huge waves. I knew what was going on, I had my head on my shoulders. He was right out to lunch.

I saw a boat out there, and I thought that if we could get out to that boat we'd be okay. I was yelling and screaming and waving but they either didn't see us or—I don't know what was going on, they didn't even try to help us. And all of a sudden, Tom Walton came flying around the corner in his boat. My dad said, "A boat's coming around." I didn't even listen to him. I just kept yelling at the other boat. I didn't listen to him 'cause I didn't think he was all there at the time.

Lauren Holman: Tom had come down the river and heard that a boat had gone down. He saw Jason on top of one of these waves, waving his arms. To this day I don't know how he did it, never mind why he did it.

Walton: There was a whole bunch of boats following me down the river because they figured I was going to try and get out. They were going to try to follow me if I went out. They didn't realize I was just going down to take a picture. So as soon as I seen these guys in trouble I threw my camera under my centre console and started yelling at these boats to get out of the way. There's not enough room for five boats at The Gap. Some of them headed back up, but I had a buddy in another boat that followed me down with a couple of my friends. He stayed there with me, and we were talking back and forth on VHF radio. I said to him, "I'm going to go get them."

I started timing waves, 'cause every third and fifth waves are the big ones. I was waiting for the big one to come so I go through it and get two slack waves to get to the guys. All the waves were so big from the storm, I just gave that up. Finally, when I had clearance to turn around from all the other boats I just headed out, eased off at the first wave as it broke right in front of me, rolled over the white water and then went as quick as I could to the next one. It was breaking too quick, so I jumped it. I was about twenty feet in the air, and came down on the back of it, landed, went to the next one, jumped it and landed on the back of it.

I knew we were getting close to where we'd seen those guys, but the big one was coming in—the fifth one, I figured—and I couldn't jump it, so I let it curl right up on me and then I shot myself right through it. I've got a spray curtain on the front of my boat, so it took most of the brunt, even though it ripped it to shreds and filled my boat up quite a bit with water. But we made it through and the guys were right there.

They were in a bad spot. They were in an area where the waves were still breaking so they were still getting drove down to the bottom even though the water was getting deeper. At the start it was fairly shallow for them, but most of the time it was twenty-five feet and they were getting drove right to the bottom every time. They'd had it, anyhow: they'd never have taken another wave and made it. They were in pretty bad shape. Every exposed part of their body was covered in blood and they were bleeding bad, 'cause the windshield had exploded on their face.

Once we had them in I jumped the next wave to get out just before it broke, then I started bilging the boat. I had two guys in shock for sure. I was close to having a third, because my partner Max was pretty shaken up, even though he didn't know it. He couldn't stop talking. He'd gone out there with me before but he'd never seen it bad. I grabbed some towels that I had under the centre console and threw them up to him and said, "Wrap them around their head and find out where they're bleeding and stop as much as you can."

MacDowell: I remember saying, "What the hell were you guys doing? What did you do? Who are you fishing with?" At the same time I was making sure they were okay. They were fishing with two or three other boats and thought the others had already gone through it. They thought they were lagging behind. Their buddies had veered off and docked at the wharf and they'd carried on. Here we are: Tom's such an expert boater and he has the smarts to stop and all of a sudden these guys don't, so you're going, "What are you guys doing? What were you thinking of?"

Lauren was in disbelief at what had happened: the water, the waves. He thought he was a good boater and it just took him by such surprise. Especially that his boat was totally gone.

No way he wanted to go back in. He wanted to go to Port Renfrew. Christ, that was an hour in rough water. He wanted to go to Bamfield and that was forty-five minutes the other way in rough water.

Lauren Holman: I was terrified. Tom said, "You're all busted up." I said, "No, no, no, let's go fishing." I said, "You've saved me, I'm saved, I don't want to go through this all over again." I pleaded with him and begged. I said, "Let's go fishing for a couple of hours—they're catching fish out there."

Walton: I wanted to get them the heck back in, but they didn't want to go back through that gap. They didn't want nothing to do with it. There were four boats out there watching this whole thing and three of them had fish on. Lauren said, "Put your lines down, fish if you want. I don't want to go back through that gap." The whole time they didn't realize they were sitting in a foot of water in my boat.

There was a few things—some broken parts—floating to the surface: a seat and stuff. I went around and grabbed that as I was bilging the boat, watching the waves the whole time—counting and watching. We got some hot tea in them. We knew they were in shock. I kept trying to phone the Coast Guard to get a helicopter or anything to help these guys out. I knew they could die if they were in shock for too long.

I just kept worming around The Gap. Then I got Lauren to sit with me and I got Max to sit with Jason. I nodded to Max and said, "Hang onto him." As soon as the big wave went past me I went up and rode on its back and took them in. Lauren looked at me and he said, "What are you doing?" I said, "I'm taking you in." He had a grip on my leg like you wouldn't believe. He wasn't going to let go. And he held his breath the whole way in—I know he did. I was patting him on the back. Once we got through I said, "It's okay, you're in."

The survivors and their rescuers (left to right): Lauren Holman, Jason Holman, Ken MacDowell and Tom Walton.
Photo by John Yanyshyn, Visions West.

Lauren Holman: He got on one of these big rollers and just went right in on it. They got us in to shore and bandaged us up, gave us more coffee, and I changed clothes with people on the wharf. There were a pile of hikers on the wharf, and they fixed us all up. Then we went for a nine-mile ride back up the lake, where there was two ambulances waiting for us.

I was in bed for eight weeks. I pulled all the muscles off my head all around, and off my shoulder. The only thing holding my head on was my bones. The doctor said he couldn't believe it. He said, "Most people get into a car accident and they're hit hard once. You were hit over and over and over. I haven't got any idea why you aren't a quadriplegic."

It was the end of the season. I hadn't caught any fish at all, hardly. I'd spent a lot of money fitting this boat up, wanting to catch this ultimate salmon, and I was prepared to take on anything. I took a chance, and I shouldn't have done it.

Walton: I hadn't had time to be scared when we were out there, but when it was over I found that my leg just wouldn't stop shaking. I had a beer—I thought maybe that would help. It didn't. So after a while, when the tide came up and things calmed down, I just said to Max, "Come on, we're going fishing." And we went back out and had a fish on in about thirty seconds.

> Tom Walton and Ken MacDowell earned National Safe Boating Awards and medals of bravery from the Royal Lifesaving Society of Canada for saving Lauren and Jason Holman.
>
> Lauren had left his twelve-year-old son Warren in the care of friends at their Nitinat Lake campground. Confused by the accident, he thought Warren had also been in the boat with them when the accident happened.

Lauren Holman: They all tried to convince me that he was on shore. I wouldn't believe this. I thought they were saying this to keep me calm. I thought that Warren was lost—that I'd killed him. I was getting pretty upset. When I saw him standing on the shore when we came back—he didn't know what was going on—and I saw him standing there with a fishing rod in his hand looking at me. Nothing hit home until I knew I could physically touch him, that it wasn't really a ghost I was seeing.

DANGEROUS
WATERS

Wrecks and Rescues
off the BC Coast

NORTH
COAST

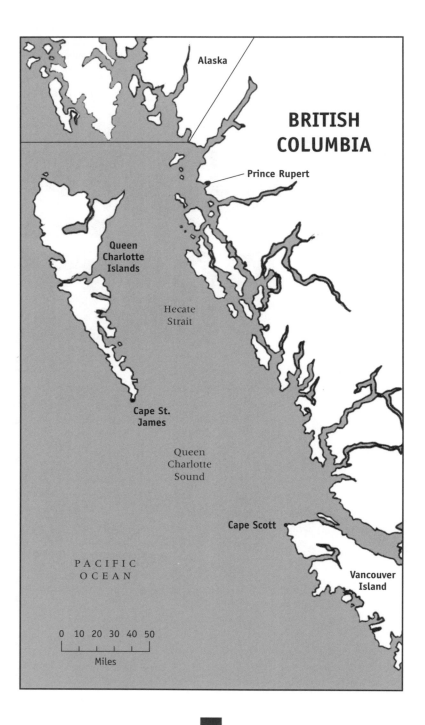

The Law of Gravity Shouldn't Allow It

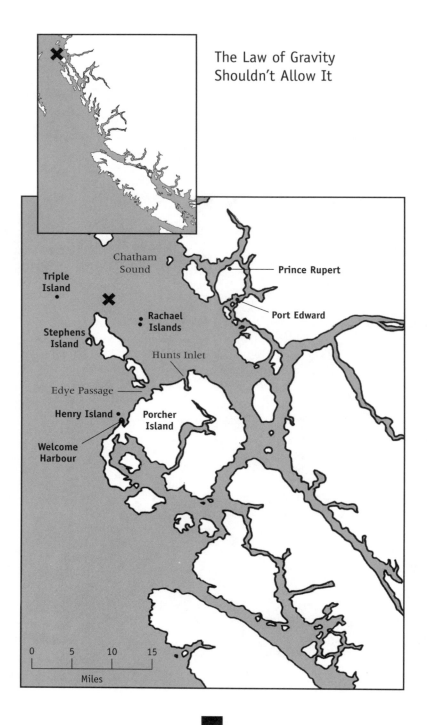

The Law of Gravity
Shouldn't Allow It

GEORGE MOORE WAS A FORTY-THREE-YEAR-OLD refrigeration specialist working in BC Packers' Prince Rupert cannery when a boat fell, more or less literally, into his hands. A group of local men had constructed a 36-foot ferro-cement hull and were moving it to the beach for launching when it slipped from its cradle and landed on a rock which punched a hole in its side. Shipwrecked before they'd gotten to the water, they lost interest in the project and offered it to Moore, free of charge. Moore was still putting finishing touches on the *Concreta* in December 1974 when he, his wife Audrey (now Audrey Samuel) and their three-year-old daughter Tracey made what was intended to be a pleasure excursion across Chatham Sound to the north end of Porcher Island.

Moore: It was just a weekend trip from Port Edward. We went across to Edye Pass, where we used to go fishing for spring salmon. It was a beautiful day when we went across. We anchored in Safety Cove. During the night the southeast wind came up. By early morning it was a gale, it was really blowing. We decided to pull our anchor and go inside a little island for a bit more shelter.

Because the boat was new and we were still building it, I didn't have no deck plates and stuff like that on it. So when we used to drop the anchor we'd throw it over the side and take the rope up to the bow and just wrap it around the cleat. When I was pulling anchor I'd just take it off the cleat and go back behind the cabin and stand midship and pull it over the side and stow it. This time the wind was blowing and the boat circled over the line and got caught underneath, wrapped around the rudder, about halfways in and halfways out.

We had the motor running, and for some reason that motor would windmill, the propeller would keep turning even in neutral, so we were creeping ahead, and the line got caught and rolled up tight. I couldn't let it out, couldn't let it in, couldn't reach underneath with anything we had on board to try and cut it. So there we were. We swung around with the stern to the wind.

The waves started spilling over the back end, 'cause the waves were getting pretty high and kept pushing us out, gradually moving us farther and farther out. After a couple of hours the anchor was just hanging, and we were in trouble.

I just had a small CB which had a range of about seven or eight miles maximum. I understand that it was Barney Wicks, the guy that ran the Gulf Oil station in Prince Rupert, that first heard me. He tried to call me and couldn't. He got me in touch with Bob Pederson, who had a radio shop or something like that, or an electrical business. He had some kind of a booster on his CB, and it was boom—like he was talking to me right there in the cabin. He came on to say that he'd relayed a message to the tug at Welcome Harbour in Hunts Inlet, and that a fishing boat was also on its way.

> The Rivtow Marine tug *Gulf Prince* was indeed close by, sheltering from the weather in a cove in the Edye Pass area. Captain Nate Turrell and a crew of four attempted to reach the *Concreta*, which was now drifting eight to ten miles north of Porcher Island in a full-blown southeast gale. Before long the *Gulf Prince* was taking breaking seas over its wheelhouse and its engine room was flooding. Faced with what appeared to be impossible circumstances, Turrell was forced to abort the attempt and struggle back into shelter.

Moore: I watched for a long time, but the wind was screaming and with snow the visibility was down to almost nothing. It turns out that the tug had been forced to turn back. She'd taken a big wave over the side or something. I never did see the fish boat. But believe me, I worried a lot about the crews of those boats that were risking their lives trying to help us.

> Time and options were quickly running out for the Moores. Their salvation appeared to rest in the hands of Captain Vince Brown, Rivtow's manager of north coast operations. Brown was in his office that morning, catching up on paperwork. Owing to the severity of the storm, other Rivtow personnel had showed up at the

company's docks to check on their vessels. Alerted to the Moores' plight, Brown got together a crew consisting of captains George Salome and Dick Northrup, engineer Tony Olsen and mate Frank Brereton.

Brown had skippered the tug *Gulf Prince* and considered it a fine sea boat. Knowing that it had been forced to abandon the rescue, he felt that only one vessel available to him was capable of taking what Chatham Sound was dishing out that furious winter day. The *Lumba Lumba* was a 90-foot personnel carrier originally built to cross the Strait of Malacca in Indonesia. At approximately one-thirty in the afternoon, with a volunteer crew in place and Brown at the wheel, the *Lumba Lumba* headed into the face of the storm.

Brown: I tried to go almost straight across the harbour to go through the Metlakatla Pass. The *Lumba Lumba* is a tremendous sea boat, and she laid right over—came very near to standing on her beam ends with the wind velocity and swell. We finally had to run down to the throat of the harbour and then tack back taking it on our quarter, and then through Metlakatla Pass.

Once we got through the pass it was really, really dirty. I would say we had a sea running at that point near thirty feet and winds were definitely gusting up to 80 plus. I think there's comments about 60 and so on, but it would have been around 80, gusting to 85 even. At times we buried the bow, and she had somewhere in the order of twelve feet of freeboard and normally skipped right over most of the swells. She buried her bow under six to eight feet of water, and we had both screws out of the water at times. I had one engine full ahead and one astern at times to keep her head-to.

Somewhere around there the anchor which was lashed forward came loose. And without a thought George Salome, one of the certified masters, went out the side door and forward and the next thing I know he was gone. I thought he was gone completely but the swell wrapped him right around the handrail aft of the starboard wheelhouse door. The handrail saved him from going overboard but he took a beating. It took a couple of fellows to get him unwrapped and secured. We didn't see it until the next day, but he was black and blue over his whole body.

He just wasn't thinking for the moment. He'd always been the type of man who responded immediately. We were very,

very lucky that we didn't lose him. But the anchor was sloshing around, and it weighed a hundred and some pounds and it was bouncing sometimes four and five feet off the deck and he felt, like the rest of us, that it could have come right through the wheelhouse window.

There was a point once we were clear of Metlakatla Pass, two props out of the water, bow buried, anchor loose, one skipper hurt, that I had some doubt about whether we were going to get back. I figured that was the time I'd better ask everybody. I was prepared to go on but I thought I'd better have a show of hands and make sure that everybody else felt the same way. And they did. There was no doubt, no hesitation whatever. So away we went.

We took an awful hammering. At times I went right to my knees. You're hanging on to something and suddenly you don't know how you let go but you did. You just couldn't withstand it, it was such a crashing, crushing kind of thing.

It was estimated that the *Concreta* was somewhere between Lucy Island and Stephens Island. That's where George Moore estimated his position. We had quite a radio system going, with the *Concreta* talking to Bob Pederson ashore on the CB, Bob relaying by phone to our dispatch, who was relaying on to me on the VHF. But it worked really well. Everybody was really cool. I can't say enough about that part.

But it was snowing and the wind wasn't easing off and the swell was getting worse, if anything, and the Moore family had a dead reckoning position only. Because of the heavy sea we'd had to tone the radar down a bit, which cut out any targets, but otherwise you couldn't see anything—the sea was just making a mess of it. Of course we weren't able to pick him up at all.

Moore: Sometimes you could see where you were, and at one point I noticed that we had drifted about nine miles, to near the Rachael Islands. I thought that by the grace of God we were going to be shipwrecked on the Rachaels, which I would have happily accepted. But the way the wind and tide were, we were drifting farther and farther from the Rachaels by the time the *Lumba Lumba* got out there. He was looking for us about a half mile from shore, and we were twice as far out. And it was getting dark.

By that time Tracey was sick, Audrey was seasick and we were bailing. These big green ones—when they'd come down on top of the boat it just sounded like thunder down inside there. I wouldn't have believed that you could pile water up that straight and that high. The law of gravity shouldn't allow it.

Samuel: I thought it was going to be my last day. When we started getting water on the boat, that was it. I was bailing—I was bailing really hard 'cause I thought it was my last day. I just told Tracey to lay still while I was bailing. She did, and she started singing "Rock A Bye Baby." She was very calm. Actually I think I was, too. I think if I'd have panicked I'd have been lost. I don't know what came over me then, but I stayed really calm.

Moore: There's a dreadful feeling that goes through you, an awful fear, when you know you're going to die. And I had no illusions about that at that point. There's also a determination in the human spirit, and I remember thinking that somehow, some way, we're going to get a chance. And you have to be ready, and when it comes, you're going to take that chance. And after that—I don't know whether it's adrenaline or what it is that goes through you, but after it passes there's a sort of calm. We had a lot of things to do out there. We were busy, really busy, and thank God we were. We didn't have time to reflect on ourselves.

The boat had an electric pump but it had been smashed. Audrey was filling a five-gallon bucket up forward with a pot or something, passing them up to me, and me emptying it through the cabin window. But you can only do that for so long. You're cold and wet and getting tired. We knew we were losing ground, that we couldn't keep going forever.

I spent a lot of time trying to figure out how we could save the little one. We thought maybe we could blow up some garbage bags and tie them up real tight and put them around her. They had told us to tie ourselves together in case we did have to go into the water.

I think one of the things that saved us that day was the fact that we had a ferro-cement boat and it was heavy as hell. It was very stable. I was amazed. It floated up and down like a duck.

Brown: Somewhere, I suppose around three-thirty or so—it was beginning to get dark—we established that he had two flares on board. I suggested as we got closer to his estimated position that he fire one off. We were all watching. And not a sign, not a peep of it.

We told him to hang on to the last one and proceeded about another half hour, out toward Stephens. Then I suggested he let 'er go. We watched and watched: not a thing. Then we just caught a glimpse, like a little candle for a moment, then it was gone. Very luckily, otherwise we'd have bypassed him, I'm sure.

When we got close and could see him there was no way you could get alongside without injuring somebody or maybe knocking them over the side. I decided to stream our twenty- or twenty-five-man inflatable raft on a 300-foot line astern of us. That was quite a scene. Sometimes I wonder if I really saw what I did. George Moore got his wife and child into the raft, and the next thing I know it was upside down on top of their boat. Within seconds the next wave rolled the raft right side up off the *Concreta*.

Moore: The *Lumba Lumba* came up along our stern and streamed out this great big life raft on a line. They were on one side of us and the raft on the other, and the line was fouling across our deck. The raft flipped over then righted itself. It was like a big rubber dinghy with a canvas top, like an igloo with opposite tunnel entrances.

The first chance I got I threw Tracey inside the raft, then Audrey and I got in. I thought we'd just drift out from behind the *Concreta*, but something happened—the *Lumba Lumba* got on one side of a wave and we were on the other, I guess—and the life raft flipped upside down and landed across our deck. Tracey fell out on the deck. I got out, and Audrey was behind me, but before she could get out, the line tightened up and flipped the raft back into the water again with Audrey in it. I yelled at Tracey to lie flat on the deck. And she did—flatter than a postage stamp.

Brown: Our guys pulled it in as fast as they could and it turned out that Mrs. Moore was in there. She was screaming 'cause she didn't know where the child was. I backed up some, got a little closer, and our guys tried to get her on board but she was hysterical for the moment figuring the child had fallen in the water.

Once we got her on board and got squared away a bit we could see George Moore on the boat, hanging onto the mast with one arm like he wasn't going to let go—which it turned out was true—and holding the child.

We tried streaming the raft again and again. We just couldn't

Three members of the *Lumba Lumba* crew, (left to right) Capt. Vince Brown, Engineer Anthony Olsen and Capt. Dick Northrup relax in the Rivtow Straits office following their dramatic rescue of the Moore family.
Photo courtesy *Prince Rupert Daily News.*

seem to get it in a close enough position and George wasn't—and I can understand—going to let go. I decided we were just going to have to wait for a break, which occasionally you'll get. It's amazing, in a sea like that once in a while you get just the right conditions. I directed our crew on the *Lumba Lumba* to let the raft line go and free us from the raft. I felt a direct rescue—our stern to Moore's *Concreta*—was the only way.

Moore: They backed the boat up to the *Concreta*. It was the only way left. And the only way you can get onto the *Lumba Lumba* is by the stern. I knew when they were coming what we had to do. And they came right up—crashed right into us. I handed Tracey up. I felt at least she was going to make it. The *Lumba Lumba* crashed right down on the cabin again. And boy I hopped up. I bet my fingerprints are still in that rail.

Brown: We had enough fuel to make the trip out and back, there was no doubt about that. But, as the engineer kept alerting me—and I knew the history of that mechanical situation—the main tanks were fed to a day tank and the day tank fed the two Cummins engines, and under certain conditions—sloppy, when the tanks got down to a certain point—the engines would tend to airlock. We were at that point, the engineer pointed out to me on several occasions. It could have been fatal for all of us, there was no doubt about it. He couldn't have got down there and even got one engine running. It would have taken twenty to thirty minutes per engine. They were a very difficult engine

Only twenty-four hours after the event, George Moore and his wife Audrey (now Audrey Samuel) describe their misadventure aboard the *Concreta*.
Photo courtesy *Prince Rupert Daily News*.

to get un-airlocked. But anyway, you're out there and you're doing it, and you just ignore that sort of thing.

After picking them up there was just no way that we could worry about the raft and the *Concreta*, so we let them go. Once we started back in toward Rupert we had quite a run because we had to run down into it, then get around and tack back with it on our stern. But we pulled in behind the Rachael Islands for damage assessment. That's when we discovered that the fo'c'sle was a shambles. Most of the woodwork was mahogany and quite nicely done, with two bunks and desks. That was a bunch of broken planks. We had pipes adrift in the engine room and some broken. A couple of waste tanks that were welded to the hull had broken their welds and were laying in the bilge.

About that time we had a call from the *Alexander Mackenzie*, which had started out but really hadn't left Rupert harbour. We confirmed that we had the folks on board and there was nothing more could be done. They were going to return to the dock and I suggested that due to this threat about the airlocking we'd appreciate them running out and we could go in the lee of them, given that they were a bigger vessel. Which they very co-operatively did.

We just got right into the harbour and half a mile from Rivtow and everybody's up in the wheelhouse, now knowing we're back home—there was a period of time out there where every one of us agreed that maybe we weren't going to get back, given the way it was—that first one engine started to go down. And it went down. Then the other engine went down. And that's where we were, with an airlock situation. We were close enough to our dock that one of our little tugs ran out and pulled us in rather than fiddle with the engines at that point.

Captain Vince Brown retired after a thirty-eight-year career with Rivtow. He now divides his time between a home in Prince Rupert and a wilderness lodge in Alice Arm. Moore is remarried, semi-retired, and living in the Sayward Valley on Vancouver Island. Audrey Samuel lives in Prince George. Frank Brereton, the man who served as mate aboard the *Lumba Lumba* during the Moore family's rescue, was one of six men to die the following year in the unexplained loss of the tug *Rivtow Rogue* near Triple Island.

Ship
Happens

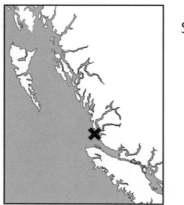

Ship Happens

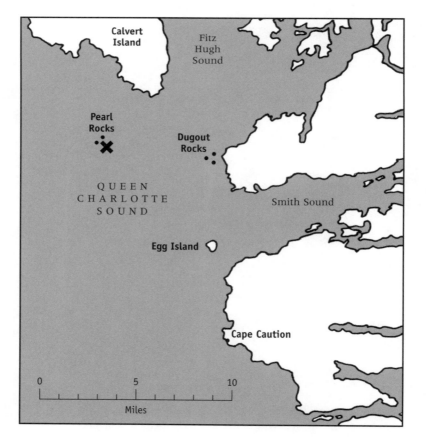

IT WAS HER GOLDEN ANNIVERSARY, BUT SHE GOT pearls. Fifty years after her launching in Bellingham Harbour, the *King Oscar*, northbound at 9 knots, made her final, fatal landfall at Pearl Rocks, a scattering of reefs protruding from Queen Charlotte Sound southwest of Calvert Island.

Originally built for the US Army, the 110-foot *King Oscar* had been christened the *FP 37*. It subsequently carried the names *Expansion*, *Dupont*, and *Twin Hill* before Art Dedolph bought it in 1988 as the *Karen Z* and, at the suggestion of a friend, renamed the vessel *King Oscar*. Dedolph, who lived most of the year in Florida, used the *King Oscar* as a packer in the Alaska salmon and herring fisheries.

Thirty-six hours before their arrival at Pearl Rocks, Dedolph had guided the *King Oscar* out of Seattle, bound for Prince William Sound. On board he had a guest, a crew of three and a deck cargo that included three smaller boats and a car. Shortly before midnight on March 29, 1992, with Pine Island just behind them, Dedolph turned the wheel over to his guest, checked the engine room and retired to his bunk.

Not long thereafter the guest turned the watch over to the cook and deckhand. Before leaving for a nap he instructed the pair to follow a tug and tow ahead of them. He pointed to an intermittent flash off the starboard bow, identified it as Cape Caution light, and asked that he be called back to the bridge when the *King Oscar* was abeam of the light. Everything seemed well.

"However," a Transportation Safety Board investigation concluded, "it was determined ... that the Cape Caution Light referred to by the guest was the Egg Island Light; the former's characteristics being a white flash every six seconds while the latter's characteristic was a white flash every five seconds."

The guest was called when the *King Oscar* was off the indicated light, but he was unable to correlate the radar

Pumping herring aboard the *King Oscar* in Prince William Sound, 1991. Art Dedolph is at centre of photo; engineer Lee Miles (far left), was also aboard when the vessel was lost on Pearl Rocks. Dedolph's son Sean is second from left.
Photo courtesy Art Dedolph.

image before him with the chart of the Cape Caution area. In short order, in visibility reduced by rain and darkness, in 30-knot southeasterly winds, the vessel overtook the tug *Storm Force* and piled into Pearl Rocks at full speed. "The master," the investigation report noted, "was awakened by the impact."

Meanwhile, for Dan Jerowsky and Rob Leonard, a trip that had been nothing but uninspiring was about to become quite exciting. The pair had spent two weeks working red sea urchins in the Bella Bella area, Jerowsky as skipper, Leonard as diver. "The price was bad, the quality was bad," Jerowsky recalled. "We were glad to come home and give it a break for a bit."

Jerowsky and Leonard were southbound, under tow in the 36-foot converted herring skiff *Cod Fin*, a boat Jerowsky ran for the owner, Glen Dennis. At the other end of the towline was the small wooden coastal freighter *Burnaco*, being operated as an urchin collector by skipper Bob Hutchinson and engineer Dave Madill. The same vessel had towed the *Cod Fin* north two weeks earlier, saving Jerowsky and Leonard the expense and effort of making the long transit to and from Vancouver Island under their own power.

Jerowsky: It was blowing really good and there was a good four- or five-foot chop on top of a two-metre swell. Rob and I were in the *Cod Fin* because with the weather conditions it was important for us to be back there in case there was a tow problem. We had already broken a towline, so we just had to be awake and keep an eye on things. It was banging pretty good. If it had have been flat we would have been on the *Burnaco* drinking coffee with those guys.

Leonard: It was so rough that the stovepipe had come off the stove. The inside of the cabin was full of smoke, so we had to

Under tow: the *Cod Fin* hitching a ride behind the *Burnaco* shortly before the *King Oscar* rescue.
Dan Jerowsky photo.

open the window and turn the stove off. It was so cold that night that when we got it all cleared out I went and jumped in the bunk to try and keep myself warm. You couldn't really sleep—it was just too rough.

Jerowsky: We were on a ship-to-ship channel rather than monitoring 16, but on the *Burnaco* they were monitoring 16. They had the initial contact. They said, "Hey, listen to this," so we switched over to 16 and listened to the Mayday.

> Dedolph's initial Mayday—"This is the *King Oscar* ... we're breaking up"— gave the men a better sense of the situation's urgency than of the vessel's location. Dedolph, unaware of the magnitude of the navigational error, identified his position as between Cape Caution and Egg Island.

Leonard: They sounded very desperate. It was a rough night. I couldn't imagine trying to figure out where they were—we didn't really know at that time. We just thought by the sound of the Mayday that they were in bad shape. I remember them saying that they thought the boat would break apart soon. It was really pounding on the rocks. They weren't sure how long the boat was going to stay together.

Jerowsky: They had an approximate position where they thought they were. But as it turns out they weren't anywhere near there. We looked for a while in the area where they thought they were and there was no sign of anything. Radio contact was still weak, so we knew we weren't in the right area.

Another vessel did spot a light which we thought could be coming from the source, so we flipped a coin and headed in that direction—actually backtracked at that point. Their radio died out on them before we came on scene, which made us wonder, "Is it over?" We didn't know what the situation was. It sounded pretty critical when we were in radio contact.

We finally found them. We saw the searchlights of the other boats. There was I believe two other vessels on scene, but they were larger vessels and couldn't do much because of the position of the *Oscar* inside this reef.

It quickly became apparent that the *Burnaco*'s initial size advantage was now a disadvantage: the *King Oscar* was aground and being pounded by surf inside a ring of reefs. The *Storm Force*—the tug Dedolph had overtaken— and the American fish packer *Tracy Lee* were also too big to get close enough to perform a rescue. The Coast Guard's *Sir James Douglas* wouldn't arrive for three and a half hours, according to radio reports. By default, the decision fell to Jerowsky, a diver and former fishing guide with experience in the Canadian Navy.

Jerowsky: I unhooked the *Cod Fin* and said, "We'll go in and have a closer look and see if we can do anything." It was at that point that Dave Madill, the engineer on the *Burnaco*, asked if he could come on board. That wasn't easy. There was a good three-metre sea in there, and with the water shoaling it made it come up even more. So it was pretty bouncy.

Leonard: There were high bulwarks on the *Cod Fin*, and Dave had to jump down inside. I had to sort of break his fall—it was quite a jump for him. In the *Reader's Digest* story it said I had to jump on Dave to keep him from rolling over the side of the boat. He wouldn't have ever rolled over the side of the boat—the bulwarks were too high. It was more to break his fall.

Jerowsky: I didn't know Dave that well, but we'd talked to him quite a bit on the trip up and I knew he knew the water. And then Rob Leonard—Rob would have gone in regardless. He trusted my judgment.

I had a big spotlight right on the bow and a remote control inside, but it wasn't working that well. So I had Rob up there manually changing the spotlight to where I requested. It was really hard to communicate back and forth 'cause the wind was howling so much. I stationed Dave in between Rob and I so he could relay messages. Then we just started going in. It really didn't look like anything, it was so dark. All you could see was this hulk—the shadow of the ship. With the lights you'd see water breaking—there's obviously a shoal—but other than that you couldn't see very much.

Dedolph: In the middle of the night, with no lights, in a pounding surf—there was a surfline just off to the port of us there—we had to holler at each other practically on the deck to be heard. Shit, it was blowing 35, 45—whatever it was. But that surf pounding made so much noise you couldn't hardly hear each other.

Jerowsky: We had a look, and it really didn't look like there was any way we could get in safely. The water was breaking all around. I had a leg on the *Cod Fin*, so if we'd hit anything and lost power, we'd have been in the same boat those guys were.

Dan Jerowsky: "Do I want to do this or not?"
Keith Keller photo.

Leonard: We went to go in on one side and it was just white water. It looked like a reef. I said, "Dan, I don't think we should go in this way."

We went around the backside. The little passage we had to get in there wasn't very wide. We had talked about it: "How should we do this?" I said, "Do you want me to swim to shore and take them a line?" Dan said, "No, I don't want you to do that."

Jerowsky: Before we'd even reached the scene, Rob and I got into our dry suits, which gives you a lot of confidence. We got lines ready and stuff. At one time we even contemplated getting a line to the reef and Rob going in the water. But it was just too wicked. It would have been too dangerous for him to even try that. This was pretty crazy.

At that point it was questionable whether I'd make the decision to go in. We had some communication with the other boats. I was at a point of indecision, really. I spent a good two minutes weighing the possibilities: "Do I want to do this or not?"

So we were sitting there sort of at the point of no return. Finally Dave asked me, "Well, what's it going to be?" To this day I don't really know why. Part of me was saying, "I don't want to go in there and get killed." Part of me was saying, "I don't want to go in there and damage the boat." Part of me was saying, "These poor guys out there—somebody's got to do something." And then part of me was saying, "What's the world going to think if I don't go?" To be honest with you. I just made the decision: "Let's go for it."

Leonard: They had thrown a line off the port bow, with a scotchman on the end. I had a gaff and I was able to gaff it. As Dan manoeuvred the boat up next to the *King Oscar*, the *Cod Fin* would rise up and I'd tighten up on the line. But you only had as long as the top of the swell. I had to tie it off really quick, then as the swell went down I had to untie it real quick—to give slack.

Jerowsky: The swell worked to our advantage. It would pick us up, right up to deck level. Unfortunately, when you get that swell coming in and hitting their vessel and the rocks, you get a backswell that wants to push you out as well. You can use that to your advantage, too. It feels like you're getting sucked in to the rocks, then right at the last moment it would push you out. It was quite a ride. At one point I could look out my window and see rocks right below the boat.

Leonard: The *Cod Fin* would come up high enough that they could jump. They were using the line as kind of a guide. One guy lost the line, and he was the one we had to grab. I grabbed him and held him. I had the line in one hand and I had to grab the guy with the other. So Dave came and grabbed him and heaved him up into the boat.

Jerowsky: Dedolph was frozen. Being an older guy and not one hundred percent, on the last pass, the swell brought us right—I mean perfectly—up to deck level, and Dave just reached an arm around him, and then as soon as the swell moves us out, he's coming with us.

Dedolph: I had a total hip replacement four months before the accident. That's why I was afraid to jump—I wasn't staying with

Rob Leonard: he offered to swim ashore with a line to rescue the men aboard the *King Oscar*.
Photo courtesy Rob Leonard.

the boat to be the captain. The captain goes down? Who the fuck wants to go down with their boat? I don't. But shit, when that boat was bouncing up and down in there ... basically I rolled over the side and Madill got ahold of me and drug me in.

Jerowsky: Once we got every-body safely on board, my biggest priority was to get the heck out of there before we did have a prob-lem. We got out of the reef area, then we could start breathing again. Then we transferred those people to the *Burnaco*, which wasn't that difficult—they went over there like rats leaving a sink-ing ship. They just wanted to get on something big. They were all quite quiet at that point. They didn't want to talk about any-thing.

It worked perfect. When I think of what could have gone wrong ... If anyone had gotten a foot in between our boat and their boat, it would have been just cut off, certainly crushed. The number of things that could have gone wrong but didn't ... you kind of think that Someone's giving you a hand up there.

Dedolph: How did it happen? The guys fucked up. You can't say anything else but that. How did they fuck up? I don't know. We were running radar ranges. They probably messed around with the radar, got it out of sync, and then were afraid to call me. And they didn't know where they were. But they're out in open water so they assumed that everything was going to straighten itself out.

With seas already washing her decks, the *King Oscar* begins to break up in the surfline at Pearl Rocks the day after her grounding. A year later, diver Rob Leonard would search the area and find nothing but a piece of grille from a car being transported on the doomed vessel (visible on the deck in this photograph).
Joel Eilertsen photo.

Christ, you go by Pine Island, you go to Cape Caution, Egg Island. When you get abreast of Dugout Rocks you turn up into Fitz Hugh Sound. I've been through there a hundred times. Those other guys have been through there. They were probably standing up there talking about pussy and scratching their ass. Who knows why the boat got off course? I thought we were on Dugout Rocks. Then when I looked around I couldn't see any fuckin' lights. I said, "Shit, where the hell are we?"

> The rescue that Dan Jerowsky, Rob Leonard and Dave Madill performed earned all of them Commissioner's Commendations from the Canadian Coast Guard.
> Leonard, who works as a deckhand on the seine boat *Prodigy* when not involved in dive fisheries,

returned to Pearl Rocks a year after the *King Oscar* was lost. Despite a thorough search above and below the waterline, the only trace he found of the episode was a piece of grille from the car Dedolph had been transporting on the vessel's deck.

The grinding moment of impact at Pearl Rocks cost Art Dedolph a vessel valued at more than half a million dollars, a vocation, an avocation, a marriage and an identity. "I've been trying to piece my life back together ever since then," he said almost five years after the incident. "From that time to the present is all a big nightmare to me."

Not long after the incident, Art Dedolph was walking down a street in San Diego when he saw in a shop window cards that featured a photograph of a large vessel that had accidentally run aground. The caption read: *Ship happens*. Dedolph bought a box to send to friends and relatives. As of early 1997, at age sixty-three, the former king crab fisherman and dragger captain was contemplating some kind of return to the Alaska fisheries.

The
*Whiskey
Jack Is*
Going
Down

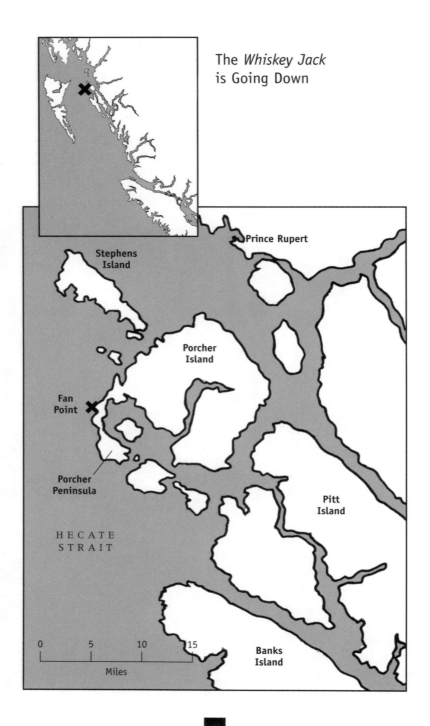

The *Whiskey Jack* is Going Down

Prince Rupert

Stephens Island

Porcher Island

Fan Point

Porcher Peninsula

Pitt Island

HECATE STRAIT

Banks Island

0   5   10   15

Miles

In 1975 Joe Fairbairn was working as a logger at Kyuquot, on Vancouver Island's northwest coast. The money was good, but the lifestyle, he felt, left much to be desired. He took scuba diving lessons during his time out of camp and, his training completed, he began diving in the fledgling sea cucumber fishery. The work appealed to him. Fairbairn spent eighteen years in the burgeoning sea cucumber and sea urchin dive fisheries first as an employee and later as an independent owner-operator. Then, one unseasonably warm and beautiful north coast evening, the whole thing came crashing to an end.

It was the second week of May, 1993. Fairbairn and his crew of two, diver Stanley Ross and diver's tender Shawn Cuthbert, were harvesting urchins near a reef between tiny Fan Island and the Porcher Peninsula, an appendage of Porcher Island, located just south of Prince Rupert. Fairbairn had just had major engine work done on his boat, a converted herring skiff he'd named *Whiskey Jack*. The shop that rebuilt his engine had not reconnected the bilge pump. Fairbairn had already missed one urchin opening because of the mechanical work; anxious not to miss another, he put off the repair.

Sea water collected in the bilge—now without a pump—as the crew proceeded with harvesting from their anchored boat. Cuthbert, new to the *Whiskey Jack*, loaded the urchin bags farther aft than he could have, Fairbairn felt, causing the boat to settle even more by the stern. Belts began to slip in the rising water, leading to the failure of auxiliary equipment.

Fairbairn: It was quite rough out the day that I lost the *Whiskey Jack*. We were working on a reef to the northwest side of Porcher Island. It was quite exposed. Being such a reefy area, we took our usual precautions entering into the area. We had the diver monitoring what was ahead of us. It was all pretty slow

Joe Fairbairn with geoducks.
Photo courtesy Joe Fairbairn.

and cautious. We often had to use these kinds of tactics to work in shallow areas.

The spot that we were sitting in was quite exposed to the weather. Most of the day it was blowing about 20 to 25. It did make for quite a lot of chop. It was fairly uncomfortable conditions, but nothing that we weren't used to, and we didn't plan on having an extremely large load that day anyways, being the first day of the opening.

The boat was holding well. I had a heavy anchor, and I had lots of scope. I think it was about three-thirty in the day that Stan came up from his diving. It was very shallow—mostly twenty, twenty-five feet of water—so he could have dove all day there. He came up and decided to call it a day. That was a little bit too early, and it was kind of choppy anyways, so we were better off just continuing working rather than trying to manoeuvre the boat and travel in that kind of weather.

So I went down and I started harvesting. I remember the anchor had slipped, so we decided to reset it. I got a signal from the surface. I came up and I reset the anchor, then I went down again. I sent a few bags up, then there was a signal to come up. I went up and I was told that the anchor winch wasn't working. I went back to the engine compartment and noticed that the water level in the engine compartment was quite high. It was up to the auxiliary belts for driving the air compressor and the anchor winch. I noticed the belts were slipping, so I thought we'd better pull up the anchor.

We had to pull the urchin product in by hand. That only took a few seconds. Then I had the two fellows, Stan and Shawn, go up to the bow and start pulling the anchor up by hand, with me manoeuvring the boat toward the anchor to make it easier for them.

The tide had been dropping. When I was under water I could see that we had lots of room. But I believe that the reef, being as exposed as it was, and the tide dropping, really tended to lift the water up quite a lot. The waves would hit the rocks and kind of backspill. And we had a northwest breeze that tended to keep us against the rocks.

My concentration was pretty much all straight ahead, keeping an eye on how things were working out on the bow, and also watching out for rocks. At some point, I believe it was before we had half the anchor up, I felt quite a sudden jarring motion on the boat that I'd never felt before. It just felt like God had come down and played with our boat and sunk a part of it. It caused me to look back.

At that point it happened again, and I could feel the stern go down and see water start rushing in over the stern. I saw the water go over top of the engine, and I knew that the water wasn't going to stop coming in—the stern was going down.

I grabbed the microphone of the VHF, and I managed to turn on to Channel 16, and I said, "Mayday, Mayday, Mayday, the *Whiskey Jack* is going down." And before I finished saying the word "down" the water had risen up over my head in the cabin. I let go of the microphone, and I had to battle with the incoming rush of water to swim out through the doorway at the stern of the cabin, which was under water.

I poked up to the surface, thankful that I'd survived. About that time there'd been another boat working in fairly close proximity to our boat. I didn't realize that they'd pulled up anchor and started travelling back. I thought that they were still close by. So I broke the surface and I looked, and that boat wasn't there. I thought, What's going on here? There's nobody there, I didn't get much of a Mayday out, I don't know if anybody heard it—I didn't have time for a response.

The two guys were perched on the bow, which was straight up and down in the water. Really there was no room for a third person up there. So here's me in the water, and all these bits and pieces of equipment and supplies floating off.

It was a 31-foot boat. The water had originally been twenty to twenty-five feet when we were working in it. At this point I'd say that the boat was probably in about twenty feet of water, sticking straight up and down, ten feet sticking straight up out of the water. As the waves would come up the boat would lift up, and as they'd go down the boat would go down and ram on the bottom. So much for my rebuilt engine.

I didn't think that we were going to be in too much trouble, but I was concerned about the fact that we weren't going to be able to stay with the boat. We didn't have any way of keeping warm. The tide was eventually going to rise up and cover up the rocks and dry areas that were surrounding us. There were some exposed rocks quite close—probably within fifty feet.

I broke in the window on the bow of the boat, and some of our flotation devices started to present themselves. First there was a couple of life jackets, two dry suits—my neoprene dry suit and Stanley's Viking dry suit, which really wasn't much good because it required a special harness, and you'd require the attachment hood to make it airtight. I'd had time earlier to get out of my suit, and Stanley had been out of his suit for probably two and a half hours, from when he'd come up. So there was two guys in long johns—the two divers—and the tender was dressed in his working clothes.

I was in that water for probably half an hour to forty minutes, retrieving things and gathering a bit of a plan together in my mind. The guys on the bow ... I was handing them the life jackets and the dry suits and stuff. Shawn said, "Why don't you take my hand and I'll try to help you up." I reached up, and the boat hit on the bottom at that time, and we both ended up getting bounced into the water. Shawn scrambled back up—I gave him a push and helped him back up. But from being halfway up, when he pulled my hand, I saw that the boat hit the bottom, leaned way over, and all you could see was this rock coming. Then I got thrown off. From that I realized that it was a very dangerous situation on the boat—it would be easy for someone to get crushed. So I looked up at the two fellows and said, "We have to make a swim for the nearest rock. Somebody's going to get hurt soon."

One of the guys said, "No, I think we should stay with the boat." I wasn't going to argue with him. I said, "This is what I think we should do." Being in that kind of a situation, it wasn't like you were the skipper and that guy was the worker. It was more like, "Well, here we are, three mice in a tub." We had pretty much equal opinions. I know there's a rule about staying with the boat, but not in those circumstances, when the boat's bouncing and the tide's dropping and somebody could get crushed.

So I swam to the rock outcropping, knowing that it's only a matter of time before my crew decided that they're going to have to do the same thing. I started swimming, and Stan threw me my dry suit. I took it, swam to the rock, dumped the water out of it and stuck it on. I couldn't zip it up myself, but that was no problem. I knew that eventually one—or two—of my crew would make it over there and zip me up.

It was a clear sky that day, and I remember thinking that it was quite a beautiful day in some respects. You wouldn't think that something like this would be happening on such a nice day.

As the minutes progressed ... it wasn't so much panic as fear beginning to develop. As you started to realize that there's no other boat close by, and we'd have to swim from here to there—which from here looks pretty far. When everything's going well that distance wouldn't look very far. But now that you're sitting there wet and cold, and the temperature of that water never does change much on an annual basis, it looked like quite a ways.

I remember that I never did feel cold at all. I spent the most amount of time in the water and I never did feel that cold. I think it would be the adrenaline—there was a lot of adrenaline pumping. But I don't think there was a lot of panic happening. We were quite controlled. It's a difficult situation in that you don't expect to be there, suddenly you are, and you have to deal with it, and you don't want to. You don't want to, but you have to. So you do an assessment. You try to figure out what's against you. You try to figure out the answers to how you're going to overcome those difficulties.

When I broke in the window of the boat I was looking for flotation devices, things to keep us warm. I was particularly looking for my little shaving kit to come popping up, which I knew to have two or three lighters in it—I was a good heavy smoker at the time. Stanley kind of laughed. He said, "I think your shaving kit's already gone floating by." It had all kinds of money in it, which I think Stanley also knew. So, in spite of what was happening at the time, I guess we had a few chuckles. Stanley and Shawn thought it was quite funny that the money had gone floating off. I was only concerned about the lighters, 'cause I knew this could really get to be a serious situation.

I got to the rock. It was kind of the back side of the rock, 'cause there was a current developing. I dumped out the dry suit, jumped into it, and walked to the other side of the rock. And just as I got to the edge I saw Stan and Shawn jump into the water. I didn't see them with the two life jackets that I'd handed up. I think they'd lost a lot of the things that I'd handed to them from trying to hold on to the boat.

What I did see was that Stanley had secured a scotchman, which is like a big orange ball that they use to mark halibut spots, or a lot of boats use them as bumpers. We were using it for a bumper and for marking our spots. So Stanley had the scotchman on some rope fastened around his waist.

Stanley came to the rock about twenty-five feet from where I was standing. I believe that panic is beginning to sink in there... I can see that Shawn has the shivers. And I don't think it was from the cold. He's starting to realize that we don't know when we're going to get out of this. He's starting to freeze up: he doesn't want to move, he doesn't want to do anything. Stanley—I believe he's starting to get panicky too, now—had this scotchman tied around his waist. He took about a minute to catch his breath. In that time I'm talking to Shawn, trying to calm him and convince him what we need to do to come out of this.

In the meantime Stan decides it is time for him to make his move. Given his fearful state, I think he was thinking if he doesn't do it now, he won't have the courage to do it later. 'Cause that's one of the things that took the most courage: to say, "We're going to have to jump back into that cold water. And we have to swim." Because you don't know how long you can stand that cold. I know I was quite afraid. I'm a pretty good swimmer and I was concerned. I didn't know if all three of us could make it, or even if I could make it. But I knew we had to go for it. It would be about half a mile, I believe.

Their immediate circumstances weren't the only conditions that conspired against the three men, as an investigation later revealed. Most significantly, the *Whiskey Jack* and the nearby urchin boat *Pacific Porcupine* had gotten into trouble at the same time. Both boats broadcast almost simultaneous Mayday messages. No one heard both messages clearly. Not everyone who heard any one of the messages responded appropriately. One of Fairbairn's own friends dismissed the *Whiskey Jack*'s distress message as a hoax. Other boats that clearly heard

Fairbairn's Mayday and could have relayed such information to the Coast Guard did not do so until the following day. Staff at the Coast Guard's Prince Rupert radio station, the investigation concluded, erroneously determined that the *Pacific Porcupine* alone had been in distress and prematurely terminated a search and rescue operation.

Fairbairn: Stanley shouted up at us, "What are we waiting for? Let's go." And he jumped in—just like that. I know that he did what he had to do. He had to try, and he had to do it then.

I had a bit tougher time convincing Shawn. I know that basically, in my mind, I'm still convincing myself. It took me a couple of minutes, and Shawn eventually said, "Okay, let's go." And we jumped in.

In the time it took Shawn and I to enter the water Stanley had distanced himself by probably fifty yards or so. I shouted, "Stan how're you doing?" He said he was doing okay. I said, "Well, I'll see you on shore."

I really had to stay close to Shawn. He tried freezing up a couple of times, saying he couldn't move and he couldn't swim. I just grabbed him and said it was okay. I had the dry suit on, so I was quite buoyant—it was easy for me to keep him floating. With enough kicking and stuff we made it to shore in it seemed like about twenty minutes of swimming.

I told Shawn that I'd have to go and look for Stan—to see how Stan was doing. Around the corner from where we were there was a large, large beach. We were at a point of another beach. So I had to go up and over a few rocks to look for Stan. That's the way the current had gone—the current was going down the beach. I came over a rock outcropping and I saw the big orange scotchman. And at the same time I noticed that there was a flock of blond hair floating on top of the water. And I could see that Stan was face down. I was shocked by the sight.

I jumped in to see what I could do. I got to Stan as quickly as I could. I lifted his head up, and his whole face was blue. I blew air in. From behind I pressed on his stomach. He threw up into the water. It seemed to me there would be a chance of flushing him out and hopefully to revive him. So I kept doing this. I kept pumping on his stomach and having him throw up the sea water, and blowing into his mouth. At the same time I was kicking my way toward shore. It was around three hundred feet, I guess.

It took me a while to get in to shore. I pulled him up onto the beach and I kept at it and at it. The sun was starting to go down and it was starting to turn into twilight. I believe that I spent about forty minutes on shore administering to him. Every now and again—I guess it was air escaping—it was that hopeful feeling that he's going to sputter, cough, and look up and make some kind of a wisecrack about the whole thing. It never happened.

I didn't know what to do. I hadn't seen Shawn then for about an hour, an hour and a half, and I thought I'd better go see what his progress was. The last time I saw him he was shivering like crazy. I went and saw him, and saw that he'd been busy gathering up twigs and stuff that could be used to make like a blanket, for bedding, to keep us warm. I gave him the dry suit to warm up, and I told him that I hadn't seen Stanley. I figured that with the time I'd spent on Stanley, he hadn't revived and he wasn't going to be reviving, and there was no point in causing alarm for the time being.

We spent the evening transferring the dry suit back and forth. It was unseasonably warm. It never gets warm up there—at nighttime it can be freezing cold in the middle of summer. We were lucky that in May we had some summer weather.

In the morning I was sleeping. Shawn came up and told me that he had some bad news for me. He'd gotten up and went looking for Stan. I told him, "I know." We just left it at that. We didn't feel good, but we had to try and figure out how we're going to try and get out of this thing.

I was quite hopeful that there would be other vessels coming around. The *Jolly Dog* had been working close by the day before, and I figured they'd be back. With the dry suit it would be no problem to swim out to the *Jolly Dog* and say, "Hey, our boat sank. Here we are."

It was a funny time then. Federal Fisheries didn't really know what they were doing with these openings. On a daily basis they could close an area, say, "We've harvested this amount of product in this area. We want you to move on to the next area." I believe that that's what happened, 'cause the boats that were fishing around the same reef as us—off a little island called Fan Island—for some reason weren't stopping in and fishing again. And I know there was lots of product. I think there was a closing.

Shawn and I watched as these boats were going by, and would be jumping up and down, waving. We were amazed that we couldn't get anybody's attention. We figured that someone would see this great big fire engine red dry suit bouncing up and down.

I remembered that there was a cabin on Porcher Island that we could possibly make our way to. We decided—perhaps somewhat foolhardily, knowing that our boat had been known to be in that Fan Island area—to walk a ways to this cabin. En route, numerous sea urchin fleet boats passed us by, and we just couldn't get anybody's attention.

Only after the vessel *Swift Invader* reported the *Whiskey Jack* overdue on the morning of May 12 were Fairbairn and Cuthbert rescued from Porcher Island by Coast Guard helicopter.

Fairbairn: It was about two or three o'clock that day—the first day after the sinking of the boat—that a helicopter broke the tree-line. It just happened to be right above the beach where we were walking. We flagged them down. They came and landed and picked us up. We told them that there was a body back by the beach adjacent to Fan Island, and that it was one of our crew members. From there we were taken to Prince Rupert, to the hospital.

They went and picked up Stanley later. After they retrieved him the coroner requested that someone identify the body. I volunteered to do that. I guess in hindsight now I kind of regret that. I think now it was another burden on my system. One eye had been picked out by the birds—it was quite a grisly sight. I was in a pretty weakened state emotionally.

It was the next day that someone from our fishing company realized that we were missing, and they decided that they'd better report that the *Whiskey Jack*'s not available. Later I found out that one of the people, who'd actually been a very good friend of mine for many years, had heard the entirety of my transmission. I believe that that person feels an immense amount of guilt. They felt somehow that I'd been joking around—they thought that it was a prank Mayday call. That was discovered in the course of the investigation. Of course I'd never done anything like that in my life.

That friend, being one of the closer vessels … it wouldn't have been that difficult for him to have turned around and come and save the bunch of us.

It's funny. When something like that happens, guilt is something that there seems to be enough of to go around. I know myself, I felt a lot of guilt. I felt guilt for owning a boat, for being ambitious—that none of this would have happened if I wasn't that way. Sometimes it is hard to accept that what happened, happened.

I know one of the things that's hardest for me, in spite of the fact that I found Stanley face down and blue in the water, is that I couldn't revive him. You see it all the time in the movies, on *Amazing Rescues* and things like that: this person that's been drowned for two hours—miraculously they're spitting and sputtering and they end up being okay. And here's this one fellow, and he's the hero because everybody loves him for saving this other guy's life. And when it doesn't go that way, does it mean that the inverse is true? That that guy is not the hero but he's an antichrist and nobody loves him because he couldn't save his friend's life? It's almost the way it seems. On one hand I would have ended up looking good if I would have saved this man. And on the other hand I end up looking bad because I couldn't save this man. I couldn't be godlike enough to pull this thing off.

Every now and again there's certain things that I see and hear that ring true. I remember Remembrance Day this year [1996], one of the soldiers who had been in the Second World War put it into words, and I realized that this was how I felt. He said that when these young men went to war, it was like they'd had their invincibility stolen away from them. A young person... before you encounter an event like I had with the sinking of the *Whiskey Jack*, you have this confidence, this invincibility, where you know that whatever comes along, you'll be able to stand up to the challenge. And then something happens, and you realize that it's not like that.

I had a number of people up there talk to me, which I'm thankful for. There was an Anglican pastor that came and visited me on a number of occasions. I remember meeting the coroner, who tried to console me with the fact that, being a fishing town and all, these things happen. And that life goes on.

Today it's hard for me to say exactly what it is that stops me from doing that again—from picking up the pieces and jumping back on the horse. I just know that I can't. The Workers' Compensation Board has said that it has something to do with the way I was before. I don't know how it was that they figure I was before. I know that I did that job for eighteen years of my life, and it brought me immense satisfaction. Today there's a lot of times when I miss it. Really miss it.

I know that there's a need inside to talk about it. I can't explain where that need lies. It's like how afterwards there were these terrible feelings of guilt within me. Psychiatrists I spoke to reassured me that the guilt was unfounded, that I did everything in my power to ensure that everybody on my crew was okay.

I have to tell it. I have to relive, I have to refeel, in order to start feeling the right things rather than just the things that aren't rational to feel. So I can start feeling purged, so I can start feeling complete again, so I can start feeling whole, so I can start feeling confident ... so I can start feeling happy. It's one way of trying to feel the things I want to feel. Trying to be the father I want to be to my son and the husband I want to be to my wife. Trying to be a better person all 'round. Trying to be a more healed person.

> Joe Fairbairn never returned to the commercial dive fishery. Four years after the *Whiskey Jack*'s sinking he was still pursuing a post traumatic stress claim with the Workers' Compensation Board. He lives in Burnaby, where he works as a school custodian.

The Storm of '85

Southeasterlies are the worst
They bring in the rollers through
Hecate Strait
So shallow
the sea stands up on its back legs
like a bear
and swats you down
Hecate, the goddess with the bad temper

—from "Southeasterly" (for Randy Morrison)
by Andrew Wreggitt

On April 25, 1985, a violent storm swept across the central and northern coast as the BC halibut fleet, between 300 and 400 boats, was five days into its first opening of the season. Weather forecasters had tracked the low-pressure system and had broadcast warnings. The system's centre intensified more rapidly than anticipated, however, producing storm conditions several hours in advance of their predicted arrival.

The halibut fishery at the time was managed through a series of brief, fixed openings which effectively forced crews to be on the grounds in often dangerous conditions. Skippers yielded to the temptation of staying on their gear longer than good judgment would dictate, risking being overtaken by adverse weather in order to take fullest advantage of the limited time allotted them.

This combination of factors—the enforced risk-taking and the premature onset of severe weather—proved to be a deadly mix. By the morning of April 26, three fishermen were dead, one never to be found. Many others were saved, often in the slimmest of circumstances, in an all-night rescue which covered hundreds of square kilometres of ocean whipped by hurricane force winds. An undetermined number of other boats managed to claw their way to shelter and thus avoid becoming more fodder for the inquiry that followed in the maelstrom's wake.

A massive search and rescue operation was necessitated by the severity of the storm, the large search area—from northern Dixon Entrance to Queen Charlotte Sound—and the fact that several vessels were simultaneously in danger. A total of twenty-five craft participated in the search operation. Among them were helicopters and fixed wing aircraft from Canadian Forces Base Comox, two chartered helicopters, two US Coast Guard helicopters, four Canadian Coast Guard vessels, one Canadian Coast Guard helicopter, seven fishing vessels and a tug.

Hey Dad broadcast the first Mayday as she struggled toward land fifteen miles west of Bonilla Island. Given that the boat was taking on water and poorly equipped with survival gear, the Rescue Coordination Centre (RCC) in Victoria tasked a large contingent of Canadian vessels and aircraft. Significantly, the RCC also requested assistance from the US Coast Guard at Juneau, Alaska. The Americans responded by sending one of their helicopters, which was about to depart on a regular fisheries patrol from its base at Sitka, 210 nautical miles north of the struggling fishing boat.

Hey Dad was escorted to safety and pumped out by the Canadian Coast Guard cutter *Point Henry*. The American Sikorsky—the first of two tasked—went on to play a major role in the operation, shuttling first to one and ultimately to four more foundering vessels, and hoisting fourteen fishermen from the lethal waters they were no longer able to avoid.

The following four stories are accounts of the harrowing hours of April 25–26, 1985.

An
Intense
Nightmare

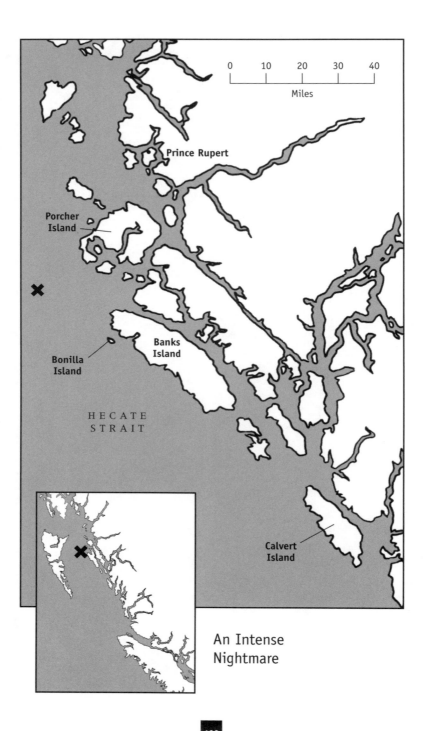

An Intense
Nightmare

"If you're going to do it you've got to fish a little weather
or you won't make it."

—Fraser Dunn

FRASER DUNN HAD ALREADY
SEEN A LITTLE WEATHER by the time he was twenty-two
and making his first voyage as skipper of his own boat.
Raised in a fishing family, with "a real hard-core fisherman" for a father, he wasn't much bothered by weather.
As he noted years later, maybe he should have been
bothered more.

Dunn had just spent the winter refitting his first
boat, the 43-foot wood-hulled *Dee-Jay*. Rounding out his
crew were his brother Scott and friends Mike McGuire
and Kevin Bouchard. The trip began about as auspi-
ciously as could be for a first-time skipper—good
weather, good fishing. Then it turned just about as bad
as he could have imagined.

Dunn: We ran up north, then over to the Charlottes, Queen
Charlotte City, and picked up herring for bait. We used fresh herring—got it off the Natives up there. Then we proceeded out for
the opening and we fished a couple of days and ended up delivering eight thousand pounds of halibut. We got some fresh bait
and ice and went out again, and we were out roughly for a day,
maybe a day and a half, and we were on some very heavy fishing, right out in the middle of the Hecate Strait. Lots of fish.
Really big-sized fish, too—hundred-pounders, an eighty-pound
average. Something like that.

It was flat, flat calm for that day. And then that night it was
just super calm. I'd listened to the weather and I believe they
were calling for 30, 35 the next day. It wasn't storm warnings.
We were twenty miles off of Bonilla. By the time you got right
in, it was a four-hour run, so you're not able to run in every
night fishing out there.

We woke up in the morning and we'd been catching lots of fish the night before so I was excited and just got on the first string. As soon as we got on it, it started blowing about 30, 35 knots. About a half hour later, it was blowing about 40—blowing southeast. A huge sea was coming in—coming from the storm. Enormous waves.

About halfway through the string the boat took a bad heave and the hold-down for the pole broke, and the pole come slamming up into the crosstree. We cut the gear 'cause we couldn't haul it any more. We had to get the pole held up, so we tied that up. It was getting real rough, so we started slowly heading in.

Before we started running we tied the hatch down, nailed down the covers—totally battened down the boat. Which was lucky we did. We were running for about twenty minutes and these waves were just smoking. It was blowing 40, 50, maybe even a little more by that time, maybe up to 60. And I hadn't listened to the weather and of course there was storm warnings out.

We were running on the stern quarter, and this big wave came along and busted on the stern. It laid us right on our side and actually picked us up. We surfed down the wave. Literally, the boat was right on its side. I was standing on the side of the wheelhouse. Often what happens then is you go into the next wave and you turn turtle. But the wave caught up to us and we fell down the backside of it. I'll bet we were doing 30 or 40 miles an hour going down that wave—surfing. The wave cleaned everything off the boat, on the deck. Everything that wasn't bolted down was gone. If anybody'd been on deck they'd have been washed over, but everybody was in the cabin. The whole boat was basically in the wave. You could just see a bit of light at the top of the window. That was the start of it and it scared the shit out of us.

That was the stern quarter, so we started jogging into it, and the waves got bigger, and the wind got up to 70 knots or 80 knots steady. My brother and I were taking twenty-minute shifts, and a guy had to work the squeegee, 'cause the whole cabin was wet. The stove was out. Just the heat from our bodies was steaming everything up. You had to work a squeegee just so you could see out the window.

You come up these waves. They're a good forty feet, fifty feet, and they were only a hundred feet apart, or less, so it was straight up and straight down. You try to get the boat straight into the wind, and you get to the top of the wave and the wind

The *Dee-Jay* sets out from Comox Harbour on its ill-fated voyage to Hecate Strait.
Photo courtesy the Dunn family.

would be so intense it would catch you—and you'd be off a degree one way or the other way—it would blow you right on the side and you'd go sliding down the wave literally on your side. And up the next one. It was just an intense nightmare.

When I was at the wheel, I could see this wave and see it start breaking. I said, "This one's coming in." It took the two front windows out. I jumped out of the way. In the cabin we had a wooden box built in—it had all the electronics in it. I jumped in behind it and reached around to keep my hand on the wheel. That wave filled the cabin two feet deep with water. And then all the water's running down on the electrical and things are sparking…

As soon as we took the first surfer wave, that was the time to tell them where we were. Since that time, the *George E. Darby* had been making its way out to us. At that point I didn't want to go into it any more, so we decided we'd run in the trough and just let the boat roll.

Captain Monty Montgomery got his view of the Storm of '85 from the bridge of the *George E. Darby*, where he spent thirty-nine consecutive hours shuttling from crisis to crisis. Forewarned of the storm, Montgomery had taken up position at the north end of Banks Island, putting the *Darby* in a good spot to assist vessels caught out in Hecate Strait. Montgomery and his crew of eighteen—sixteen plus two cadets—had escorted one boat to shelter and been tasked on four other incidents before turning their attention to the *Dee-Jay*.

Montgomery: The first five incidents took up most of the day and well into the dark. When they were finished we headed over toward the *Dee-Jay*. By now the sea had built up. The wave-rider buoys were indicating fifteen-metre seas, so he was in a pretty rough situation out there.

Dunn: This would probably be about two o'clock in the afternoon when we took the windows in. It was probably four hours since we cut the string. We had to batten down so the water didn't keep coming in. I usually carry a sheet of plywood with me in case that happens—you pound it over the windows. Getting that job done was just unreal 'cause the wind wanted to rip the plywood away. Mike was the guy who did most of that. It was incredible.

We had to tie up a pole at one point. The first one we got tied in. The other one bust and let loose. It was slamming up into the crosstree, ripping the aerials off. It wouldn't break loose. And the whole boat's shuddering—scary as hell. That went on for hours.

I was talking to the *George E. Darby* the whole time. And when we took that window in, every piece of electronics on the boat got smoked except one VHF radio, and it was on the backside of that electronics panel. Somebody'd put it there for that reason. If it wasn't for that we would have been dead.

I'd just bought the boat. I'd only just fished it four days when this happened. That winter I'd rebuilt the main motor and done lots of getting it ready—maybe four months' work on the boat. Got it seaworthy—lucky I did.

At about five o'clock the *George E. Darby* seen us. We could see this boat coming. And these waves were burying him. It's got maybe a hundred-foot mast and they were busting right over that—the spray. It was incredible, watching that boat.

The *George E. Darby*: "severely hampered by hurricane conditions, shallow water and rocks." The vessel took a pounding that damaged its bottom and injured Capt. Monty Montgomery.
Painting by Graham Wragg.

Montgomery: We had to run right into it. The *Darby* never was a racehorse of the sea. She had a blunt bow and boy, she used to pound something awful.

You could see by the course he was steering and the set of the wind—although his radar wouldn't indicate it because of it being such a low profile to the sea—I could see that eventually he was going to end up running over Rose Spit. I started trying to convince him that he should start altering course to starboard and head around Rose Spit. He tried, but he said it stopped riding easy then.

Finally it got to the stage where the water was starting to shallow up. The *Darby* drew seventeen feet of water. With a fifteen-metre sea and a seventeen-foot draft I couldn't afford to go much farther. I advised him that he had to haul up there or I couldn't stay with him.

In the words of the federal investigators who later studied the Storm of '85, the *George E. Darby* was "severely hampered by the existing hurricane conditions and restricted by shallow water and rocks."

Dunn: He was following us for three hours, four hours, and it was getting to be about seven-thirty at night when he told us he couldn't follow us any more 'cause we were getting pushed into the shallows of the Hecate Strait. I said, "Let us on the boat. We want off—we're not going to make it."

He said, "I can't do that." He couldn't pull us out of the water.

I said, "Hold on a minute. If you've got to turn out, I'll turn out." I basically had no idea of where I was. All I had was a VHF. I had no electronics whatsoever.

Montgomery: He finally did haul up, and when he hauled up—it was riding pretty wild. I could see that from where we were. I tried to stay upwind of him, although it's tough to hold position with a larger vessel sheltering a smaller vessel. I tried to stay upwind of him as much as possible to break the sea for him.

Eventually the report I got from him was that one of his outrigger poles had carried away and jill-poked back through the wheelhouse. So now the vessel was open to the sea. We put out a call for assistance at his request. I readied two volunteers—rescue swimmers—to, if necessary, go in the water and try to recover them on a line. That's pretty hairy in that situation. One was a female cadet who volunteered. One was a seaman. This was just at the beginning of the rescue swimmer program. They hadn't had the training yet, but they were strong swimmers and they had wetsuits and all that gear.

There was a US Coast Guard helicopter in Sandspit, but he was having radio problems. He launched, and he said he would attempt a rescue, but he would only attempt it if we stayed on scene to give him a reference. It wasn't a case of illuminating, it was a case of providing a reference point.

The problem he had was that he couldn't communicate directly with the fishing vessel, and he couldn't communicate directly with us. So, an Aurora from Canadian Forces Base Comox came and orbited overhead, and the transmissions went from the fishing boat to us to the Aurora to the Coast Guard helicopter. Back and forth.

It took the helicopter a while to locate us. I put spotlights on the clouds overhead and that's how they found us. I had Night Suns—very high-powered lights. He came over and we held position as close as we could without causing any further damage to the vessel—two or three hundred feet.

Dunn: The chopper from Alaska was flying down the middle of the Hecate Strait. He was flying to save the guys on the *Traveller*. He heard me talking to the *George E. Darby*, and he took a look at the boat and said, "You guys'd better get off." I said, "Yah, okay."

He said to throw the life raft in. The boat's just alive—I'd knocked it out of gear. Where do you put the raft? Where do you throw it off?

I threw it off the stern and hung on to the rope. Kevin jumped in, which is about a 200-pound man. Scott probably weighs 250—he jumped in. Mike, he's probably around 250. So they all jump in, and this big wave comes. The raft comes shooting along the boat and I was running along with it, trying to push it off and jump in. The hold-down for one of the poles had a hook in it—like a turnbuckle—and that grabbed the raft on the way by and it ripped a chunk out of it about a foot long and it's deflating like crazy. I'm saying, "Get out, get out!" Mike's climbing out slowly and he's got his hands up on the cap rails. Scott and Kevin see what's going on and they go up each side of him like a ladder. We all pulled Mike onto the deck like a big halibut. After that we were all just laying on the deck laughing. It all just got to the stage where it didn't matter any more.

The chopper's watching all of this going on. By this time it's dark—we're working on his floodlights. So the guy says, "Jump off, one at a time." But you don't want to get off the boat when it's just sitting there—the boat's going to get you. The rigging's going in the water, the cap rails—it's going to cream you. You want to get away from it.

I said to Mike, "Mike, you've got to be the first one off. You're the strongest, you're the best swimmer. You've got to do it." This is kind of an experiment, eh?

I get the boat going ahead. Mike's standing there at the stern, hanging on to something. He's waiting for the signal. We're telling him to jump, and then it doesn't look good and we're telling him not to. Then we tell him, "Go for it, Mike!" And he jumps.

A Sikorsky helicopter was used to rescue the crew of the *Dee-Jay*.
Painting by Graham Wragg.

We've still got the boat going. We had it going maybe two, three knots to try and get it away from him. He's in the water, and the chopper tries to drop its basket. But the wind just whips it right up. It looked like it was heading for the prop. So they throw the chopper sideways and suck the basket in. Then the guy goes straight up. And we're going, "What the hell's going on—are they leaving?" We're thinking about trying to turn around to pick Mike up. 'Cause we can't directly talk to the helicopter and this is all happening so fast.

He went way up, then it seemed like he put the bird out of gear and free-fell—dropped—then took the winch out of gear, I guess, and stopped the chopper and shot the basket into the water. Good pilot. And doing all of that right above our rigging. He had recorded 80 to 90 knots on his chopper, which is over a hundred miles an hour. I think it was just about the highest wind airlift in history. It was incredible, how hard it was blowing. Your face, everything that was exposed, hurt for a while, then everything got numb.

So he shoots the basket into the water. And there's a big whip in the line because of the wind. He pulls it over and Mike gets in it pretty quick. You get ahold of the cable and pull yourself in, then they reef you up real quick so you don't get whipped into the bird.

Kevin was next. He jumped off. That went smooth. Then Scott jumped off. That was funny. Before he left he said, "You better not stay with this boat 'cause it's not going to make it." 'Cause it was my first boat and I didn't want to lose it. Everything from the cupboards was on the floor: pots, pans. Everything got turned upside down. There was a bottle of rum laying on the floor. Scott grabs it, takes a swig, smashes it on the stove and fucks off out the cabin: "Fuck you, boat!"

He jumps off and they pull him up. Then I've got to get off the boat. I didn't want to leave it in gear because I thought the boat could come around and get me—nobody driving it. I knocked it out of gear. I stood on top of the halibut winch, took my pants off and put my fins on and waited for a big wave to come. I dove into the wave, and when I popped out I was one hundred, two hundred feet away—gone. So I was fine.

When they dropped the basket for me I got ahold of the line okay and I was pulling myself in. I could swim really good with my fins on—I had pretty good control actually, and the life jacket was keeping me buoyant. And it was a short time so you could still move, you weren't getting the hypothermia right away.

I got ahold of the cable and was pulling myself into the basket and my fins got stuck—I couldn't get them in there. I finally get in there and I'm going through the waves. I had to give them the up signal, 'cause they knew I was having trouble. Finally I give them the up signal and get reefed up.

Montgomery: The skipper rolled into the net but he hadn't even made it into the chopper—the chopper was still overhead—when the *Dee-Jay* rolled and the lights went out.

Dunn: I remember the wind caught me and I got slammed into the chopper. When I got in there it was unreal—the chopper was dropping and bouncing. Right away there were two people who ripped your clothes off and put you in a survival suit—something like that. On the way back they strapped us in, it was so intense in the chopper. It's an incredible job that those people did. Without them there's no way we'd have made it. And the *George E. Darby*.

It took me years to get over it. I'm still not over it. I don't take any chances at all. I learned my lesson the hard way about how you've got to respect that sea. It can be just incredibly mean. I'll still go out and fish in 30-, 35-mile-an-hour winds, but anything more than that I go in. I study the weather forecasts all the time—I know what it's doing. I understand it—what fronts are, a cold front, what it does. I watch my barometer. I'm really on the ball.

Fishing would be a lot easier for me if I hadn't had that accident, let's put it that way. It's been eleven years now. For the first seven years…I should of went and got some counselling. I don't think it would have hurt. I think that probably would have helped. I didn't. But who's to say if it would have helped or not? Time heals things. I haven't hit the beach or had a problem of any sort since then—touch wood.

I used to downhill ski—I did a little bit of racing when I was younger. I had a real fast motorcycle. Used to race dirt bikes. Used to do lots of wild things. After that my whole life changed. I drive real slow. Life is good, and I guess I figure I came real close. It was long…we were out in that Hecate for just so long. It sticks in your mind. I think it was nine hours since we took that first bad wave.

I've seen sixty, seventy a few times through the years. My dad was a real hard-core fisherman. We were brought up in it and weather never bothered me. It should have.

I kept telling everybody, "We're going to make it, we're going to make it." Nobody said anything. Nobody really believed me. There's a good chance we weren't. We fought right to the friggin' end. If we hadn't been young and in good shape—strong guys—something would have happened. I had a couple of minor cuts and that was it. Nobody got hurt.

When you're in your early twenties … I guess that's why young guys go to war. You're kind of fearless. That's what you needed to be in that situation.

Fraser Dunn in 1985.
Photo courtesy the Dunn Family.

Despite the size of the *George E. Darby*—175 feet—the ferocious pounding took both a human and material toll. Captain Monty Montgomery was hospitalized for a compression fracture to the spine; the *Darby* had its half-inch steel bottom set in to the point that it had to be dry-docked for repairs. Montgomery has retired from the Coast Guard, and is living in Qualicum Beach.

When Fraser and Scott Dunn returned to Hecate Strait a month after losing the *Dee-Jay*, it was in the company of their parents, Fred and Maggie, aboard the boat they had cut their teeth fishing on, the *Marnie*. On that trip they hooked and recovered the string of halibut gear that Fraser had cut off when he decided it was time to run for their lives.

Fraser Dunn now lives in Port Alberni, and fishes out of French Creek on the troller-longliner *Polar Jo*. Scott Dunn owns the Port Alberni-based dragger *Beaufort Sea*. Mike McGuire and Kevin Bouchard, having survived the *Dee-Jay*, went into other lines of work.

Miss
Rachel
(and Other
Crises)

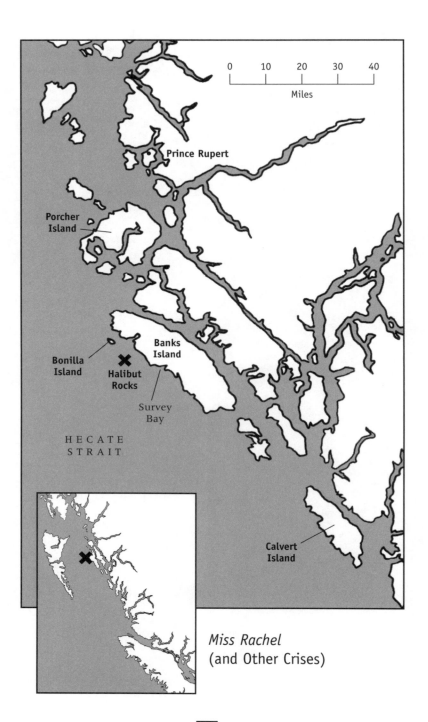

0   10   20   30   40
Miles

Prince Rupert

Porcher
Island

Banks
Island

Bonilla
Island

Halibut
Rocks

Survey
Bay

HECATE
STRAIT

Calvert
Island

Miss Rachel
(and Other Crises)

MARINE RESCUES ARE NEVER SCRIPTED. MUCH OF THE work done by rescue professionals—the Coast Guard, the armed forces—is preparation for the real thing, and they make every effort to be prepared for every foreseeable circumstance. But their business by nature demands reacting to the unforeseen, and to working in conditions for which there can be no dress rehearsal. It goes without saying, too, that the more treacherous the conditions, the more unpredictable the rescue. At the point where people and materials are stretched to their limits, improvisation takes place. Luck also happens; sometimes it's good.

On a shelf in the living room of Wayne Watson's waterfront home sits a small metal shackle twisted out of shape to the point where it would be reasonable to question whether it could withstand significant strain. Watson picks it up, turns it over in his fingers. "I collect junk," he says dismissively, tossing the shackle back in its place.

Watson is a professional fisherman. He has fished for tuna, for herring, for salmon and for dogfish, among others. He has had more than one narrow escape on the water. He is also a director of a fishermen's insurance co-operative. Overall, he is well placed to know that his story is only one of hundreds of close-call tales fishermen could tell if they had the time and the inclination, and he wonders aloud why he should offer this one up as something special. And yet there on the shelf is the shackle, and here he is, alive to tell the tale.

Accompanying Watson on board his *Miss Rachel* for the opening of the 1985 halibut season were deckhands Rick McIntosh, Colin Simpson and Alain Bellemare.

Watson: They had forecast a big storm, which we knew was going to be severe. We were not really that far from land—about two hours' run from shore. When it reached the point that I felt there was a chance of getting injured, we decided to pack up our gear and head 'er for shore. I had planned from the morning on running in when the wind got up to what was dangerous. Whether we left it too long or not—who's to say.

Bellemare: I still remember ... I still see Wayne ... we pulled that one line and then it started to blow more. And Wayne goes, "Ah, one more." So we pull one more line. And he goes, "I think we can pull one more." By then it was so rough, you're in the front of the cabin and you're running, and every wave hits the cabin and it's complete green water. You see nothing but straight water.

Watson: What had happened was, there's a reef that sticks out from these Halibut Rocks—really shallow. When you run in to this harbour we were running in to—Survey Bay, on the outside of Banks Island—you run pretty close to that reef. I would guess the wind was blowing close to 50 when we were running in. I don't remember whether the tide was ebbing or flooding, but we were being set down on this reef. And I was having to turn more and more into the southeast to clear that reef.

It finally got to the point where we were just burying in water. I probably missed a kelp patch and hooked it with the stabilizer. Kelp patches are sometimes the size of a house, although that early in the year they're not that common.

It couldn't have happened at a worse place, 'cause we were right at the reef. I was working hard to get around it 'cause it's really shallow and there's rocks there that break. All of a sudden the pole broke. And we had lots of heavy rigging—big rigging and big stabilizers to help us while we're working.

I kicked it out of gear and ran up to the front and got the anchor down, which probably took me thirty seconds. I had a monster big anchor. I used it on the herring and I used it on early halibut trips. It was a bit of a brute to get up and down, but we always got big winds in the spring.

Right away I knew what had happened. I hollered at the guys, "See if you can get all the ropes and rigging in so we don't get it in the wheel." 'Cause we could have ran in without the pole, but we can't run it with stuff like that in the propeller. Though what happened in the end, even the pole was jammed between the rudder and the propeller. It sucked up all the cables and the chain and the rope. And the pole was sticking out—we looked kind of like a speared whale.

Wayne Watson on the bow of *Miss Rachel*—launch day, 1977.
Photo courtesy Wayne Watson.

By the time we got straightened around and laying into the wind on the anchor, we started trying to remove that stuff. We tried to get the pole out. We tried everything. We put blocks up on what was left of the pole and tried to pull—'cause we had to pull the pole away from the boat. And with one pole still down and a big, heavy stabilizer, it made the boat list pretty good, too.

It got to the point where we couldn't work any more, so we decided it was time to call for help. I'd been talking to my friend, Jean Beaudet, the lightkeeper at Bonilla Island, and I finally phoned him and said, "I think you'd better add us to the list of casualties." Something like that. I don't think I put out a proper Mayday. He phoned the Coast Guard and told them the situation we were in. We were fine at the time. They had lots to do anyway.

Finally the wind got so bad that we decided we were in trouble. There was a danger that we could be drug over the rocks. We

CCGS *Point Henry.*
Painting by Graham Wragg.

were hanging right off the rocks. I considered us to be in a Mayday situation. They decided to send a boat down and take us off, but I guess the wind kept getting progressively higher and higher and higher, and by the time the boat got there—we were in shallow water, probably 4 fathoms, 5 fathoms of water—and I think the wind came up 75 or 80 at the peak. So it was ... wrinkly.

Bellemare: Wayne decided to phone the Coast Guard, to tell them we were in trouble. The Coast Guard boat *Point Henry*, out of Prince Rupert, said, "We're leaving and we'll be there in an hour and a half." There was also the question of sending a chopper, but I believe the chopper was into another rescue.

So we stayed there on the anchor. And it got rougher and rougher and rougher. I said, "What have I got to do? I've got an hour and a half. Why don't I start to write the story?" So I started. I wrote, "Here we are in the middle of Hecate Strait. We're stuck in a storm..." I spoke way less English at the time so it was quite a bit of effort for me to figure out all that stuff. I think I even slept a little bit, just putting my head down on the table, because I was so tired from fishing.

The Coast Guard arrived and they started talking to Wayne on the radio. And it looked like they didn't quite have it together, the Coast Guard. I don't know whether they were scared or whether they weren't used to being out in that kind of rough weather. They tried to figure out a plan.

> Captain Carl Safianuk and his crew aboard the 67-foot, Prince Rupert-based cutter *Point Henry* had initially been advised that, owing to their vessel's size and the unusually severe conditions, they would likely not be sent out into the full fury of Hecate Strait. As one Mayday broadcast after another was sent out, however, rescue co-ordinators were left with no alternative but to send the *Point Henry* into the teeth of the intensifying storm.

Safianuk: When we arrived there the seas were making up to the point where they were twenty, thirty, to forty feet high, and the velocity of the wind was around 80 knots. Once it set in that way it just continued to blow and with the size of our cutter, we were being tossed around like a cork.

What that meant was a lot of care to keep control of the vessel. It was constantly being picked up and set to one side, then heaving over the other way and pitching and tossing. You've got a limited amount of control as to exactly where you place your vessel. You've got to look ahead and make your approaches slow and make a lot of allowances for the forces—the wind—and the vessel being tossed about.

Bellemare: At the same time the boat arrived, the helicopter arrived. There was a question that the chopper would send a man on the cable to get us. But they decided not to do it. They decided it was going to be best if the Coast Guard just came with a Zodiac to get us. They launched the Zodiac and they came beside us, and we were there in our survival suits on the *Miss Rachel*. Wayne turns to me and he tells me, "You go." I think because I was the youngest he sent me out first—me and Colin. He and Rick stayed. They would take two guys in the first trip with the Zodiac and two guys on the next trip.

McIntosh: There was two Coast Guard guys in the Zodiac and there was only room for two more. Wayne was in the wheelhouse, so I put Colin and Alain in the boat and away they went. Those poor guys, you've got to give them credit—they were in more trouble than we ever were. God, you should have seen 'em. The waves were breaking... these huge, huge waves rolling down on them.

Anyway, they got over to the *Point Henry*. It had a stern launch and retrieving apparatus. In Victoria Harbour it probably worked a hundred percent every time, but out on the high seas ... the stern of the *Point Henry* was going about thirty feet in the air and the Zodiac was still down in the water. It was pretty hard to put them together. They finally tried. They got the bow into this little slot where it was supposed to go. Alain grabbed ahold of something and held on. But as the stern went up again and the Zodiac went back down, he was just left hanging there. Then the *Point Henry* came down on the Zodiac and that was the end of that.

Coast Guard Zodiac approaches the stricken *Miss Rachel* in an attempt to rescue Wayne Watson and his crew.
Photo by 442 Squadron, courtesy Rick McIntosh.

Bellemare: I think what happened is the battery got totally wet and shorted something out. Because it was under water. The engine quit. I remember turning around and the Coast Guard guy had opened the cover to see whatever he could do with the outboard. And of course the thing just got instantly swamped full of water and was never going to work again.

As the engine quit, the Zodiac was still in the direction to meet with the Coast Guard boat. So the guy with the Coast Guard tells me, "Jump!" I knew that I had one second to do it. Because then the Zodiac was going to bounce back and drift away. I thought, Go for it! I jumped, but I'm the only one that made it, because Colin wasn't on his feet, and the Coast Guard guys let me go off first. So I was the only one to get on the Coast Guard boat.

Then the Zodiac drifted away. And it was going so fast... you wouldn't believe it. The *Point Henry* tried to catch up with it but it was impossible, 'cause it was going so fast. So they came with the helicopter.

> Among the craft tasked to aid the *Miss Rachel* was a Labrador from Canadian Forces Base Comox's 442 search and rescue squadron. The six-man helicopter crew had spent the day being bounced—often literally— from rescue to rescue. They were refuelling at Prince Rupert, thinking their day was done, when called to the assistance of Watson and his crew.
>
> On board the Labrador, along with aircraft commander Captain Bob Grant, a co-pilot and two flight engineers, were search and rescue technicians (SAR Techs) Master Corporal Jim (Gator) McLusky and Corporal Brad Gough.

Gough: With the SAR Techs on board, there's a team leader and a team member. And I was brand new pretty well—less than two years in the trade. The team leader will usually do the calls first, and that was Gator McLusky. Gator opted to go down first.

People are not comfortable in a storm like that. And most people don't want to be in the water anyways. It's uncomfortable, and a lot of people are non-swimmers. I've been stuck twice like that in a bad ocean, and it's surprising how much water gets forced down your throat. Plus you spend a fair amount of time under the water. Even though you have positive buoyancy, you spend a fair amount of time under water because of the waves smashing on you.

Optimally the engineer would like to put you right beside the Zodiac if he could. In calm weather it's not a problem. That night was quite bad. So Gator went down to get the first guy, but Gator didn't feel there was enough room in the Zodiac for him to get in. So when he got over to the Zodiac, he got to the first guy and he just pulled him over the side. What happened was, they got separated from the Zodiac. Gator's still on the cable of the helicopter. He's in a wetsuit and stuff, so he's pretty buoyant. But any casualty in the water…they only have one thing left to hang on to, and that's the SAR Tech. And that's what happened to Gator. The guy grabbed ahold of Gator, and they were both drinking a lot of water, because Gator was trying to get the hook hooked up, and it's not a smooth procedure.

They finally got up. Gator was going to go down and get the second guy. He tried the same scenario. He pulled the second guy over. And that was catastrophic. They got hit by a monster wave. The Zodiac went one way, they went the other, and the guy grabbed ahold of Gator around his helmet. And he was a big guy, and Gator was underneath the water the whole time. I could see Gator hitting the guy in the face and the head, trying to make him let go—he was drowning him—but there's no way a panicked individual's going to let the SAR Tech go.

I was telling the engineer, "Wheel him in! Wheel him in!" 'Cause he wasn't going to let go of Gator anyways, even if they hoisted him up. Miraculously, Gator did get the horse collar onto the guy, and they got him up. Gator had drank so much sea water by that time, he was sick to his stomach. He handed me the horse collar and said, "Go for it." Which, when you're new in the trade, that's not a problem. When you're brand new to the trade, you know you're invincible, you can't get hurt, you can do it all. And you want the opportunity to show that. So it was like, "Thanks there, old timer. Have a seat and I'll show you how it's supposed to be done."

I had the opportunity of viewing two of the hoists from the safety of the helicopter, and I'd thought up another plan. I told the engineer, "Put me down by the Zodiac, and I'm going to climb in and take the guy right out of the Zodiac. And that way, even if we get ripped out of the Zodiac into the ocean, I've already got the guy hooked up, and just wheel us in."

At this time we were into low fuel. We've got two tanks on the helicopter, and at 350 pounds you get lights on as an indicator. We were already in that state.

So damned if I didn't go down and that plan worked really well. So now I not only thought I was good, I knew I was good. So when the aircraft commander said, "We've got time for one more hoist—do you want to go down and try and get the guys off the *Miss Rachel*?" I was more than willing to give it a try. That's where things really went bad for us.

The most dangerous part of our job, the best chance we stand of getting hurt, with all the parachuting and everything that we get done, is getting put onto a boat in rough seas. There's so many variables there. Especially on a smaller vessel—anything less than about a 90-footer. In rough seas like that, especially at anchor, it's phenomenal how much that boat gets rocketed around the ocean. And here you are in a helicopter that's an unstable platform, with a guy hanging down on a cable. So it's a real ugly time. There's a seventh wave theory. There are people that don't believe it, people that do. Usually they seem to feel that there is a small rhythm to the ocean: you get the one big wave that will come in a certain rhythm. So we try to time, if we think we can see it, that you let the boat take the one big wave, and then it should sit a little bit more stable for a while. That's when we try and get on the boat.

We have a slightly different procedure for getting onto a boat. We have 250 feet of rope that we have on a specially coiled system that we call a bird's nest. We hold on to that in our hand, and it's hooked onto us or the hook—whichever we want—with a thing called a weak link. It breaks at about a 200-pound pull. That's 'cause you don't want to have a hard rope tying the helicopter to a fixed object, where things are going to get ripped. So with the weak link, the rope will break off if anything gets snagged, and the helicopter's still fine. What our intent is—if we have the opportunity to brief the people on the vessel—is to tell them we're going to throw this rope down to them, and for them to take the rope and steady the SAR Tech. But it was so rough out, it was very difficult for them to try and do.

I got the rope on to the *Miss Rachel*. They were having a tough time, 'cause with their boat going up and down in these monster waves, and the helicopter getting buffeted around, sometimes I'd get knocked away and the rope gets ripped out of their hands. And sometimes we'd come back together again and they couldn't get the slack back in fast enough. And also, you don't want to get a rope tangled up around your feet, 'cause the next time things pay out you might be getting snapped off the boat.

One thing that people don't understand is, they think the helicopter just flies over and looks down and stays there. Actually it doesn't work that way. The way it's designed, once you're hoisting a person down, the pilot can no longer see what's underneath him. He's going on the engineer's calls. And it's a finesse call: two feet this way, two feet that way. When that thing's getting knocked all over the sky, it's not a great scenario. When we're doing bush work, if the pilot can look out at a tree it's easy for him to hold a position. Out in the ocean ... now he's just looking at moving water. The engineer calls to him, "Right five." What's five? It's very tough.

So at that time the pilot called the *Point Henry* over to the one o'clock position—the nose of the helicopter being 12 o'clock, the ass end being six—off in the distance a little bit, to use them as a hover reference. If they station keep, then he can station keep. Once they moved off into the distance, that's when we tried again to get on to the *Miss Rachel*.

In ideal conditions, from the time the SAR Tech goes out the door, an absolute maximum of thirty seconds and he should be on the boat. That would be a long hoist. Lots of times it's done within ten seconds. This time it was in the three- to four-minute mark, I would say, and I was still hanging down underneath the helicopter. And I've got the big oscillations on—I've got a monstrous swing on, and there's no way to take that swing out. Plus you're spinning around on the hook, too, 'cause the hook is on a swivel.

He finally got lined up on the *Miss Rachel* and flew me ahead into the boat. Fortunately I didn't get hurt at that time. I hit the rigging about six feet off the main deck where the two guys left on board were waiting for me. The vessel was up high on a wave, and I just hopped down.

Watson: The SAR Tech came down right between us and landed on the deck. It was probably close to the worst of the storm about then. He was standing between us, and I said, "Rick's going to go first." He had this harness, and he'd just started to explain what to do with the harness ... and he disappeared. He got jerked up so fast that he seemed to vanish. He was gone.

Gough: One of the older guys, he had turned around with his back toward me. I grabbed him and turned him around and said, "Face me." That's all I had a chance to say. I could see the boat was going down on a big swell, and I could see the helicopter drifting back, and I could see the cable all paying out tight. So I knew where I was going: I could see I was getting snapped off.

I tried to run to jump off the back of the boat. My leg hit a big bollard on the way, so I thought I'd broke my leg. I gave the signal to bring me up. And on the way up I had a real bad oscillation on. The fishermen still had the rope, but they couldn't keep the swing out. The helicopter was very high, because the waves were so bad. If the water itself goes into the engine intakes, you've lost your engines. So we were hoisting from around eighty feet. And of course, the way the pendulum effect is, the more cable you have out, the worse the pendulum swing. And I had a bad one on—the worst one I'd ever had.

We work out of the right side of the helicopter, and the aircraft commander is in the front right seat. What happened was, when I was about twenty feet below the helicopter, the oscillation was so bad, I got swung right over to the other side. I thought I was going to go right up into the rotors, 'cause I was going over there with such a velocity. I was looking at the first officer—who's in the left front seat of the helicopter—eyeball to eyeball from about five feet away.

The weak link had snapped, so I didn't have the rope on me. But what happened was, when the cable got caught in the hinge of the door underneath the helicopter, it just cut like butter. It took me about a full second to realize that I was free falling. Because we train every day almost, and you use that gear so much—you become so dependent on it—it's hard to believe that it's failed you. But it did.

Bellemare: I was on the Coast Guard boat watching this, and what came next was so incredible…I never forgot that moment. They were lifting up the guy and he was about a hundred feet in the air and clack—the cable broke. And vroom—he fell down and hit the water.

McIntosh: I couldn't believe my eyes. This poor guy that was trying to save us come tumbling out of the air and landed in the water about seventy-five feet behind us.

Sgt. Brad Gough.
Canadian Forces photo.

Gough: I free fell back into the ocean. I did six years in the navy when I first joined up, and I remember an old salt on board the ship telling me if you ever get knocked off a high point of the ship into the ocean, adopt a ball position, because it offers less of your body to the water. I didn't do that. I'd contemplated before being in the air—free fall—and I felt I could land on my feet like a cat does when you hold them up in the air and drop them. I remember trying to kick myself, to kick myself around, and nothing happened; traction was really bad. So I was flailing through the air and was in a horizontal position when I hit the water. That was a mistake: if I'd adopted a ball position I might not have got hurt quite the same way.

It was like walking into a room and somebody turns off the light and hits you in the face with a pillow. It was black. It helped that the sea was rough, 'cause if it's flat it's just like hitting concrete. I broke the surface again. I disconnected the hook and threw it away—no need for that any more. I kept the fluorescent indicator on the back of the horse collar to help them try and spot me in the ocean. We also wear a Mae West life preserver, and I inflated that a little bit to try and keep out of the water. You do get popped under the water quite a bit, but you know you're going to surface again if you just hold your breath for a while.

I broke some ribs, partially collapsed a lung. That was from the hook, I believe, 'cause I still had the hook and twenty feet of cable with me when I hit the water, and the hook is fairly weighty. I thought I had lost my right eye, because my visor had got smashed and cut me on the eyebrow. I couldn't see out of it. Plus I was having respiratory distress from the lung. I could feel that there was blood coming out of my mouth.

I knew that I was in a bad spot because the helicopter had no gas left to try and get me out. We do have a backup winch on board, but we didn't have it rigged up at the time. Since that accident, it's standard operating procedure to have the backup winch rigged at all times when we're going for a sea rescue. And the *Point Henry*—because they'd been sent off for a hover reference—was quite a ways away.

Because Bob Grant was a good friend, he stayed in position—which he shouldn't have done, 'cause he was jeopardizing five other crew members plus the three people we'd picked up. Bob should have actually landed and let me fend for myself there. It would have been the smart thing to have done. I'm sure glad he didn't; it's really hard trying to pick a head out of the water in conditions like that. Bob stayed on scene over top of me until they could get the *Point Henry* over to me, then he just zipped over and landed.

We had a problem there, too. The *Point Henry* had lost some of their crew members—they were in our helicopter. They'd been beaten about so bad … their cabin area was just a mess. I remember, when I finally crawled into it, I was crawling over piles of stuff that had fallen off the shelves and everything. It was bad.

Bellemare: The *Point Henry* was completely upside down. There was thousands of suits and things—an overload of equipment. Survival suits everywhere. My first reaction at the time was I was not so thrilled. I found the Coast Guard didn't have the training that they should have had. I know when I wrote my story I put them down quite a bit. But then I had a second thought about it: those Coast Guard guys were really risking their lives out there.

Safianuk: At the time that all this was happening the conditions were so severe—the boat was rocking so violently—that the magnetic compass got fouled in the gimbals and we couldn't use that. Spray from the seas was getting into the wheelhouse, and my electronics were all starting to fail. The gyro was gone. I was left only with one radar—and I'm thankful to this day that we had the one radar still operational.

Gough: When the *Point Henry* got over to me they threw me a Kisby ring—a lifesaving ring. I got my head and arms through—at least I was attached to the ship. But when he tried to pull the rope in, he didn't have the strength to pull me up out of the water; it takes a lot of strength to lift a guy up out of the water freehand. In the interim I got washed around to the other side of the *Point Henry* and I was getting beat against the side of that by the ocean. Finally they walked me around to the Zodiac launching pad, which was vacant now, and they walked me up on that. I remember when I did crawl up on the back of the *Point Henry* I thanked them and said, "Now, if you'll just leave me alone for a little bit, I'd like to just stay here for a second on my hands and knees."

I spent the next four hours in the cabin area of the *Point Henry*, licking my wounds. They told me it was just a cut above my eye, and the blood dripping down from that was the reason I couldn't see. That was comforting. I'd never had lung damage before. We're trauma trained, but I thought it seemed like an excessive amount of blood that was coming out of my mouth. With the pain of respiration, I was trying to think: How bad is the damage here? But it turned out that the lung reattached itself a couple of days later, so it wasn't that bad of a deal.

McIntosh: Wayne and I—we were still on the *Miss Rachel* all through this—we decided that we'd try to send a buoy, a scotch-man, back on our halibut line, and the *Point Henry* would send us a life raft. We sent one back and…that poor *Point Henry*. Boy, those guys were taking a shit-kicking. It was just burying itself in those big rollers. And of course when it came up on the other side, the wind would hit it and it would fall off one way or the other, out of control.

Watson: The waves were big enough, and there was enough white water, that as the Coast Guard boat come up to the crest of a wave the wind would turn him and the white water would just engulf him. It was a terrifying thing to watch. I wouldn't have wanted to have been on the boat. He'd just turn and fall sideways and be engulfed in a mountain of white water thundering down. You'd see him turn around downwind of us and come jogging back up to us. Then he'd hit one of these big whitecaps and it would just bury him.

McIntosh: The first time they ran over the scotchman and chopped it off. We hauled the line in, stuck another one on, sent it back. By the time they'd made a big circle and came back probably half an hour had gone. The next time they got it. They launched one of their life rafts, a raft probably twenty feet long with a cover on it. They attached it to our groundline and then tried to get away from everything. The *Point Henry*'s stern went up in the air and came down on top of the life raft, spit out a bunch of splinters, and that was the end of that.

Bellemare: Finally it was discussed: what should be done. I remember the Coast Guard guy asking me for my opinion. I told him. I said, "We've been at it for hours and hours and everything we tried didn't work. It's getting dark. What are we going to do in the night? Somebody's going to get hurt." Plus we had a person that apparently had broken ribs on board. That guy was such a professional. He was always smiling. He had military training that included paramedical study. I came to see him once in a while to try and take care of him, but there was nothing to take care of: he was totally together. He knew he had broken ribs and he must have had great difficulty breathing.

It became dark. The Coast Guard guy gave me the radio and I said to Wayne, "Wayne, that's it. We tried all day and nothing happened so we're going to have to let you go." I think he kind of felt lonely. He said, "Okay—you guys can't make it, you can't make it."

Watson: Rick and I said, "Well, we'll ride it out." There was nothing we could do. The only real danger was going on the beach. The boat seemed secure enough. It was taking a tremendous beating, but the engine was running and it was dry. It was sitting at a hell of an angle and the waves were roaring over it. We sat at the back of the cabin. We didn't want to sit at the front 'cause so much water was hitting the windows that it was hard to believe that they would withstand it. They did. But boy, we sure took a hosing.

McIntosh: Wayne and I were sitting there gabbing. We were about two miles above the rock pile that was downwind of us. It was called Seal Rocks—quite a big rock pile. And all of a sudden—if you're at anchor in a gale your ship holds directly into the wind. Well, all of a sudden we were broadside. And we knew exactly what happened: the anchor let loose.

Watson: We got up on the bow. We had the regular anchor, which was maybe 170 pounds, and we managed to shackle it on to what was left of the chain and throw it out. Rick couldn't even face the wind on the front—he had to face back. I could face the wind 'cause I had glasses on. His eyes couldn't stand the spray. Just like pellets.

McIntosh: We crawled back into the wheelhouse. We didn't expect it to hold, really—it was just a little shackle. We were looking at one another, and we decided, Jesus, we must be close to those rocks. 'Cause it took us fifteen minutes or so, even longer, to get the second anchor down. Wayne looked into the radar. And he was silent for a couple of minutes. Then he said, "You've got to see this." I went over and took a look, and we were about a mile downwind of the damn rocks: we'd drifted right down through them. Right between them and out the other side. Didn't even know it. That would have been a quick ending if we'd have hit those rocks.

Watson: The other anchor didn't quite hold us; after we got through the reef we were dragging. As the biggest waves would come it would drag a bit. I talked to an American helicopter that had been rescuing guys. He was down in Sandspit. He offered to come and get us. I said, "I've just seen a helicopter rescue. I think I feel safer here."

He had a little chuckle. He said he'd sit on the ground there at Sandspit. He had to fuel up anyway, and I think they had a bunch of survivors aboard—I think he'd picked the guys off the *Bethune* and the *Dee-Jay*. We packed our flares in our survival suits, and we decided if it looked like we were going on the beach we would give him a call and jump overboard. Then he'd come and get us. We had flares and we'd give him our position from our Loran.

I've been on Bonilla. Both my wife and I stayed there one March in 75- and 80-mile-an-hour winds. We went out to that exposed southern beach and watched the waves come in. You could never go ashore there. You'd never survive that.

Sometime during the night I think we fell asleep. And the wind started to go down a little bit. Through all that violence, we'd noticed that the pole was gone. We looked out the back. The three-eighths stay wire and three-quarter-inch Samson rope was still in the propeller, but the pole was gone—the rudder moved.

I started revving the engine up and throwing it in ahead and throwing it in astern. By then the *Darby* was on its way. He'd actually started out earlier but they couldn't make it across the straits. He would have never got in that shallow water. If it was rough out in the Hecate Straits it was a hell of a lot rougher in where we were. But they were coming across that morning, and by the time they got over toward Bonilla we had freed it up enough that we felt it could run. You could tell there was still rigging in there. In fact, the pole was still there. When we got into Rupert and I threw it into reverse to stop at the dock it stalled the engine again 'cause it sucked all the rope back in it. The tip of the pole was still there, and all the rope and cables were hanging down.

Bellemare: The next day in Prince Rupert we looked and looked, and finally we saw the *Miss Rachel* coming. You could tell it was them because there was a broken pole. As normal fishermen, as soon as they arrived at the dock, bing, bang, boom: they had the parts ordered, the aluminum was down, they loosened up the prop and within a few hours we were back on the road.

I had a great time. That's the greatest thing I ever did. At the time I was twenty-one. I didn't care if I would die. Now I've got kids and it's different. Now if something happens I get nervous 'cause of the kids. At that time I had no concept—I was glad to go. And I thought that Wayne was such a good seaman. I totally trusted him and thought it was just fine to go back. If we survived that we'd survive anything.

Alain Bellemare had been a commercial clammer before signing on for this, his first trip as a commercial deckhand. He now lives on Cortes Island, where he fishes prawns from the *C-Fin*. Watson has since sold the *Miss Rachel*. He is now a partner in the combination troller-prawn boat *Midnight Dancer*.

Rick McIntosh, who has worked with Watson for more than three decades, fishes prawns from his boat *H P 1*. He lives in Lund, pretty much just around the corner from Watson. Simpson, owner of the fishing vessel *Central Isle*, lives in Cumberland.

Corporal Brad Gough, now Sergeant Brad Gough, is once again based at Canadian Forces Base Comox. In recognition of his effort in the *Miss Rachel* incident, he was named RCAF Association Airman of the Year. Gator McLusky, now Warrant Officer McLusky, is a SAR Tech

Capt. Carl Safianuk: "We were being tossed around like a cork."
Photo by Virginia Kimmett.

based in Greenwood, Nova Scotia.

Captains Grant and Safianuk were among the vessel and aircraft commanders who received commendations for the jobs they performed during the events of April 25 and 26, 1985. Both have since retired.

Jean Beaudet's perch on Bonilla Island, however isolated from the rest of the world, was located in the eye of the April 25-26 storm. Twice during the night that the *Miss Rachel* spent at precarious anchor just off Bonilla's shore, the lightkeeper recorded thirty-one-metre waves coming from a monitoring buoy located ten miles southwest of Bonilla.

Beaudet spent that day and night at his radio, relaying urgent messages and broadcasting weather bulletins every fifteen minutes. The constant contact he maintained with the *Miss Rachel* reflected more than professional duty, however: Wayne Watson was his best friend. Their daughters, Rachel Watson and Isabelle Beaudet, had grown up together via what Beaudet describes as "a lightkeepers' relationship": by phone and letter and rare visits. Wayne Watson delivered to Isabelle her first cat, a gift from Rachel, during a Christmas visit to Bonilla.

And so Beaudet spent the night of April 25 wondering whether his friendship with Watson was about to come to a violent end on the shore of his own light station. His fear was never so real as when Watson radioed Beaudet to say that the *Miss Rachel*'s anchor chain had broken.

The *Miss Rachel* crew (left to right): Rick McIntosh, Colin Simpson, Alain Bellemare, Wayne Watson.
Photo courtesy Rick McIntosh.

Beaudet: I thought, Geez, they're gone. I was very, very scared. And he was scared. It was getting to the point where I thought he was going to die, and I think he thought he was going to die, too. Wayne was my best friend, so it was a very touchy situation. It was a very emotional experience. You could hear the wind and waves over the radio. And people were dying.

> Beaudet's wife Lina was also a close friend of the Watsons. Unable to act directly on behalf of the *Miss Rachel* crew, she sought intercession elsewhere.

Beaudet: That's the first thing that went through her mind. Those were friends there, so we were pretty desperate. Lina, I would say, is a strong believer, and that's the first thing that went through her mind: God, if they make it through, I won't eat chocolate for a year.

> At a reunion between the *Miss Rachel* crew and the Beaudets after the incident, the four men presented Lina with a yard of chocolate. Lina kept her promise.

When
Jean Was
Young and
Foolish

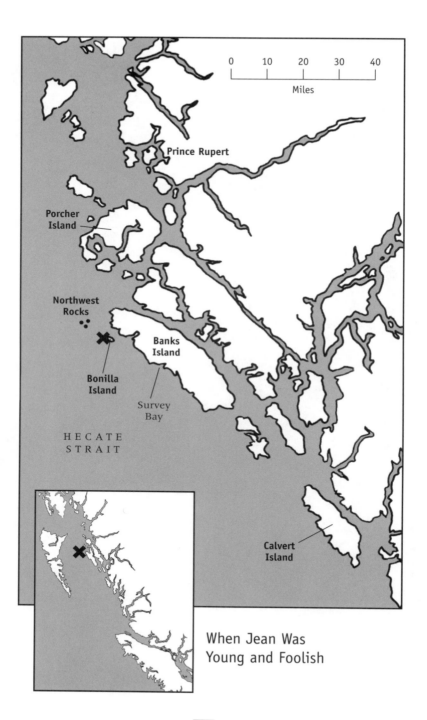

When Jean Was
Young and Foolish

JEAN BEAUDET DIDN'T WANT TO WAIT FOR HIS reunion with Watson, who returned to Bonilla the night after repairing the *Miss Rachel* at Prince Rupert. Despite the fact that the wind had come back up to about 50 knots, Watson tried to get out to the gear he'd left behind two days before when running from the storm.

"We tried buckin' but we were just getting beat to hell," Watson recalls, "so we said, 'To hell with it,' and we went back in and anchored in behind Bonilla—spent the night there."

Beaudet went out to the *Miss Rachel* in his ten-foot inflatable and arrived without incident. The get-together was a joyous affair until, reminded by his wife that he'd stayed too long in the falling light of a north coast evening, Beaudet attempted to return home.

Alain Bellemare: Jean leaves the house and he comes to the boat. We were bullshitting and he was so happy that we were there. We were talking about all those things. And then: *"Miss Rachel."* On the radiophone. It's Jean's wife.

Wayne comes and says, "Hi!"

"Is Jean on board?"

"Yes. He's on board."

And she goes, "Can I please talk to him?"

Wayne says, "Yes, go ahead."

And she started to give him shit because when he arrived on the boat he didn't phone her. He was supposed to phone to say that he arrived. She gave him shit, but in French, so nobody understood anything. But I do. And he just kind of holds the phone on the side. And she's going, "I don't want to be bachelored," and all that. Da da da da da da da. She just doesn't stop.

Jean goes, "Okay, now Alain heard everything."

"I don't care!" Da da da da da da. She went on and on and on. She was really mad.

Bonilla Island.
Terry Weber photo.

Beaudet: My wife was always telling me that I should always call when I was getting at a destination and when I was leaving from a destination. I guess I was pretty young and foolish and forgetting about that most of the time.

Bellemare: So Jean had this lesson. When he was going back to the house, he phoned his wife. He said, "I'm leaving now. I'll be there in three minutes. I'm all ready to go."

Beaudet: After a while my wife called Wayne and said, "Has Jean left yet?" Wayne said, "Lina, I think we're in trouble if he's not there yet."

Wayne Watson: She got excited and said, "Should I phone the Coast Guard?" I said, "Take your hand-held radio and go see if he's fighting with his Zodiac." He had to pull it up the beach each time, and in that kind of wind ... he could have been on that beach fighting to get his boat back up. She went down there and said there was no sight of him at all.

Beaudet:　She had noticed that my dog was at the end of the island, looking away and barking. She thought it was strange, so she called Wayne and said, "I think we should look for Jean." Wayne, being the seaman he was, said, "Okay."

Watson:　I pulled the anchor up and we charged off in the dark—tried to decide how far he could go. We drove out there full bore for about half or three quarters of an hour. I figured I was going to search back toward the beach.

Beaudet:　Because we were shielded from the weather, I didn't know that the wind was picking up. When I left Wayne's boat it was near dark. There probably was three- or four-foot seas, but we were dealing with that quite often. It was no big deal. But on the way back the wind had picked up again, and it became a little more hectic—more than that little boat could handle.

I went around the west side of the island, and there was really big breakers. I took a few, and then one was really big. It exposed too much of the bottom of the Zodiac to the wind. It took the boat and blew it away.

Because I was living in isolation and I had done that all my life, I always had the bowline tied to my waist, so I fell in the water but the boat stayed with me. I just got back to it and held on to it. I was drifting away.

It was pitch dark, and I was seeing the lighthouse going away, then suddenly I saw Wayne's boat going away. I said, "Well shit, I guess I'm in deep trouble."

I tried a couple of times to get on the Zodiac, but the sea was washing me off all the time. The boat was upside down in the water, and because the engine was laying on its side it was easy for me to get on the boat. I was just climbing on the engine and getting on the boat, but every time I was doing that I was washed off because of the waves. I thought, "If I keep on doing this, I'm going to lose all my strength and get real cold." So I preferred to stay in the water.

Wayne went about three, three and a half miles away. I was seeing his big spotlight looking in the water. The Zodiac's pretty small, and we had maybe six-, seven-foot seas there, so I didn't think he was going to pick me up. But he did.

Rick McIntosh: We went out, turned west and started to zigzag, flashing these spotlights around. And I'll be damned if that reflector stuff on his shoulders ... if it hadn't been for that reflector stuff he probably would have been long gone out to sea. We spotted him a good four or five hundred yards off to starboard. His boat was upside down and he was on his knees. He had the bowline tied around his waist. He was one happy boy to see us.

Beaudet: He made a pass at me in those great big waves—great big breakers. The boat was going up and down—great big whiskers around the boat. He made a first pass at me and said, "Jean, can you grab ahold of the boat?" I thought I could, but I guess after about forty-five minutes in the water, in April, you're not very agile any more. I had a cruiser suit on. I guess that's what probably saved my life—the fact that I was dressed properly.

After the second pass a few guys on board the boat picked me up, got me on board, and got my motor and boat on board. I think Alain was quick enough that he started my engine right away, 'cause my engine was upside down in the water.

They had blankets in the oven, so they warmed me up, and the guys came in the sack with me and warmed me up. Alain was the guy who spent the most time in the sack with me, and Wayne was taking pictures. About two o'clock in the morning I started to feel good again. It was a time of close calls, that weekend.

Bellemare: It was so funny. If his wife wouldn't have given him shit like that he would have never phoned before he left, phoned his wife and said, "I'm leaving now." If she wouldn't have done that he wouldn't have called, and we would have realized too late, and he would have been out and gone. Or if Wayne would have turned the radio off.

Beaudet: We discussed it quite often, Wayne and I, whether I'd have survived without him there. It was ridiculous, because I had always been in this kind of conditions, and I thought I'd make it to Northwest Rock and grab on to the beach or something like that. But there was no hope of that at all. I was already

Together on the light: Lina and Jean Beaudet with their children
François and Isabelle, photographed in 1984 at Bonilla Island.
Photo courtesy Wayne Watson.

so weak when they picked me up, and I still had two or three
miles to do. And in those great big breakers against the rock, I
had no chance. Not a big chance, anyway. Wayne saved my life
that time, there's no doubt in my mind.

Jean Beaudet went on to put in twenty years of light-
keeping service, sixteen of them on Bonilla Island. He
subsequently moved to the Georgina Point light station,
at the eastern entrance to Active Pass, until the Coast
Guard's destaffing program brought his career to an end
in November of 1996. He, Lina and their son François
live on Mayne Island.

Randy's
Story

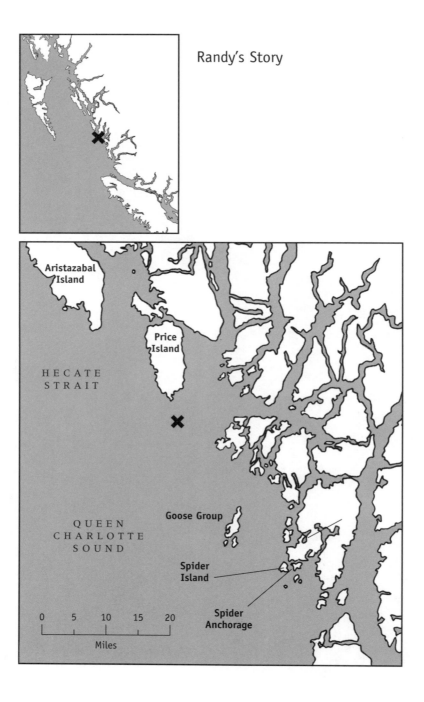

Randy's Story

I cannot stop thinking about Randy Morrison
Storm force winds,
his skipper mad as Ahab,
pulling up halibut skates
in the mouth of a gale
White needles of rain,
the swell breaking across the boat
until finally she lists over drunkenly,
both of them pitched into the sea
A single moment, grasped
like a lungful of air,
the skipper without a survival suit
Randy says
"You're a dead man. I'm sorry.
Goodbye."

—from "Southeasterly" (for Randy Morrison), by Andrew Wreggitt

RANDY MORRISON WASN'T SUPPOSED TO HAVE BEEN ABOARD the *Pacific Traveller* the day the small troller-longliner succumbed to the Storm of '85. Though he was a seasoned fisherman, Morrison was called in at the last minute by skipper Leonard Egolf to replace his regular deckhand, who'd come down sick and had to be taken ashore on the fourth day of the halibut opening.

Morrison, who lived in the Comox Valley at the time, joined Egolf in Port Hardy on the morning of April 24. The pair left at noon, returning to fishing grounds on Goose Bank in northern Queen Charlotte Sound. Upon arrival they shut down for a few hours, resting while the boat drifted.

April 25 dawned clear and calm, but with a forecast that called for southeasterly gales. Egolf and Morrison began setting their lines.

By ten that morning they had three strings of gear in the water. On the radio they heard that the gale warning had been upgraded to a storm warning for that afternoon. According to the report of the investigation that followed, "The crew considered that they still had enough time to pull the strings back on board and seek shelter at Spider Anchorage some twenty-five miles away." Egolf was thirty-three years old. He was an experienced fisherman, doing what fishermen have always done: push their luck.

Morrison: The weather bulletin said it was gonna be blowing southeast later on—winds wouldn't come up strong until later in the afternoon. So the guy I was with, the skipper, said we could pick up all our gear. So we picked up two strings. We debated on the third, then we picked it up. That put us up to about one o'clock in the afternoon. Started heading for land.

We couldn't run full speed because of the wave size. We had to quarter into the waves. The boat was rolling, the waves were getting bigger and bigger. They were starting to stack up like mountains.

We were rolling around so much that all this gear in the cockpit—hooks and gangen and netting and spare line—got tangled up in the steering gear. It caused the chain on the steering to pop off. When that happened the boat leaned over; we no longer had steering. The boat heeled over on its side.

The skipper had his window open on his side and I was sitting on the galley table. Water came right in through the window. He righted the boat—he sort of turned it around into the wind. We jogged into it a while there, and we tried to fix things up a bit. The anchor had come loose, and he was up on the bow trying to straighten out the anchor.

We'd taken a couple of waves over the stern. The whole cockpit was full of water. All the junk in the back and the floorboards were floating around in the cockpit.

He got the steering fixed up. We cleared all the junk out—put it in different spots in the boat. We started to get underway again. We ran for maybe another hour or so. We changed our course this time—we took the sea on the stern.

I guess we were about eight miles off shore—something like that—and the damn chain come off the steering again and got all bound up in there … something got all bound up in there. Netting or something like that.

The boat heeled over the same way again. And more water came in through the window. At that point I was freaking. I'd put my survival suit on in the meantime, while we were running. But the skipper hadn't put his on. I kept telling him, "Put your damn survival suit on." But he wouldn't do it. He thought it was too bulky to work with. I guess he figured he could fix the boat and get everything going.

Waves were coming into the stern. It was just incredible. By that time they're up to twenty-five, thirty feet.

I'm standing at the back of the wheelhouse, holding the door open. The boat was over on about a 45-degree angle. The rail was under water, and the bulwarks were about a foot and a half high. They were right under water. And there was water coming right over the side of the boat. I'm yelling at the skipper, "Get your damn survival suit on. This is the end of us here." He just looked at me like—I don't know if he was in shock or what it was. He just kept trying to save the boat.

After the cockpit was filled up with water and water was coming over the side of the rails, I told him to phone the Coast Guard. But he wouldn't. It was like he was confused, or he was panicking. I just don't know. I didn't know him well enough to know, to know what his feelings were and how he reacted to things like that.

I told him to call the Coast Guard. He didn't know exactly how to do it. I said, "Put the channel on 16. Call 'Mayday, Mayday, Mayday,' and give your boat name and position." So he did that. Then I said shortly after that, "Put your survival suit on." His survival suit was right at his feet. And he wouldn't put it on.

He came out of the wheelhouse again, and he had a hammer and nails and a couple of boards that he was going to nail over the cockpit that was already full of water. He must have been in shock. Experienced fishermen don't get in confusion like that.

Shortly after that the boat went right over. It was up to the stack—the exhaust pipe—in the water. The mast was in the water. Slowly it went over. It was over on its side for a while. The side of the wheelhouse and the top sides of the thing—the way the boat would sit in the water—was sticking out of the water, so we could walk on it.

It was a heavy-duty boat. It was built well and well put together. There was just a bit of haywire in it—old antiquated stuff that should have been repaired years ago and wasn't. After the boat had gone right over we stood on the side of the boat. We hung on to the side of the boat for maybe a couple of hours.

We were heading for night. I thought that the skipper, Leonard, doesn't have a chance. It would have been better for him to just shoot himself or whatever. It would have been the same effect. He's a dead man. He's got no survival suit on, the wind's howling and screaming, you can't look in the direction of the wind because the rain would blind you. When the rain was hitting your face or any exposed part of your skin it felt like somebody shooting needles at you. You couldn't face the wind.

The waves were breaking over the side of the hull. We were hanging on. I guess Leonard lost it maybe twenty to thirty minutes ... I've got no idea. A series of waves broke over the boat. Leonard went one way, toward the bow of the boat. I went the other way—I got blown right off the boat. I was about forty feet away. I tried to get back to the boat. I got back near the stern and I tried to grab on. I could see the waves were going to try and beat me against the side of the boat. I just let go, and I drifted.

I drifted ... I thought, This is it—I'm a dead man now.

I was thinking about all my unpaid bills, thinking about dying, what it was going to be like, where I was going to go, how it was going to happen ... I just resigned myself to the fact that I was going to be dead. And I thought I was dead. The last little while of the next day ... the last few minutes ... I thought I was on the verge of death. I'm sure of it.

The salt water had swollen up my eyes. I couldn't open my eyes and I couldn't see for a couple of days afterwards.

The next day I did have an experience with ghost boats or something like that. I couldn't open my eyes, so I didn't know where I was or anything like that. I could see things ... boats around me, with men in them. Rowboats—old rowboats. They were calling to me to get in the boat. I'd go to reach for the boat and my arm would go right through the side of the boat. That was wanting to be somewhere else, maybe. I don't know.

While Morrison drifted, the crew of the Bull Harbour-based Coast Guard cutter *Racer* was plowing north under the command of Captain Geoff Sanders. Sanders, now a skipper on the Campbell River-based cutter *Point Race*, had been tasked to search for the *Pacific Traveller* and another of the many overwhelmed halibut boats, the *Galleon*. Sanders steamed north through the night at

The Coast Guard vessel *Wolfe* finds the overturned hull of the *Pacific Traveller*.
Painting by Graham Wragg.

reduced speed to avoid damaging his ship in the storm-generated seas.

Daylight brought word that a search aircraft had found the *Galleon*, smashed in and awash, with two bodies floating in survival suits nearby. No one will ever know exactly what transpired aboard the vessel during its final hours. Early in the evening Prince Rupert Coast Guard radio received a message that the two-man crew was having difficulty with a stabilizer. Two and a half hours later they issued a distress message, their last communication. The crew of the *Racer* pulled aboard that grisly cargo, then continued on to search for the *Pacific Traveller*.

Sanders: The seas were still fairly rough then, probably about ten feet. It was just the remainder of the swell; the skies were clear and the storm had passed through by this time.

We were going in toward the search area because they'd decided they wanted to use our diver to go with the diver off one of our other ships, the *Wolfe*. They'd found the wreck of the *Pacific Traveller* by then and they wanted to search and see if anybody was inside.

We never got there, because as we were steaming toward it, one of my guys noticed something in the water.

The guy Sanders referred to was seaman John Wilson; the something was Randy Morrison.

Sanders: There was a fair bit of swell activity. We watched the spot for a moment and sure enough, we came to the top of a wave and Randy Morrison's head came to the top of a wave. He was maybe a thousand feet away at most. It wasn't a long ways away.

We headed over there. At first we thought he was dead because he wasn't responding when we headed over. When we got there I blew the whistle, and then he started waving his arms. The reason he didn't respond to us at first was because he had so much water washing over his face the salt had gotten into his eyes and crusted his eyes and he was blind at that time. So he hadn't responded because he hadn't realized there was anybody in the area.

We got alongside of him and recovered him out of the water. He was a big guy. It took a lot of work to get him out of the water. He of course was very weak so he wasn't really able to help. And his suit was full of water. It was a fair grunt to get him in. We put our scramble net over the side and had a couple of our guys halfway down the scramble net hauling on him. They got a rope around him and the rest of the guys hauled on him and got him on board that way. When he got on board he was pretty much just lying on deck. He wasn't doing too much.

Our paramedic on board started working on him and I high-tailed it toward Bella Bella, which is where the nearest hospital was. We got about halfway there and they decided to send a helicopter over to finish the job so we could go back and look for the other person. So we did the transfer—he was hoisted into the helicopter—and we went back out.

Capt. Geoff Sanders at the wheel of the Coast Guard cutter *Point Race*.
Keith Keller photo.

Our divers looked around, couldn't find anything, so we took the vessel under tow for Bella Bella. We were relieved of the tow by a commercial tug once we got into calm waters.

At that time it was getting pretty late in the day. We searched until nightfall. The whole crew had been up for probably thirty-six hours by then, so everybody was pretty wiped out. We anchored for the night, or tied up, and went out the next morning and assisted the aircraft in doing the search until it was called off. They called it off after about another twenty-four hours.

Dreadnaught
to the
Rescue

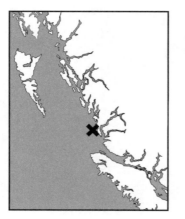

Dreadnaught
to the Rescue

IN 1926, AT THE AGE OF THIRTEEN,
LEO Butcher left his home in south Vancouver on the
Union Steamship Company's *Camosun*, determined to
experience firsthand the alluring upcoast territory he'd
heard described by a family friend. The steamer deposit-
ed Butcher at Alert Bay where he boarded temporarily—
and illegally—on the Alert Bay reserve. His first neigh-
bour, just across the reserve boundary, was the Indian
agent William Halliday.

Butcher earned his first pay that same year, 25 cents
an hour, for doing cleanup at the BC Packers wooden
box plant on the Alert Bay waterfront. After drawing
wages in a variety of coastal jobs, he built the first of
many boats and embarked on a commercial fishing
career which lasted until 1978. Butcher now lives in
Nanaimo. In 1938 he lived on Malcolm Island, where he
built a boat he named the *Dreadnaught*.

Butcher: I was living at Mitchell Bay and fishing out of Bull
Harbour, Hope Island. That spring I built this 26-footer, a dou-
ble-ender V-bottom, all fir construction, solid as a block of wood
and a good sea boat. I was salmon trolling at Bull Harbour for
about two months, I guess, and I decided to cross Queen
Charlotte Sound because I wanted to fish out of Hakai Pass.

I left early one morning and went in a straight line across. I
was running broadside of a six-foot groundswell. It was about
fifty fathoms apart and coming from the south-southwest and
my course was almost northwest. I'd crossed the sound and was
abreast of a long sand beach on Calvert Island when I noticed
smoke coming up from about the centre of the beach, so I
changed course and headed there to see what it was about.

The beach was shallow a long way out so I had to stop outside of the surf quite a ways and turn to face seaward in case a
big comber broke outside of me. I stopped in about two fathoms
of water, so I'd have been about a hundred yards from the beach.
Just then a man came down to the surf and waved me on to the

west. I couldn't hear him and he couldn't hear me because the surf was too loud. He waved me down the beach to where some rocks were, so I could pick him up off the rocks. I turned around just in time to see this breaker outside of me. I put a little fuel to her and throttled up and then slowed down just before we hit. It was just like going through the side of a barn, right into it and out the other side. It hit like a bomb but didn't break any windows. It filled up the

Leo Butcher aboard the *Dreadnaught* at Mitchell Bay in 1938.
Photo courtesy Leo Butcher.

afterdeck and the cockpit but I closed the door just before it hit so it didn't fill up the cabin. That was a lucky thought.

After that I took off to the west to where this rock was. I could see that I couldn't take him off there because there was too much of a slant on the rock and I couldn't get that close. He would have gotten washed off.

There was this ravine that went back into the mountain and it went about halfway up the mountain. He had to go up to the top before he could cross the ravine to come down on the other side. It was a couple of hours later before he got there. This little point of rock on that side of the ravine had almost like stairs, about three feet apart. He came down to a point where he could jump into the boat when I came in.

There was a big ground-swell there—it was the open sea—and the swell would race right up this ravine—a gut, you could call it—get to the far end and back out again, back and forth. So I came into the ravine, up alongside the cliff, the "stairs" where the guy was waiting, at about 3 knots. But the surge carried me flying by him and halfway into the gut. I went into reverse to try not to get thrown up into the head of the gut. I went full speed reverse, but the water settled down and let me down on the edge of a submerged ledge, and as the water went down farther the boat fell off the ledge onto its side in the water. Then it righted itself. The engine was still in full speed reverse and when I hit the water, the

The shipwrecked fisherman leaps onto the *Dreadnaught*.
Painting by Graham Wragg.

prop threw forty feet of foam ahead of the boat and I went sailing back out. I went back past where he was standing ... and he wasn't there any more. I had lost him. I thought, My God, I might have chewed him up with my propeller when I backed out.

I stopped the prop and went out on deck to see where he was, and darned if he wasn't on top of the wheelhouse, on his stomach, hanging onto the handrails on both sides of the top of the wheelhouse. And he was soaking wet. He turned around and sat up and he was grinning. He slid down onto the deck and he was crying. Laughing and crying, tears coming down out of his eyes. He had jumped on when I went flying by and hung on when the boat fell into the water. He didn't say too much, and I didn't even ask his name.

I gave him something to eat, sandwiches and cocoa, and said, "Where's your boat?" He told me where the boat was, so I said, "Let's go see it." He said, "No way." He was quitting fishing as of now and he didn't want to see the boat at all. He had come from Winter Harbour to fish Rivers Inlet and had run out of gas near Calvert, and a southeaster had drifted him west and close to this little nook where he had enough gas to run in and beach the boat.

He had been four days going about five miles from where his boat was to where I picked him up because of so many ravines running up the mountain. He was headed for Cape Calvert where he could flag a boat. That was, I'd say, about four or five times the distance he had already come. The going would probably be better along most of the west side until he got to the south end. There it would be harder again. He would never have made it, because the big black wolves there, all over the place, would have chewed him up before he made it. Besides, he had no grub, no food.

I talked him into showing me where the boat was, to see if we could salvage it. A few miles to the west was a sheltered nook that ran in a ways and to the left, and there was the boat, up high and dry on a sandy beach with the stern buried in sand to the waterline. The tide was low and coming in so I ran my boat bow-on onto the beach and tied it to a tree. I told him we could save his boat by digging it out and towing it off.

I had a 1928 4-cylinder Chevrolet in my boat—good power. So we each took a pen board for a shovel and dug away the sand and waited aboard my boat for the tide to come up. I had a towline on his boat all ready to haul.

Well, as the tide came in it was something horrible to see. The doggone surge washed all the sand back in to where we'd dug it out, just settled it in again solid. There was no way I could pull out that boat. I tried but it just wouldn't budge.

So I told him the only thing I could do was to go up to Welcome Harbour and get the packer and tow it out of the sand. I took him into Hakai Pass and into Welcome Harbour and talked to the skipper on the big *Sea Gay*. He said, "All right," so we went back around and he sent his crew ashore with an inch-and-a-half towline, passed the line under the stern, wrapped the whole stern with his towline and he pulled it off like it was coming out of butter. He towed it by the stern all the way to Welcome Harbour and it never broached at all, it went right straight behind him. I went on up the pass and fished out of Goldstream Harbour. I never seen the guy again. I don't know what happened to him or his boat.

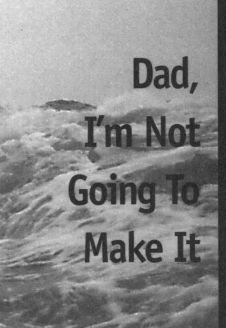

Dad,
I'm Not
Going To
Make It

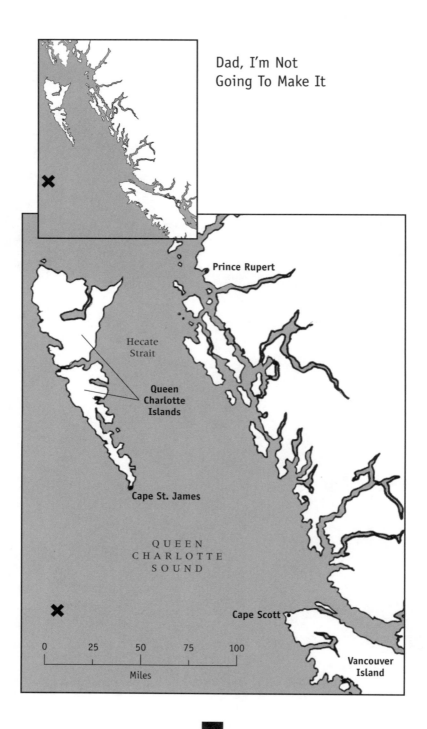

Dad, I'm Not
Going To Make It

Prince Rupert

Hecate
Strait

Queen
Charlotte
Islands

Cape St. James

QUEEN
CHARLOTTE
SOUND

Cape Scott

0   25   50   75   100

Miles

Vancouver
Island

"Every sailor ... the thought is a nightmare: being in the ocean, your ship sinking, and you hope to God that somebody's going to look."

—Bill McMunagle

TUNA FISHING IS A LONG-DISTANCE AFFAIR, A CHASE. The boats, many of which fish out of southern California, spend the majority of the season out of sight of land, fishing the South Pacific in winter, working their way to Hawaii by spring, then continuing north on both sides of the International Date Line. The movements of albacore tuna change from year to year, and in 1990 the best catches were being made off Canada's west coast.

In late September of that year, Barry Holmberg was in his twentieth year of tuna fishing and his second season aboard the 70-foot *Quicksilver* which, like Holmberg, sailed out of San Diego, California. Holmberg and the other four men aboard the boat delivered fish to Westport, Washington, then ran two days to a position southwest of Cape St. James. For safety and efficiency, tuna boats tend to travel in company, and the *Quicksilver* was one of approximately a dozen loosely grouped vessels that were having a last shot at what had been a poor season.

The reward was minimal: the crew of *Quicksilver* had taken forty-two fish the first day, forty-three the next. In the face of heavy weather on the evening of September 28, skipper Charlie La Gamma, a fisherman since age twelve, decided to shut down early and give his crew a good night's rest. Holmberg's twenty-three-year-old son Rob cooked a big spaghetti supper that night. It was Rob's second trip fishing tuna. "He liked it," his father recalls. "We were having a good time."

Being far from land, the majority of tuna fishermen simply shut their engines off at night and drift until morning. Some deploy a sea anchor, a parachute-like device that opens under water, holding the vessel's bow to the wind and reducing its drift. Many fishermen are wary of sea anchors, feeling that their potential risks can outweigh their advantages. *Quicksilver* appears to have been the only vessel of its group on a sea anchor that night.

Barry Diehl, a California-based tuna fisherman, was another member of the fleet working the open Pacific more than 115 kilometres west of the Queen Charlotte Islands. Diehl had fished on the family-owned *Defiance* for fifteen years, having received his ocean operator's certificate when he was eighteen.

Diehl: We were seventy miles from a little port on Graham Island, on the western side. The day before the storm, in the morning, we all kicked around the idea of going in and ducking out. But all these storms had been going over the top of us. They'd come across, hit that high pressure, and shoot north. If we'd left at nine in the morning we could have got in at seven o'clock at night. But we decided not to. If we had taken off, we would have missed a day's fishing. When I first started fishing, when the wind used to blow like that, we'd all go in and have a good time. But the way fishing has gotten, you have to stay on the grounds to make it pay.

When you get into that time of the year, not only are you helping each other catch fish, you're watching out for each other. We'd always make it a point every evening to check in. You leave your radios on at night, just in case such a thing happens. Every night, right at shutdown time, everybody'd call in. It's kind of an informal thing: how many fish you had that day, where you're shut down at, what's your position. We always write this down, so if this kind of thing happens you have a general idea where the guy is.

What was funny about Charlie was, we got his evening position but he was having a lot of trouble with his Loran C. It was cutting in and cutting out. So he didn't always know his position. That evening, when he shut down, he put out his position.

Holmberg: Everybody was asleep except for my son. He was on watch. We were drifting. The captain had shut the main engine off and put the sea anchor out. Shouldn't have done that—should have left it running.

I was laying in my bunk. I wasn't really sleeping, I was just kind of twilight sleeping. I heard the sea anchor chain pop. It's got a harness on both sides of the bow, and it's got a metal cleat at the middle of the harness. I heard that hit the bow. I knew that wasn't right 'cause there should be tension on it.

I got up. I had just underwear and a T-shirt. I went into the galley and my son was screaming, "Let's go, let's go!" I went up top. My kid threw me a life jacket, one of the old ones—it had one of the pads missing on it. The new ones were down below. I was trying ... like, "What the hell are you doing?" The captain gave out a Mayday with no location because the Loran wasn't working.

Diehl: My bunk is right by my radio, and I leave my radios cranked up. I heard it when the Mayday came out: "Mayday, Mayday, Mayday. *Quicksilver*. Mayday, Mayday, Mayday." Just like in a textbook.

Dick Gaydoshe on the *Millie G.*, another of the California boats fishing with our group, was the first one to answer him. Dick came back and said, "Charlie, where are you at?" And he said—he had kind of a comical little chuckle, just out of frustration—he goes, "I don't know." His Loran C. had quit working. At that point we lost him.

Holmberg: Charlie said, "Oh, fuck, we're not going to make it." 'Cause when the sea anchor went the boat had broached sideways. All the water from the bait wells went to one side and it couldn't roll off fast enough. He's yelling, "Start the main!" But you've got to go down to the engine room to start the main.

I ran back down below. I had to go through the bunk room but that's about as far as I got. I yelled to Bill and Manuel, "Let's go! We're going down!" The boat was sideways. Water was coming in the galley door, which was supposed to open sideways; now it was going up and down. There was a big spaghetti pot there so I grabbed it to jam the door open for the guys. I guess they didn't make it.

I ran back up top and the boat was going over. Charlie passed me and fell in the water. My son ran into me and I rolled over and we both went in the water behind him. The captain was freaking—he didn't know what to do. I started yelling, "Let's go, let's go!" We swam out as hard as we could to get past the rigging, 'cause the rigging was coming over. I turned around and looked. The boat was waterline, belly up. And bloop, bloop— gone.

> Gone too, having been unable to escape the foundering vessel, were deckhands Bill Taylor and Manuel Saldana.

Diehl: Dick came on and said, "Do we have his position?" Dick had been fishing a long time, and he kind of designated some things. Somebody got ahold of the Coast Guard. We figured our positions; we figured how much each one of us had drifted; we approximated where he would be.

I woke the crew and we fired the boat up. I'd say we had 70 knots or better of wind, and a driving kind of a hail-type rain. The boys, they wanted to stay outside to look, but there was points where they had to come inside 'cause the rain was driving so hard it was hurting them.

I've seen over 100 knots in the South Pacific. But in BC, it's funny—it's different up there. I think it had to do with the current; it was a very steep sea. It was dark, and with the driving rain, you couldn't see the waves coming. And we couldn't make any kind of speed. We were going faster than an idle, maybe making 3 or 4 knots. So we had to be very careful ourselves. It was such a steep sea. I couldn't tell you how high it was at night, but in the daytime I believe they were 20 plus.

Holmberg: I was looking for Bill and Manuel but couldn't see anybody. It was blowing so hard you couldn't see, couldn't breathe. Tough to swim in that. Me and my son had life jackets. The captain was stark naked—didn't have nothing. He had a jacket but he didn't put it on for some reason. He started saying, "You guys'll make it but I won't." We're trying to tell him, "Shut up, man—shut up and swim!" We found a hatch cover and put him on that. We found a couple of buckets. We tried turning them over and sitting on them full of air. Couldn't do it, it was just too sloppy. Every time you'd come up and go to take a breath, boom—you'd get hit with a swell in the face.

We were all three together. Charlie, he lost it. He was numb or whatever. He was still alive. We were trying to hang on to him. A swell would hit us like a washing machine. And either

Barry and Rob Holmberg struggle to keep skipper Charlie La Gamma afloat on a hatch cover from the sunken *Quicksilver*.
Painting by Graham Wragg.

my son would come up with him or I would. Until this one time—this gigantic one got us. I came up spitting and sputtering, and I looked at my son and said, "You got him?" He said, "No, do you?" I said, "No." He was gone.

We just tried to stay afloat. We saw lights going by. I felt myself fading real quick—going, going. We were both praying, screaming. We were yelling at the top of our lungs at the lights going by but nobody could see us.

We just kept drifting around, floating, trying to swim. I told my son—I didn't think I was going to make it—I said, "If you see a light and you want to swim toward it, Rob, go for it." So he did. I didn't know he was going to take his jacket off, but he did. He started yelling from a distance, "I can't make it." I said, "Well get your butt back here." He got back, but he was totally out of wind. I was fading in and out. I was gone, I thought. We had my jacket—we were sharing that.

Diehl: The two boats ahead of me had found debris, and they were putting out positions as this was happening. So we'd get focussed—get the search going. Of the first three boats in the general area, we were the only one that had a spotlight. We were working the spotlight, and the first thing we saw was a life jacket—actually the reflector, because the visibility was very limited with that driving rain. We approached it real slow; all it was was a life jacket. Turns out that was probably Barry's son's jacket—the one that he took off.

The next thing we found was the raft—inflated, totally upright, light on. Everything was perfect. And nobody in it. That was frustrating. We went right up to it—it took a little bit to do this—and grabbed it and looked inside.

At that point—you're seeing more debris floating—we found the bait skiff, capsized—nobody there. Didn't look good at all.

Holmberg: All of a sudden I felt a spotlight hit me. Just as I turned around to tell him, "Rob, there's a light," his eyes rolled back in his head and he said, "Dad, I'm not going to make it." And then we got hit by a gigantic swell. I felt him with the back of my hand. I scrambled for him, but that was it. The next thing I remember it was eleven o'clock the next day.

Diehl: We came to Barry next. We seen a reflector, and there was somebody in it. But the hard part was, the wind was blowing so hard, and the seas were so big … I did not want to get upwind of this guy, 'cause I knew we'd have blown right over the top of him. So I'm downwind of him, trying to get to him. It seemed like it took forever. I didn't know what kind of condition he was in. I knew the water was cold; the water was 60, 61 degrees, ballpark.

We had a guy standing by with a life jacket—I had a guy willing to go in. But I really didn't want to put a guy in the water—it was very tough conditions. We got close enough, we threw him a life ring, and he grabbed it. We got him to the boat. And when we got him to the boat, he was not functioning. I don't know how he even got ahold of the life ring. He told me later that he was floating in and out of a kind of sleep—hypothermia.

When we got him on the boat he was not talking. His eyes were open, but he was not moving. His arms and legs were locking up. They carried him in, and his arms and legs were kind of bent; it was like they were already stiffening up on him.

Holmberg: They said my whole body was just shaking completely. They poured the water out and kick-started me. They said they put me on the floor in the galley, turned the oven up all the way and opened the door. They had a guy on each side, on each arm and each leg, and they brought me back around.

Diehl: The BC Coast Guard was great. They had a plane out in no time. I'd say in less than an hour they had a plane out that was dropping these lighted flares to light up the sky to see if we could see any more—to see if they could see any more. And a ship was there within hours. It was unbelievable. They were really on the ball.

> Two Buffalo aircraft and an Aurora anti-submarine warfare plane from Canadian Forces Base Comox had joined the search, as had the 1,500-ton, 235-foot Canadian Navy Auxiliary Vessel *Endeavour*, of which Bill McMunagle was master. The *Endeavour*, designed by the Department of National Defence to perform oceanographic defence research, was hove to in rough seas sixty kilometres south of Cape St. James when it was tasked to join the *Quicksilver* search. McMunagle was also designated on-scene commander—the link between searchers and the Rescue Coordination Centre (RCC) in Victoria. Diehl acted as communications link between the *Endeavour* and the tuna fleet, which played a major role in the fifteen-hour search effort.

McMunagle: It was foul weather, absolutely dreadful. It was a howling gale. We could not go at full speed or we would have done ourselves an injury. At the best speed we could with the weather conditions prevailing, we got there at six-thirty, seven in the morning.

We had certain communications difficulties; we had difficulty contacting people. But we managed it. Diehl was doing a super job with his friends in the tuna fleet. They knew what they were doing and the capabilities of their craft. They were combing up and down—that's all they could do. They were constrained by the weather, but they were all frantically doing their very best at conducting the search. They did a great deal of hard work and took a great many risks.

The oceanographic defence research vessel *Endeavour*, under Bill McMunagle's command during the *Quicksilver* search.
Painting by Graham Wragg.

Diehl: We kept searching into the morning and into the day. We didn't find anything else. Barry really wanted to find his son. He was just beside himself. We'd all been talking, among the boats, and we decided it would be the best thing for Barry, with the shock, the hypothermia, if they airlifted him off.

> A Labrador helicopter from Canadian Forces Base Comox's 442 Squadron was tasked to proceed toward Diehl's vessel, the *Defiance*, which in turn steamed toward northern Vancouver Island for the deep-water rendezvous.

Diehl: I thought that as steep as the seas were, they weren't going to be able to airlift him off. The wind had backed off tremendously, but the sea was huge. But they said, "No problem." This guy really handled the chopper well. It was really smooth. We went with the swell, just idling. He brought the chopper right over top of us. They lowered the guy in a little seat thing, and they got Barry in there and took him up. I was really surprised they were able to do that so easily.

We had been gone from the search area for a couple of hours when they called the search off. None of us quit looking, but you have that shitty feeling in your gut that, hey, we're just wasting our time. But nobody gave up. The Coast Guard told us when they thought the search should be called off. None of us wanted that responsibility. You always think, What if...? If there is somebody out there and you're calling off the search...

McMunagle: It went on until about five o'clock in the afternoon. By that time we had had to send some of the fishing boats away because the weather was going to get dirty again and they had a long way to go. About five o'clock we were told to stand down on the search. There was obviously nothing more we could do. Nobody was going to be picked up.

You never like to think that it's too late, that you're never going to get them. I've been shipwrecked myself once, and I know perfectly well that there comes a point in time that you just have to say, "That's it. He's gone—they're gone." There's no point risking people for a body.

> McMunagle was referring to his firsthand experience of an immensely powerful storm that struck western Europe on January 31, 1953. McMunagle was a cadet aboard the steamship *Clan Macquarrie* when the vessel was driven ashore on the Isle of Lewis, ten miles from the Butt of Lewis lighthouse, whose anemometer was carried away at 135 knots. McMunagle and the other sixty-odd people aboard were rescued by breeches buoy.

Diehl: It kind of puts things in perspective. We weren't catching a whole hell of a lot of fish. All it was was a scratch. It had been a tough year. At the best we were catching a ton a day, which is the equivalent of $1,900, before expenses.

So we all left—we called it. For myself, I guess I was kind of naive that way. I always thought that we were on top of things. I never imagined one of my co-boats going down. Just didn't. We always worked real tight together. It put things into perspective for me: no matter what, it can always happen. Mother Nature was showing us what she can do. I thought, Here we are, we're making just a pittance, and we lost a boat. That was it. We just called it.

Holmberg: I was a basket case for two years, until I met my wife. She brought me around. I didn't care about anything any more. I didn't care about living. You get to that point: "To hell with it." That's where I was at.

Six years to the day—September 28—I finally got back in the water. I couldn't even get in a swimming pool for a while. I just couldn't get into the water. My first dive, I thought about everything. But it felt good—I overcame it finally.

In February 1997, shortly after giving this interview, Barry Diehl was tuna fishing off New Zealand when, in the space of five minutes, the *Defiance* filled with water and sank. Diehl and his crew had survived a violent storm the previous day, and speculate that the *Defiance* may have broken a weld which subsequently opened. Though one crew member drifted alone for two hours, all five people on board were rescued by a New Zealand-based tuna boat. Diehl recently purchased a former University of Washington Bering Sea research vessel, which he is converting for tuna fishing. At last word, he was debating whether it would be renamed *Defiance* or *Defiance II*.

The
Very Last
Voyage
of the
Deanna

Gaye

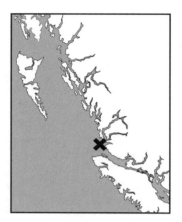

The Very Last Voyage
of the *Deanna Gaye*

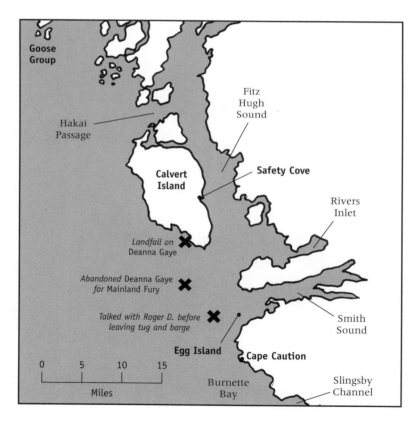

Goose Group

Hakai Passage

Fitz Hugh Sound

Calvert Island

Safety Cove

Rivers Inlet

Landfall on Deanna Gaye

Abandoned Deanna Gaye *for Mainland Fury*

Talked with Roger D. before leaving tug and barge

Smith Sound

Egg Island   **Cape Caution**

| 0 | 5 | 10 | 15 |
Miles

Burnette Bay

Slingsby Channel

ROGER SKIDMORE AND HIS
BROTHER FORESAW BIG THINGS for themselves in the
shipping business in 1977. They owned a barge which
Skidmore towed up and down the coast north of Lund—
Desolation Sound, the big mainland inlets, up into
Johnstone Strait—delivering logging equipment to the
area's gyppo camps. They were laying the ground floor
for a lucrative future, but in the meantime they were
barely making ends meet.

Skidmore, who was thirty years old at the time, had
other occupational aces up his sleeve. He was a fisherman. He was attempting, without benefit of prior training, to become a machinist. He built fuel tanks and
machined various boat parts, learning as he went.
Lacking the requisite training, Skidmore eventually
decided that, in his words, "I was pretty hopeless at it."
He was open to all job prospects. Enter Roy Johnson.

Johnson, in addition to being a prawn fisherman,
was involved in a host of other coastal activities.
Skidmore remembers him as "quite a crazy character." A
friend of Johnson's was going bankrupt in the logging
industry, but for the time being remained in possession
of all the equipment. "Roy had propositioned him,"
Skidmore explains, "saying, 'Give me the equipment.
We'll beachcomb up the coast, get a log barge full of logs,
bring it back and maybe we can bail you out—make a
bunch of money on it.'"

The friend had two choices: agree to the plan or lose
everything to the bank. He turned the works over to
Johnson: a 36-foot tug called the *Mainland Fury*, a barge,
trailers, a boom boat, a skidder, a Trojan—a large rubber-
tired log moving machine—and enough associated
equipment to keep the operation afloat. So they
thought.

At the last minute Johnson's cook backed out, creat-
ing a job prospect for Skidmore. "Sure, I'll go," he said.

"And if I don't like it I'll just leave. I'll take my own boat with me."

Skidmore's "own boat" was the *Deanna Gaye*, a converted 30-foot Winter Harbour troller belonging to friends, the Robertsons, who had fallen in love with the beamy little work boat and, with much help from Skidmore, had breathed new life into its abused hull. Unwilling to sell the vessel when work forced them away from the coast, they left it in Skidmore's care. For a while Skidmore used the *Deanna Gaye* to tow his own barge until, in early February of 1977, he, Johnson, Roger Dowker and two other crew members left Lund on what was to be the definitive beachcombing expedition.

Johnson's plan was to stockpile beachcombed logs at several sites on the central coast, load it all onto a log barge during a second lightning tour, then whisk south to sell the bounty in Vancouver. They were shooting for a million board feet.

Skidmore: We landed at Burnett Bay, which is a huge, beautiful white sand beach just south of Cape Caution on the mainland side. Lots of southeast exposure, so they had a lot of logs. They picked the right tide, drove the barge up onto the beach. It had a landing ramp and the Trojan just took everything off, put it above the high water mark. It was the highest tide of this particular cycle so the barge just went up in the lee of a little point and stayed aground.

My boat and the *Mainland Fury* went around up into Slingsby Channel, which as the crow flies is only a couple of miles. But it's around some points and up a channel. We found some anchoring spots in there. I didn't do any of the beach work, I just looked after my boat. And the tug, 'cause they couldn't leave it out where they were working, where it was very unsheltered. Also, the tug leaked and had to be pumped out regularly. The VHFs wouldn't go over the hill to talk to each other so we had to go through the telephone at Holberg, so we only had occasional communication.

Finally Roy phoned and said to have both boats in front of Burnett Bay by two o'clock the following afternoon. The tide was just right—the barge was starting to float. We loaded it up, yarded it off, and took off for Egg Island. Egg Island, then Fitz

Hugh Sound and up into the Inside Passage, then we'd probably end up going out Hakai and head across to the Goose Islands. Or, if the weather was really good, we could just make a beeline across to the Goose Islands.

As it turned out there was not a good weather forecast. From Cape Caution to Egg Island to Fitz Hugh Sound is maybe about twenty miles, so it's not a big distance to cover. But we got hit with the wind as soon as it started to get dark. The wind increased to more than 30 knots southeast. And we had these big freshets of tide out of Fitz Hugh Sound, Rivers Inlet and Smith Inlet all coming against us, so it made for real lousy, lousy weather. That famous Queen Charlotte slop—it was cresting at at least twelve feet. And it socked in—rain and sleet. As the wind got stronger and stronger the barge wanted to go broadside to the wind all the time and it was making steerage really difficult for the tug and barge.

Roger Dowker and Roy were on the tug. I started out on the barge with the two other guys, but when the weather started to get crummy I hopped on the *Deanna Gaye* and just chugged alongside them. I know we passed Egg Island on our way for Fitz Hugh Sound—we could see the Egg Island light as the weather proceeded to sock in, so we were somewhere in between. I sort of had an idea of where we were, I thought.

Our communication between the two boats was no good because the VHFs were on the tug and barge, so the tug and barge could talk together but I couldn't talk on the *Deanna Gaye*. I just had a Mickey Mouse [CB radio]. After circling the tug and tow for a couple of hours I came as close to the tug as I dared. I asked Roger, "Do you know where we are?" I thought he said, "No." He wasn't sure.

I said, "I'll go and find out, come back and tell you." He turned to Roy and said, "Roger's heading into the anchorage." I found this out later. They thought I'd buggered off into one of the anchorages I was familiar with—a smart thing to do in that little boat in those conditions. It was now gusting to 50 and 60.

So I disappeared over the horizon. I was trying to get a bearing on where we were heading to. I guess it was around midnight when the rain eased off and I was able to make out some land. As I moved in I could see breakers both port and starboard. I switched on the sounder and found I only had 15 fathoms under me, and I knew that if I didn't get the hell out of there soon I'd have none at all. I realized I was about a quarter of the way up the outside of Calvert Island. Instead of the southeaster taking us north into Fitz Hugh, on the inside of Calvert Island, the freshets had ended up taking us on the outside of Calvert Island.

They still had time to turn the tug and barge in around the inside of Calvert, so I headed back to tell them. I could see their lights occasionally. I took a compass bearing and started back. Going back was way worse than going with it. The little boat, like a little duck, was really good in a stern sea. But bucking into it was way worse. I was bucking fifteen- to twenty-foot swells with continual breakers. Up, up, up, and then crashing down into the trough and then the same thing, wave after wave after wave.

Around two-thirty in the morning I noticed a big bunch of lights right where the tug was. I didn't get a good view of it. I'd lost my glasses in a Sportyak—a little plastic dinghy sort of thing—when I was going into the beach at Burnett Bay. I could see fine during the day but my night vision wasn't all that great. They've got all these huge spotlights on the front of the Trojan for working at night. I figured they were rearranging the tie-downs on the barge, getting things right, and they'd started the Trojan up 'cause they wanted the light. Then I didn't see the lights any more.

It was about this time that I got seasick. It was probably fear; I normally never get seasick.

I was slowly getting closer and closer, keeping an eye on things in the boat, when I started noticing that I was taking on water. The bilge pump had been keeping up just fine, but it kept getting a little worse, a little worse. My thought was I'd sprung a plank and it was slowly opening up a little bit more all the time—the boat was taking a hell of a pounding. I started blinking my light at the *Mainland Fury* to get their attention.

As I got closer and closer to the tugboat I kept getting swept by its spotlight. I'd think, Great—they're still buggering around out there. I kept going, kept going, and the water kept getting worse and worse and worse.

In this little boat, the engine was up in the front. From the floorboards to the bilge was probably only eight or ten inches. There was no hold or anything. As the water got deeper and deeper in the boat it started to get picked up on the flywheel. It sprayed water onto the top of the engine, onto the muffler, and so it was coming up and fogging up the wheelhouse window. I had a hard time trying to cope with this water coming up, getting more panicky, flashing at the guys: "I'm coming, I'm coming!"

The engine was running on maybe half the cylinders 'cause the head was all full of water, the spark plugs were shorting out. It wasn't a diesel—it was just a little old Ford Falcon gas engine, and it was shorting and puffing and snorting. I kept playing with the throttle, trying to keep it going.

Finally, I just smashed into the side of the tugboat and leaped up onto it. I just put the engine in neutral, ran from the helm and jumped. Saved at last! It couldn't have been seconds after that the engine packed it in. I didn't tie the *Deanna Gaye*, I didn't have time. It was just, smash, off onto the tug, and it drifted away. I knew it was going down anyway, 'cause by the time I jumped there was a foot of water above the floorboards, which means there must have been a foot and a half or two altogether. I was more interested in saving my life than I was in saving the boat.

Right away on the tug, my supposed salvation, I went into the wheelhouse. Nobody. Off to the right there's a sort of a cubbyhole. There was a big coil of rope, and Roy's big German shepherd, Puppy, was tucked in the corner there, looking at me. There's a big hatch that goes down to the engine room, so I opened that, looked down. The sight was unbelievable. It was just awash with water and whatever they had to live: toothbrushes and sleeping bags and blankets and life jackets. Everything just slooshing back and forth in the hold.

The tug was just about sunk, but it was a diesel, too, so you don't have to worry about the engine until the water goes through the air breather. It was a big GM V-8, so the intakes were up pretty high. But it was running and in gear and it was going around in circles. It dawned on me: that's why I'd kept getting swept by the spotlight when I'd been coming toward it.

I went out to the back where the barge had been tied. The cable was just hanging off the back. It wasn't tied to anything. The barge had taken off. My only thought at the time was that they must have thought they'd be safer on the barge than they were on the tug. I assumed they were right, even though the barge was nowhere to be seen. The barge didn't leak. Maybe if they sat there they'd end up crashing on the beach and finding someplace to hole up on Calvert Island. There is a cabin up at the top end of Calvert Island for people who have had shipwrecks in the past. You can make your way up there along the shore if you happen to be healthy enough to get there. I didn't really think about it too much. Just that the dog was there and they weren't and I hoped they were okay.

There was a big power take-off pump on the front of the engine, so I went down to the engine, put the pump on and pumped the boat out. But it leaked like a sieve anyway.

I turned the boat for Egg Island, which I could see. It was seven or eight miles away. The fuel pressure was zero—the filters were clogged solid. It was sucking enough to idle, but once you put any throttle to it, it gasped. The *Mainland Fury* was a yarder from Howe Sound or up the inlets. It was never meant to be out where it was, and once it was it churned up all the garbage that had been sitting happy at the bottom of the fuel tank, made muck out of the fuel. I kept idling toward Egg Island, and then the engine just packed it in.

The VHFs were there but I got no return. I Maydayed and Maydayed. I guess that as I gave up on the Maydays it sounded like there wasn't a Mayday any more. I don't know what they assumed at the other end: "Mayday, Mayday, Mayday. This is the *Mainland Fury*. Is anybody going to come and rescue me? Can anybody hear me?" I found out later that they had heard the Mayday, but they'd discontinued it, saying it was a drunk at Sointula or Alert Bay or something because everybody was rescued. Coast Guard had picked up the Mayday but had disregarded it because nobody was supposed to be there.

The batteries were just about cooked, anyway. I'd left the pump on to keep the boat dry. So when the engine packed it in, it started to fill up again. It proceeded to slowly sink, but in my estimation it would be after daylight before I would have to worry about abandoning that boat. I'd noticed that the Davidson life raft was still on the roof, so I wasn't really worried about dying at that point. The tug would sink out from under me eventually, but at least I'd be in a raft. So I sat on the floor and waited for dawn. Between the Mayday attempts and a stimulating conversation with the dog I managed to maintain some semblance of sanity.

Before daylight came I was sitting in the back of the wheelhouse, staring out the front window, and I saw the dog looking past me out the back. And there was this light. I looked out and there was this spotlight shining. I got out on the back deck and this big spotlight was shining down on me, so I realized that it was something big. I was waving—waving frantically so they

Roger Skidmore and Puppy, illuminated by a spotlight from the *Alaska*.
Painting by Graham Wragg.

could see me. I looked down to keep the glare of the spotlight out of my eyes and saw a life ring on the back deck belonging to the *Queen of Prince Rupert*. That started to answer my questions about what happened to the guys on the tug.

The freighter came up alongside and the captain said over a loud hailer, "Are you okay?" I thought he wanted to know if I was physically okay, so I said, "Yes." He'd come too close, so he backed off. In the dark it looked to me like they were satisfied that I was okay and they were leaving. And I thought, I didn't do that right. I said, "No! No! I want off!"

They moved off about 500 yards, then slowly came up again and stopped alongside again. He said, "Do you require any assistance?"

"Yes!"

"Do you want to be rescued?"

"YES!"

Twenty years after his return from "the haywire mission we were on," Roger Skidmore stands aboard his boat *Tinkerbell II*. Tied alongside is the double-ended cod boat *Empress of Finland*. Skidmore is currently restoring the venerable *Empress*, owned by his wife and fishing partner, Claire Guest.
Keith Keller photo.

They backed off and waited for dawn. Dawn up there in February must have been about eight o'clock in the morning, so they proceeded to rescue me about seven, in the morning haze. They took the boat up in front of me in the wind, made a wind-break, then drifted down on top of me. They put a couple of Jacob's ladders over the side of the boat, then they had the main steps that they use when they're at dock.

While they were getting positioned I put a sling around the dog so they could hoist it up. I missed the Jacob's ladder, then I got the ladder and I was up it with the rope in my teeth. I gave it to the guys who were out on the walkway. The dog had run around to the other side of the tug and become tangled in the rigging. But the freighter was so big, it was way over the tug's rigging, so they were able to pull the dog right up out of the mess it was in. And we were saved. They took us to the officers' mess.

I had a coffee. Puppy had roast beef and short ribs.

It was the *Alaska*, which is a big train car carrier from Alaska, on the way to New Westminster. It never bothers with the Inside Passage, I guess, no matter what kind of weather it's in. It's a huge boat, I think in the 500-foot range. Big stuff. They were just plowing their way through and stopped to take a look. They'd monitored the rescue of the other four guys by the *Queen of Prince Rupert*, and were just making a visual check on the supposedly derelict tug which was now a hazard to navigation.

When they were ready to leave they spotted the *Deanna Gaye* not too far from the *Mainland Fury*. It was sunk—just the nose was sticking out. So I would have been toast if I'd stayed on that boat.

Once I got on board I found out what had happened to the other guys. The BC Ferries—the *Queen of Prince Rupert*—was coming through, and they found the tug, got ahold of Roy Johnson and asked him if they required any assistance. He talked it over with his crew members and said, "Fine, yes, we want to be rescued." So the lights that I'd seen—that I thought was the log loader on the barge—had been the BC Ferries enacting the rescue of those four guys.

They had driven the tug up under the big loading ramps of the ferry. The ferry would hit the tug, driving it down into the water, giving the crew the chance to get onto the back of the ferry. They did that twice. The second time the last two guys jumped up, trying to bring the dog. But the dog held back, and the ferry disappeared, leaving the dog on the tugboat. It was Roy's dog, and I guess he was pretty broken up about it, but there wasn't much he could do: the big ferry can't manoeuvre in that kind of conditions to go back and rescue a dog. At that time the BC Ferries docked at Kelsey Bay, not in Port Hardy, so that's where those guys ended up.

The *Alaska* phones the Coast Guard and says, "We've got the last guy off the boat."

"What other guy?" There'd been no mention of me, because the other guys who'd jumped on the BC Ferry hadn't bothered to worry about me. I was off in some anchorage someplace, so they thought.

So Coast Guard is going, "Who's this fifth member? Nobody told us about somebody else on the boat." I guess the police met the four at Kelsey Bay saying, "Hey, who's this other guy?" And they're going, "What? What are you talking about?" Then,

"Well ... that was Roger Skidmore. He wasn't supposed to be there. He was gone off to Safety Cove or Jones Cove or one of the little anchorages on the coast there." They got that all cleared up.

I ended up down in New Westminster. My brother lives there, so I spent some time in Vancouver with him. I didn't get back to Lund until about a week later. We met at the Lund Hotel and compared stories. The interesting thing in this is that you could probably take the five people involved and get five contrary stories. Each person saw it as if they were the saviour, or they knew what they were doing or didn't think they knew what they were doing, or whatever.

I was never really part of that crew of four. I never did get to be a cook, because I was up babysitting the tugboat and they were out doing their beach stuff. I was sort of an afterthought. I had a ball for the week that I was up in the inlet where I was taking care of the boat: jigging ling cod and turbot, dinkin' around 'cause I didn't have anything else to do.

There was no more information on the tug or the barge. The freighter had made a reckoning on the barge, and it was hell bent for leather in the wind, heading up off Hakai Pass toward the Goose Islands. Shortly after I got to Vancouver, a fella from Bella Bella called me asking where the barge was. He told me that he had an airplane and he was heading out to look at it.

I've got a sneaking hunch that somebody found the tug, and they found the barge and everything, whistled it up to one of the logging camps in the inlets, and all that stuff went to work in somebody else's name and that was the end of it. The guy that owned it was giving it all back to the bank anyway, so it was easy for him to say, "It got lost at sea as far as I know."

A tug that size, it could have taken maybe twenty-four hours for it to sink—plenty of time for somebody to get on it with a scow pump, pump it out and disappear it. It was a good little work boat. And the equipment that was on the barge at the time must have been worth at least a half a million bucks.

The loss of the *Deanna Gaye* marked a turning point in Roger Skidmore's life. Shortly after returning to Sevilla Island he married, quit the barge and machining businesses, and left Lund for good. He now lives in Comox, where he and his wife, Claire Guest, fish prawns and shrimp from their boat *Tinkerbell II*.

Daryl's Ghost and the *Salty Isle*

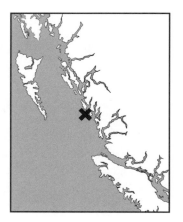

Daryl's Ghost
and the *Salty Isle*

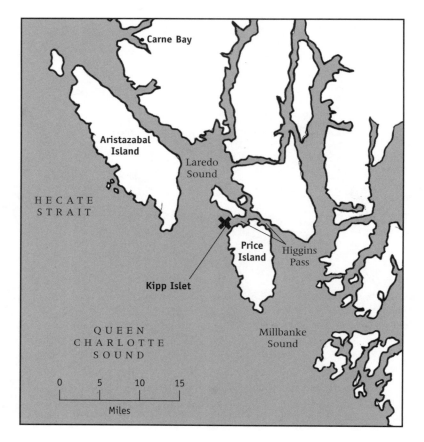

THE 73-FOOT VESSEL *SALTY ISLE* WAS BUILT IN 1954 in Peterhead, Scotland. Launched as the *Fertile Vale*, she worked in the North Sea until 1976, when she crossed the Atlantic, passed through the Panama Canal and began working in Canada as the *Choice One*. Her subsequent owner, Hirk Roland, decided on a further name change and made the event into a contest. The winning entry was provided by an old tow-boater, Daryl Georgeson, whose suggestion played on the name of his island home, Saltspring. Some old maritimers believe that it's bad luck to change a vessel's name, and Georgeson died shortly before the loss of the *Salty Isle*. The *Salty Isle* was lost on the day of Georgeson's memorial service.

Ron Bellrose's relationship with the *Salty Isle* began when he worked for Roland first as deckhand, then as skipper. It was year-round employment, packing sea urchins, geoducks and sea cucumbers in winter, herring in spring, then gearing up the boat to head offshore for tuna. Bellrose purchased the boat a year and a half before having it pounded out from under him one stormy night in February 1995, on a reef approximately 40 kilometres northwest of Bella Bella. On board with Bellrose were his partner Eileen Hare and his deckhand, Mark Barton.

Bellrose: The *Salty Isle* was a strange boat; it was a real love affair with that boat. People that worked on it, after working on it a while, became really possessive. It just grew on you. It was never a question of whether I would get it, it was a question of when.

We had taken a load of sea urchins out of a place called Grants Anchorage, in Higgins Pass. It was winter time, February. When we went in to get that load it was snowing, zero visibility. You couldn't see the bow of the boat. It's a real horrible place to go into, reefs and rocks everywhere, and you have to twist and turn. There's no lights or anything. It's nuts. You'd never go in there unless you were being paid to go in for some reason.

Anyway, we went in there in zero visibility, and on the way out the next day with a load I laid a plotter line on our plotter— a track, using a Global Positioning System, a satellite system. I figured we went in there in zero visibility and we came out in good visibility. We know the place pretty good, we'd got a plotter track coming out. I thought we had it covered.

We went up to Prince Rupert, then came back to get the next load. We had groceries for the [urchin dive] fleet and whatnot. It was blowing southeast 40, 45 knots—it was a very shitty day. I called ahead on our way there. I was talking to people, and they were saying that the fleet wasn't fishing 'cause it was too rough. So we figured if they're not fishing, what's the use in pounding our way down there. So we stopped in a place called Carne Bay and anchored.

We couldn't get the anchor to hold, and we anchored about four times before we could get it to hold. It was just screaming, blowing about 50, 60 miles an hour through there. We figured we'd stay the night and go on the next day, but eventually the wind came down. It was only blowing about 20, 25. It looked like it was getting fairly nice, so we thought we might as well go and get to Higgins Pass before dark. They'd have their groceries and whatnot. So we headed out.

On the way down to Higgins Pass the wind increased in velocity again. Of course when the wind picks up and you're bucking into it, it slows you down. Once we were about three quarters of the way there it became apparent that we weren't going to make it before dark. But that wasn't a big deal because we'd been in there in zero visibility. We kept going. As we got nearer to the place, the wind had picked up to about 40 knots and it was raining.

As we made our approach to Higgins Pass it really started to rain heavily. Torrential rain. And that wipes out your radar picture. You can hardly see anything on the radar. Bucking into a southeast wind going into that place, you angle down so that you've actually gone past it, then you turn and you head back with a following sea.

When we turned and went up, that's when it really started to deteriorate. You could see barely anything on the radar. But we did have the plotter line, and we were following down our plotter track. But the wind had picked up to about 50 knots at

Two days before being reduced to splinters at Higgins Pass, the *Salty Isle* rests at anchor in nearby Grants Anchorage.
Photo courtesy John Parkin.

that point and there was a huge sea starting to build. And as it was getting shallower the seas were getting steeper. You end up in a position where you can't just back up and change your mind. You're committed. You're going in there.

Even on the plotter line it was getting hairy, but I still thought we'd make it. As it turns out, the Global Positioning System was about a hundred feet off. They don't guarantee it for more than that accuracy. And we didn't have a hundred feet of leeway there. We were off course by about a hundred feet and thought we were on course.

The deckhand had a searchlight ahead of us, and I could see in the searchlight the colour of the water—you could tell there was a reef there. We went astern on the engine but the next thing you know we were on the reef. The propeller was damaged right away, of course, and we were just screwed. As soon as we touched the rock I knew where we were. And I knew that if we were on a rock in those conditions, it was all over. We had that advantage: there's no screwing around thinking you're going to be okay, fight your way out of something. I knew we were toast right away.

From there the wind picked up in velocity and the seas built until there was about a thirty-foot sea crashing down on the boat and the wind's howling, almost a full-blown hurricane. It was pretty nuts.

The dive fleet that the *Salty Isle* carried groceries for was securely moored deep inside of Higgins Pass that night. The fleet had been in the area for several days, diving for sea urchins and geoducks. With storm force winds forecast for the night, the dive boats had dropped anchors, strung beach lines and, in John Parkin's words, "everybody rafted together and we just sat it out."

Parkin, who lives in the Comox Valley, is owner-operator of the dive boat *Aquastar*. With him was Greg McKay, a diver who lives in North Vancouver. On vessels anchored nearby were Stan Hutchings and Doug Stewart, Fisheries observers monitoring the specialized dive harvests.

Parkin: They were just coming back toward Higgins Pass to pick up the next day's product. We'd heard the other packer slightly ahead of him, the *San Juan*. He was just coming through Higgins Pass and the *Salty Isle* was maybe a couple of miles behind him. *San Juan* got through Higgins okay and then the *Salty Isle* started coming through. I guess it was around eight o'clock we heard Ron on the *Salty Isle* talking to Kerry on the *San Juan*, saying, "Kerry, Kerry, I hit a rock." We heard a little bit of talk. We couldn't hear exactly what was going on, but everybody's ears perked up. It was really howling out there. About thirty seconds later on Channel 16 we heard, "Mayday, Mayday, Mayday." This was the *Salty Isle*, hit the rocks. Everybody thought, Holy cow, what a night to be on the rocks.

Hare: When we went into the pass I was napping. In my dream I had dreamt about putting my survival suit on. And I got fed up in my dream, and I said, "I don't need this: I know how to do it," and threw the dream away and woke up. A good thing. I guess it was about three minutes before the action started. I got up and went out and looked at the radar. I looked at our position and everything looked horrible but okay. I thought, Everything's fine—looks good. I went back to lay down. Even before I got to lay down I heard this smash and Mark said, "You'd better get your coat and boots on." Another smash, and Ron says, "Forget that, you'd better put your survival suit on."

Bellrose: I immediately told them to put their survival suits on, and I called a Mayday. We carried an inflatable life raft on the roof, but once we hit the first reef the boat was laying over on its side. It was listing to port about 45 degrees, with these huge seas breaking right over the top of the boat. With rocks and reefs all around, and a dropping tide. The rocks are covered in barnacles—if you try to just swim off to the beach your odds of survival are pretty slim.

As far as launching the life raft goes, I climbed up onto the roof and was hanging up there, flapping like a flag in these huge seas, and I knew if we tried to launch that raft somebody would probably get washed overboard. And if we did manage to launch it, it would be the leeward side, and it was just a mess. It didn't look very practical to me. I figured somebody'd get lost trying to do it. We just didn't bother trying.

Instead I tried to figure a way to get us to the beach on a line. During all this time I'm talking to the Coast Guard and I'm talking to other boats around there. People have come out of the anchorage in their boats and they could see us with our lights on, and we're firing flares, but they can't get close to us because the wind has driven us up onto this shallow reef and we're getting smashed to pieces.

Parkin: We all untied—about four or five boats—and started heading out toward the entrance of Higgins, this little islet called Kipp Islet. This was maybe twenty minutes from where we were tied up, right at the northwest entrance to Higgins. As we get closer and closer to the outside the swell is big, a big swell rolling in there. It was pouring rain, pitch black. I'm sure it must have been a moonless night, because it was pitch black. Just before we got to where the *Salty* was we could see the mast, and we could tell it was on the rocks by the way it was moving, jerking. We tried getting around the front side where he'd run aground, but there was no way. There was just a huge swell, at least a ten- or fifteen-foot swell and probably a six-foot rough chop on top. It was pretty big—way too big for the *Aquastar*, or any of the other boats that were there. Plus it was completely dark. Radar was useless because of the heavy rain squalls. And herring balls in the water—it was herring season, and you don't get accurate depth readings when you've got a million herring under you.

Everyone was kinda running around in circles, trying to decide what to do. Then we realized that they'd run aground on an island. The *Aquastar* is a pretty small, mobile boat. It only draws about a foot and a half of water, so I said to Greg, "Get in your suit, I'm going to see if we can get around the backside of the island, put you ashore, see what's going on."

Greg got into his dry suit. Stan Hutchings was in his jet boat and Doug Stewart was in his jet boat. They were shining their spotlights to try to show me where the beach was. I finally figured out that we could get around the lee side of this island. We got on the lee side and Greg got together a big coil of rope and a flashlight and a hand-held radio. Stan took him ashore in his jet boat. Meanwhile, I'm trying to anchor the *Aquastar* behind this island so I can get over and help. But it was blowing so hard—it must have been blowing 35 or 40—and I kept dragging anchor. Finally I just drove the *Aquastar* up onto the beach pretty well and just threw the anchor into a pile of boulders and let it drift back. Then Doug Stewart kept the *Aquastar* off the rocks with his jet boat, acting kind of like a little tug. He kept in radio contact with us.

Greg took off. He'd been across the island for about ten minutes when I tried calling him on his hand-held, Channel 68. There was no response. I was wondering what was going on, 'cause he was supposed to call me when he got to where the *Salty Isle* was.

McKay: There was diesel everywhere. I tripped and fell—broke my radio. At one point Ron threw a rope with a life ring on it, trying to drift it around. It got washed out again. There was rope everywhere. It was pretty shitty. There was nothing that anyone could do. You just sit there and watch helpless as the boat gets destroyed. The mast snapped—a sixty- or seventy-foot mast. The rigging fell all over the boat. The noise was incredible: the wind and the waves and the noise from the boat itself, all the creaking. It was unbelievable. I was there for about twenty or twenty-five minutes on my own, and then John and Stan showed up.

Parkin: Finally we get there and it was unbelievable: waves hitting the side of the *Salty Isle*, spray everywhere, and waves going right over the wheelhouse. The lights were still on. The mast light was on and part of the wheelhouse lights were on. By the time I got there, I think it was the foremast had already come down and there was wire and rigging all over the place. I could see all kinds of stuff hanging into the water and lights flashing under the water. The first thing that went through my mind was that somebody was trapped under the hull wearing one of those little life vests with lights that go on and off automatically. That's what we thought at first, but Greg said, "No, no, I saw all three of them on the deck."

We couldn't hear Ron. We were only seventy or eighty feet away but it was blowing so hard and making so much noise—the wood splitting, the grinding and groaning. Shipwrecks are really noisy. It was hard aground but it was half on the rocks and half in the water. The swells were hitting it almost broadside.

We were standing there thinking, Jesus, what are we going to do? There was huge surf so we couldn't get too close on the rocks—it would have swept us out to sea. Stan had to be real careful 'cause if he got swept out we'd never see him again. We could see that the life raft was inflated on the bow but it was all tangled in the rigging. When the mast fell over it fell right on the life raft.

Ron lowered a rope over the side on the end of a life ring or something and tried to drift it out toward us, but the way the wind and the swell were working it drifted away from us, toward a big gully. We were all just standing there for at least an hour and a half, running back and forth on the rocks, trying to see what we could do.

Bellrose: I could see them on the beach and I thought maybe we could drift a line in to them. So I tied a line to one of our life rings and tried to float it in to them through the surf.

Hare: The first life ring went around the other side of the boat and came back to us.

Bellrose: It was like being in a pot of boiling water and you're trying to drift it to the edge of the pot. And all the time that this was happening the boat was disintegrating.

McKay: Finally Ron threw over a big rope that did make it to shore, and we got ahold of that. That washed up with a wave. We grabbed it and I grabbed another chunk of rope that had washed up and tied that onto it to lengthen it a bit. We were holding on to the rope and trying to get close enough to Ron to yell. He was up on the bow and me and Stan were holding onto the rope.

John had his dry suit on as well; Stan just had normal raingear. John was working his way down the rock, trying to yell at Ron, see if maybe they could slide down the rope, maybe pull themselves in that way. A big wave came in and just completely swamped John. He went right off the rock, but he was holding on to the rope. We were still holding on to the other end of the rope. John was completely submerged. All I could see was his head sticking up out of the water. The wave crashed right over top of us but didn't wash us off the rock. It went out again and John just fell on the rock and scrambled back up.

Parkin: We decided we needed some more help, so I went back up onto higher ground and pulled out my VHF, and I called the guys on the other side of the island. I said, "Look, we need more flashlights out here and more divers with dry suits 'cause it's deteriorating here pretty fast." When I went back to where Greg was on the edge of the rock, the *Salty* had jerked and pulled the rope right out of Greg's hands—he'd lost the rope. There was no way he could hold it.

McKay: We just sat there for another hour or so as the boat was disintegrating in front of us. We could see the wheelhouse come loose from the boat. The boat was facing sort of bow toward the shore and the waves were hitting it on the port side. We could see the wheelhouse opening up and coming slamming back down. They were still huddled in the stern area on the starboard. When the boat rolled over on its port side and the wheelhouse opened up, their legs and bodies were falling into the big hole left—down into the engine room. When the boat rolled back over, the wheelhouse would come slamming back down and they'd pull themselves back up—pull their legs up—

and the wheelhouse would slam back down right beside them. That was when they thought they were all going to die, crushed to death.

Bellrose: It was like a giant Pacman trying to chew you up. You're hanging onto the rail, then the wave hits and stretches your body. As it stretches you the wheelhouse lifts and you're stretched underneath it. Then you scramble back out and wham: this thing comes down. And that's over and over and over again that happened.

Hare: I thought we were dead. It's not a scary thought. It's just: Well, this is what's happening ... okay, if that wheelhouse comes down again, that's it.

Bellrose: Finally a big enough wave came, and up went the wheelhouse, and it tore all of us off the rail, and we were sucked right inside the ship. At that point I thought the wheelhouse would come back down and that's the end of us. But the wheelhouse was carried away.

Parkin: I thought, Jesus, maybe they're all toast. Everything on the boat went black and our flashlights were running out after all that time. All we could see was this big, gaping hole in the *Salty Isle*, where the wheelhouse used to be.

McKay: We thought we'd just witnessed three people dying. We were just, Oh my God. For almost ten minutes we didn't see anybody, and we thought it was all over. We sort of scattered around after we saw them disappear. Maybe we could fish up a body or something.

Bellrose: So we were all underwater down in the guts of the ship, tumbling around. And when I tried to move I realized my foot was caught. I figured, So this is how I'm going to go. But then I got my foot loose and I thought, Maybe I'm not going to go after all. I popped to the surface and there were these two sitting there on the surface.

Hare: A few months before that Ron had had the boat strengthened. And he'd had wires—

Bellrose: —three-quarter-inch steel rod, right from one side of the hull to the other, with giant turnbuckles so you can tighten the whole ship—

Hare: —those wires were how Mark and I got out of the ship. We were down underwater and I got an end of one of them. That was how I pulled myself out. Mark as well. We both had one of those wires. But then I didn't have any strength left to get up on what was left of the deck. Eventually the waves changed somehow, from a slightly different direction, and I found that each wave helped me get up a little bit. One washed me up over what was left of two stanchions. I don't know how these guys got out.

Barton: The strap I ended up following had been sheared off, so I was only holding on to a foot of it or so. But when the wheelhouse started to come back down I was able to kind of squeeze myself down. That's what I used to stop from getting crushed. The wheelhouse is kind of washed off and we've been washed into the engine room. How much of it came back I don't know, but I know I was being crushed for a minute. I thought, Oh, so I'm going to be crushed to death. Then all of a sudden it washed away again and I was free. I came up and Eileen popped up. The first thing out of her was, "Where's Ron?" I just started to turn around to figure where he might be when he did surface.

Bellrose: We came up to the surface and we're hanging on to the edge of the boat. And by that time the bulwarks were gone, the wheelhouse was gone, everything was gone. There, fifteen feet away, was John Parkin.

Parkin: Shining a light along the edge of the bulwarks, which were getting all smashed off, I see these little reflective stripes that they have on the shoulder of their survival suits. All three of them had survival suits on, thank God, or they'd have been toast for sure. So I saw these things, and it looked like someone was jammed or trapped on the deck against a stanchion. I guess what they were doing, they were all just wrapped around the stanchion to hold on, 'cause the boat was rocking—huge waves just washing right over it.

I could see they were all there, so I yelled to Greg, "Come over this way." And when I look down, there's the rope that Greg had originally—it drifted back right in front of me again. By now the *Salty* was about twenty feet away from me, and there was all kinds of surge and stuff in between me and the *Salty*. I jumped down into the surf—it was about up to my chest—and scrambled back up onto the rocks between the swells. And I had the rope again. I was yelling as loud as I could, "Grab the effing rope!"

Bellrose: Poor John, he's standing on the rock, and he finally sees the three of us appear, and he's just screaming at us to jump. He's thinking that now's the time to get us down the line. We're all so shell-shocked at this time that we just look at him and we jump—the three of us. So now he's got all three of us at once. He didn't mean for us to jump at the same time—it's a wonder we didn't pull him right in the ocean.

Parkin: They all jumped in at the same time and just about yanked my arms out of their sockets. Then Greg and Stan came up behind me and grabbed the rope. The three of them swam out to the rock and we just basically grabbed them and—it was about a little six-foot cliff—pulled them on top of the rocks.

The *Salty* was moving. The waves were pounding it more and more and it was moving toward the rocks. It was getting ground away and the keel was pretty well gone at this point. We thought, We'd better get up on higher ground 'cause this boat's going to be where we are in no time. And sure enough, we got up about twenty feet on the shore and a big wave picked up the *Salty* and smashed it right on the shore, right where we'd just pulled them up, and smashed it right in half. It was incredible, it happened so fast.

The first thing they all wanted to do was get their suits unzipped, 'cause they had them zipped right up into their noses. So we got them unzipped a bit so they could breathe better. Eileen was a wreck. She was in shock, I guess. It was a pretty terrifying thing and I guess she figured they were going to die. Ron was pretty dazed too. Everyone was pretty dazed. Eileen couldn't walk 'cause she was so scared and cold and everything. So Stan pretty much carried her, it must have been 250 yards, through the dark on his back over these slippery jagged barnacle-covered rocks. Greg and I helped Ron and Mark across. They were okay—they could walk.

It took a long time and it was a pretty quiet walk. It wasn't like a big rush. Nobody talked the whole time. About halfway

Commercial diver Greg McKay examines the *Salty Isle*'s battered remains. Less than twenty-four hours earlier, he had helped save the lives of three people aboard the vessel.
Photo courtesy John Parkin.

back one of the divers showed up with a handful of flashlights, so he helped us get them across the island. Finally we got back, and Doug Stewart's jet boat took Ron, Eileen and Mark to the *Gemini* [the packer *Pub Nico Gemini*, anchored in Higgins Pass] and they got hot showers and everything.

Bellrose: When you think about it ... they pulled us up on those barnacle-encrusted rocks, we all crawled across the rocks, across the island in pitch black, screaming wind and torrential rain, and after all that nobody even broke a finger. Them on the beach being tumbled in that surf—it was amazing.

Parkin: It was like the *Salty* knew it was going to die and it didn't want to take anybody else with it. Throughout that whole thing, nobody had so much as a scratch. I cut my thumb. A little abrasion on my thumb—that was it. You see the rocks: jagged and covered with barnacles and seaweed, and everything covered with diesel fuel. You couldn't get a slipperier, more hazardous environment. And in total darkness. It was unbelievable. I get more injuries when I go out and cut the lawn.

Bellrose: It's like she delivered us all to the rock. Once we were off the boat and safe the boat sank within seconds. It was gone as soon as we got on the rock.

Hare: As far as I'm concerned, she brought us in as close as she could. She was going and she knew it. And she tried to tell me.

Occasionally I felt like there were ghosts on the boat—people who had worked on her in the past. I'd said to Ron that day, "Somebody's sitting in your seat again." Maybe it was Georgeson. I don't know.

Parkin: About two days later the seas calmed down so we could go back and have a look at the site. We'd just gone back to geoduck diving the next day. We had a quota to pick, so five hours after this was all over Greg was back in the water. Eileen had lost this beautiful Native gold bracelet that she wanted back—that was all they wanted back. Ron had bought it for her and it was a special thing.

> As the *Salty Isle* was home as well as employment for Bellrose and Hare, the vessel's loss cost the couple many personal possessions. Aside from the clothes and survival suits on their backs, Hare's wallet was the only item saved during the ordeal. Barton went back into Bellrose and Hare's cabin three times during the early moments of the shipwreck in an attempt to find the purse that contained the wallet. He came up with the wrong bags on his first two attempts, threw them on the wheelhouse floor, then went back a third time and recovered the right one. Only after the incident did Hare realize that one of those bags tossed aside contained the gold bracelet Bellrose had given her two weeks before.

Greg McKay (left) and John Parkin
relaxing on shore.
Photo courtesy John Parkin.

Parkin: We were the first ones to dive on the site. Greg's the main diver on the *Aquastar*, so he went down there. It was only about eight feet of water. He said it was just unbelievable: the bottom's littered with all kinds of shiny objects. It was like trying to find a needle in a haystack: everything from hose clamps to knives and forks. You name it, it's down there.

He looked for an hour and a half, two hours—couldn't find her bracelet. Then he says over the radio, "You're not going to believe it. I've found a bottle of wine down here." Apparently it was jammed under a piece of ballast. It still had the label on it. That was the only thing that wasn't broken on that whole wreck: a bottle of red wine. We gave it to Ron and Eileen a couple of weeks later when they took us out for dinner in Vancouver. We said, "Here's another survivor of the *Salty Isle*."

On the evening of February 18, 1996, Ron Bellrose, in the company of Eileen Hare and Mark Barton, uncorked and emptied the bottle of vintage South African cabernet that McKay had found among the debris on the bottom of Higgins Pass. Bellrose and Hare had been saving the wine to christen the boat they knew they would soon buy, but chose instead to commemorate the first anniversary of the loss of the *Salty Isle* and, significantly, the fact that they had escaped going down with their ship.

Bellrose and Hare have since purchased the *Melville*, a classic wooden longliner which they are using in the albacore tuna fishery.

Index

Page numbers in bold type indicate photograph.